161 511239 6

D1141846

ciad pythefnos

W orking with Adult Abuse

fore the due date to avoid overdue charges

cyn y dyddiad a nodir ar eich llyfr os

osgoi taliadau

by the same author

Training Manual for Working with Older People in Residential and Day Care Settings
Jacki Pritchard
Foreword by Luke Bond
ISBN 978 1 84310 123 9

Working with Elder Abuse
A Training Manual for Home Care, Residential and Day Care Staff
Jacki Pritchard
ISBN 978 1 85302 418 4

The Abuse of Older People
A Training Manual for Detection and Prevention
2nd edition
Jacki Pritchard
Foreword by Eric Sainsbury
ISBN 978 1 85302 305 7

Becoming a Trainer in Adult Abuse Work
A Practical Guide
Jacki Pritchard
ISBN 978 1 85302 913 4

Good Practice with Vulnerable Adults
Edited by Jacki Pritchard
ISBN 978 1 85302 982 0

Male Victims of Elder Abuse
Their Experiences and Needs
Jacki Pritchard
ISBN 978 1 85302 999 8

Elder Abuse Work
Best Practice in Britain and Canada
Edited by Jacki Pritchard
ISBN 978 1 85302 704 8

Support Groups for Older People Who Have Been Abused
Beyond Existing
Jacki Pritchard
ISBN 978 1 84310 102 4

Good Practice in Adult Mental Health
Edited by Tony Ryan and Jacki Pritchard
ISBN 978 1 84310 217 5

Working with Adult Abuse

A Training Manual for People Working with Vulnerable Adults

Jacki Pritchard

Jessica Kingsley Publishers
London and Philadelphia

Crown copyright material is reproduced with the permission of
the Controller of HMSO and the the Queen's Printer for Scotland.

First published in 2007
by Jessica Kingsley Publishers
116 Pentonville Road
London N1 9JB, UK
and
400 Market Street, Suite 400
Philadelphia, PA 19106, USA

www.jkp.com

Copyright © Jacki Pritchard 2007

The right of Jacki Pritchard to be identified as author of this work has been asserted by her in accordance
with the Copyright, Designs and Patents Act 1988.

All rights reserved. No part of this publication may be reproduced in any material form (including
photocopying or storing it in any medium by electronic means and whether or not transiently or incidentally
to some other use of this publication) without the written permission of the copyright owner except in
accordance with the provisions of the Copyright, Designs and Patents Act 1988 or under the terms of a
licence issued by the Copyright Licensing Agency Ltd, 90 Tottenham Court Road, London, England W1T
4LP. Applications for the copyright owner's written permission to reproduce any part of this publication
should be addressed to the publisher.

Warning: The doing of an unauthorised act in relation to a copyright work may result in both a civil claim for
damages and criminal prosecution.

Library of Congress Cataloging in Publication Data

Pritchard, Jacki.
    Working with adult abuse : a training manual for people working with vulnerable adults / Jacki Pritchard.
        p. cm.
    Includes bibliographical references.
    ISBN-13: 978-1-84310-509-1 (pb)
    ISBN-10: 1-84310-509-8 (pb)
    1. Abused men--Services for--Employees--Training of--Great Britain. 2. Abused women--Services
    for--Employees--Training of--Great Britain. I. Title.
    HV6626.23.G7P78 2007
    362.88--dc22

                                        2006100085

British Library Cataloguing in Publication Data
A CIP catalogue record for this book is available from the British Library

ISBN 978 1 84310 509 1

Printed and bound in Great Britain by
Printwise (Haverhill) Ltd, Suffolk

This book is dedicated in memoriam to my grandmother, Dorothy Kendall, whom I miss terribly. She was always the first person to read a book when it was published; this time round it will feel very strange her not being here to comment.

Contents

Acknowledgements

Whenever I finish a book I always reflect on the fact that I could never have written it in the first place if I had not had the privilege of working with so many helpful people through whom I have learnt so much. As always my knowledge has come from working with survivors of abuse who have willingly talked to me about their experiences. Workers from many different organisations who I meet through training, research or consultancy work have also been very open with me about their practices and the things they struggle with. So the whole point of writing this book is to aid any worker who in the future may need to help and support a vulnerable adult who is being abused. So my thanks and appreciation must go to all the survivors of abuse, workers and organisations I have worked with in the past; they know who they are.

In addition I need to thank particular organisations and individuals who have agreed to me reproducing their tools and forms in this manual: Lincolnshire County Council Adult Social Care (in particular Peter Sadler); Rochdale Metropolitan Borough Council Adult Care (especially Pam Lloyd-Hughes); the North Wales Forum (Arwel Owen); and the South East Wales Executive Group (Liz Majer and Bill Garnett).

Special thanks are also due to Tony Richardson (Fluid Medium Ltd) and Steve Fabian for all their advice, support and humour when filming the videos.

A Note on the Text

The following symbols have been used throughout the manual for ease of recognition:

Case examples

Handouts

Exercises

Case studies

Role play

Suggested videos

All pages marked ✓ may be photocopied for training pages, but may not be reproduced in other forms without the prior permission of the publisher.

Glossary of Terms

For the purpose of this manual the following definitions will apply:

Abuse
Abuse will include child abuse, domestic violence, elder abuse and adult abuse

Abuser
Someone who inflicts abuse on another person

Adult abuse/ protection/work
This includes prevention, investigation and intervention in working with adults who are the victims of abuse (physical, sexual, emotional, financial, neglect and discriminatory)

Agency
A government office or department providing a particular service

Care worker
A person who works in a home or day centre

Day centre
Any day care facility

Domestic violence
Physical, emotional, sexual violence experienced either by a woman or a man

Elder abuse
Any form of abuse which has happened to a person over the age of 65 years

Home
This manual is aimed at all homes where care is provided, so the use of home may refer to residential or nursing home, regardless of size

Organisation
A body of people with a particular purpose. Within any sector (statutory, voluntary, independent) which could be involved in adult abuse work

Participant
Person on a training course and who may participate in a training exercise. A worker who may be receiving training on a formal training course or on an 'in-house' basis

Service user   A person accessing services provided by health, social services, an independent or voluntary agency

Training officer   This term is used to include anyone who has responsibility for organising training within an organisation or specific work setting; for example, staff within traditional training sections, deputy managers in residential settings and development officers with a responsibility for training on adult abuse

Victim   A person who has experienced abuse at some point in their life. The term is not used in a negative way. Nor does it imply personal incapacity

Worker   Person at any level working in any setting/organisation within the statutory, voluntary or independent sector

Chapter 1

The Purpose of the Manual and How to Use It

I think it is important to explain at the outset why I wanted to write this training manual and at this particular time. I have been training all sorts of workers across the sectors for the past 17 years and, while I am giving my course participants lots of useful information, I also learn a lot from them. I find out what training they need because they tell me what they struggle with in their day-to-day work. The world of health and social care is changing rapidly and it is often hard to keep up with new information and changes in practice. Endless guidance, standards and targets seem to be being produced. It is important that workers do keep up to date, but very often they just do not have enough time to do this. It also seems that many workers in more senior positions are being given the lead to train staff on top of their normal jobs; sometimes they may not have any experience or idea about how to deliver training. From all my years of training I think I have gained a clear insight into how people learn best and I like to be able to produce training materials which will help other people in their learning.

My specialism is in working with adult abuse and it is an area of work that is gradually developing (although in my view this has taken far too long). Back in 1996 I wrote *Working with Elder Abuse*, which is a training manual for home care, residential and day care staff (Pritchard 1996). Over the years people working in other specialisms (and doing very different jobs to home carers and care workers) have told me how useful the manual has been. So I wanted to update it (although the original is still relevant and of use to workers and trainers). Before I got round to doing that, I decided to produce some training videos on working with adult abuse; six videos form the Working with Adult Abuse Series (see Appendix 5). I believe that workers need a variety of training materials in order to learn and for training to have a real impact. Having done that it was the time to write a training manual which will be of use to anyone working with vulnerable adults (not just older people).

In recent years many organisations seem to be getting their act together to deliver some form of basic awareness training on adult abuse. This has become more imperative with the introduction of the Care Standards Act 2000 and setting of standards and requirements for learning (Skills for Care 2006). However, there are so many aspects to working with abuse and these are often not addressed on basic awareness courses – purely because of lack of time. Many organisations just do not have the resources (or budgets) to deliver more in-depth training. So that is the main reason I wanted to write this manual. I want it to be a resource that covers the basic information any worker should have but also to go into much more depth and address some of those topics that often get missed out.

I think it is also important to say here that I still work with victims myself. To be a good trainer I think you have to know what it is like to practise in the real world. Many of the examples and case studies presented in this manual are based on real situations but obviously details have been changed for anonymity.

My terminology

I want to make it clear at the very beginning of this manual that I am going to use certain terminology, which some readers may not like. I am *not* talking about political correctness here, but rather I am referring to the fact that there is a lot of debate currently about terms we should be using in adult protection work. I discuss terminology in the forthcoming chapters and emphasise how important it is to speak in plain language so that workers understand each other – and even more crucially the service users understand.

I am very clear in my own mind that we all should be working in ways which incorporate and promote the principles and practices promoted within the Department of Health's guidance *No Secrets* (Department of Health 2000a). Therefore I shall use the following terms which are used in *No Secrets* and *In Safe Hands* (National Assembly for Wales 2000): *adult abuse, adult protection* and *vulnerable adult*. Policies and procedures around the UK have different titles so in this manual I shall use the term *vulnerable adult/adult abuse policy and procedures*.

In October 2005 a national framework for standards for good practice and outcomes in adult protection work was published called *Safeguarding Adults* (ADSS 2005). Some argue that the term 'safeguarding' should replace 'protection' and that 'safeguarding adults' should replace 'adult protection work'. I personally do not have a problem with the term 'safeguarding' but I do not believe there is anything wrong in using the terms 'adult abuse' and 'adult protection work', which are very clear in their meaning.

I know I have been criticised in the past for my use of the term *victim* in my other works. I choose to use this term after working for years with victims of abuse where their use of terminology has been discussed with them – either for research purposes or in the support groups I facilitate. Both men and women have said they do not have a problem with people using the term 'victim' because, as one woman put it, 'I might be a survivor now but I want people to know I have been a victim too.' Therefore, I am not using this term in a negative way nor does it imply personal incapacity.

Who can use the manual

Adult abuse still remains very much a taboo subject in our society. People do not naturally think about an adult being abused; the exception might be when thinking about domestic violence situations and the victim is thought to be a woman. Therefore, it is vital that awareness about adult abuse is raised not only within society but also amongst everyone in a work situation who may come into contact with a vulnerable adult. Just a few examples of workers who may benefit from using this manual are:

- social workers, care managers, senior managers
- care workers and residential managers
- domiciliary care workers and managers
- support workers
- nurses, doctors (in the community and hospital based)
- health care staff
- probation and prison staff
- police
- volunteers
- advocates
- hospice workers
- managers and workers who have responsibility for training
- training officers
- NVQ assessors and verifiers.

Anyone who works with vulnerable adults needs to be trained on the subject of adult abuse because a high percentage of these adults will have been abused in the past or will be living in abusive situations currently. Adult abuse, although an upsetting and emotive subject, needs to be at the forefront of everyone's mind; one never knows when you are going to come across it. It is an issue for *everyone* in our society; it deserves the attention that child abuse and domestic violence have gained over the past 30 years.

The manual and the videos

This manual can be used as a stand-alone training tool to cover all sorts of different courses on adult abuse. I mentioned above that I have directed and produced a series of videos (see Appendix 5). These videos can complement the materials in this manual. A trainer should become familiar with the content of a video before using it in training. This is because the videos can be used in a variety of ways. Some trainers may choose to show the video from start to finish at some point during a training course; others may choose to show parts of a video at different points in the session –

perhaps when introducing one aspect of the topic under consideration or between undertaking exercises. At the end of each chapter in this manual I have indicated the main video(s) which can be used for the particular subject under consideration.

Content of the manual

I have developed this manual to coincide with the way I think training should be presented to workers. I think there needs to be a progression from basic awareness through to more specialist training. I feel a good training programme should be developed in modules. We do not live in an ideal world, so often there are many constraints on training officers when they are developing a programme; the major one being budget. Nowadays, many Adult Protection Committees (or Safeguarding Adults Boards) have Sub Training Groups who decide what is needed locally. This manual offers guidance on what should be included in any comprehensive training programme.

Chapter 2, 'History, Current Guidance and Principles', gives a brief overview of developments in the UK from the time we talked about 'granny bashing' through to now when we talk about 'adult protection' and 'safeguarding adults'. In an era when we are plagued by litigation, it is vital that workers know what law and guidance they are functioning under; this chapter gives an overview together with a discussion of the fundamental principles underpinning adult protection work.

Chapters 3, 'What is Adult Abuse?', and 4, 'Recognising Adult Abuse', have been written to present essential information for a basic awareness course but also for workers who have little or no experience regarding adult abuse. They are lengthy chapters which go into great detail about definitions, exactly what constitutes abuse and how to recognise it. Chapter 5, 'Handling Disclosure', is devoted solely to the topic of handling a disclosure, because I feel strongly that this is one of the subject areas that is not addressed in training courses adequately. Anyone could receive a disclosure at any time and it is important that workers do not contaminate evidence before a proper investigation gets under way.

The next two chapters, 'Investigating Adult Abuse' and 'Case Conferences', take us on to the investigation process. Many readers might initially think they will never be involved in an investigation, that they will only refer on to their line manager or social services. I implore these readers *not* to skip these chapters. Many workers may be involved in sharing information or supporting a victim (or abuser) while an investigation takes place. Risk assessment is another subject area that is not given enough attention so this is why Chapter 8, 'Risk Assessment and Developing Protection Plans', is devoted to it and the development of protection plans. Protection plans must be developed and written clearly, which leads the reader nicely to the whole issue of recording in Chapter 9, 'The Importance of Recording'. I do worry constantly about the fact that many workers have never received proper training on how to record. Chapter 9 takes the reader back to basics and then relates the theory to adult protection work.

The final three chapters, 'The Abuse of Older People', 'The Abuse of Younger Adults' and 'The Abuse of Black and Minority Ethnic People', have been written with the sole purpose of providing more case materials. For the trainer they will be useful for developing exercises and using on their courses. For the general reader the scenarios presented will give a clearer insight into how, where and when abuse happens.

Layout of the chapters

I do think variety is needed when training people in order to keep their interest. Therefore, each chapter contains an assortment of materials:

- discussion of the subject
- case examples
- key questions
- key learning points
- suggested reading

- related videos
- exercises
- handouts (which can be used as overhead projections – OHPs)
- role plays and case studies.

For the reader's ease, exercises, handouts, role plays and case studies have been located at the end of each chapter. The reader is alerted to the appropriate exercise ✍ or handout 📄 by the correct symbol and page number within the body of the text. Exercises, handouts, role plays ☺ and case studies ∽ which can be photocopied are marked by the symbol ✓. However, they cannot be used or reproduced in any other format as copyright belongs to me.

Equipment needed

For the trainer who is going to use the exercises on courses the following equipment will be required:

- TV/DVD/Video Combi (optional)
- flipchart stand
- flipchart paper
- flipchart pens/markers
- pads of A4 paper

- pens
- adhesive notes
- blu tack
- adhesive tape
- scissors.

 Handout 1.1, p.22

Additionally, trainers may wish to supply their care workers with:

- folders for handouts
- A4 lever arch files for notes.

Using the training materials

This manual contains both exercises and handouts which can be used by:

- those providing a training course

- managers working with a group of staff or in individual supervision sessions

- individual workers.

Exercises

The exercises which are included in the chapters can be adapted to suit the needs of the training situation. I was very conscious when writing the manual of the fact that some workers will be reading it individually for their own professional development or because they have to deliver training; other workers might meet with a manager in small groups to train, whereas others will be trained in larger groups on formal training courses (for example 16–20 participants). Consequently, I was careful to develop the exercises so that they could be adapted to suit the size of the group. Also, managers may choose to adapt some exercises to be used in supervision sessions on a one-to-one basis.

Each exercise gives guidance about:

- the *objective* – what the exercise aims to achieve

- the *participants* – how they should work; that is, individually, in pairs or small groups (i.e. four or five participants)

- *equipment* – which the trainer may need to prepare beforehand (see below)

- *time* – this is a rough guide about how long the work will take the participants; it does *not* include time for feedback. The trainer should decide about the duration of feedback depending on the agenda for the course. The trainer should always make it clear how long will be given for the tasks to be undertaken and for feedback

- *the task* – what the trainer will ask the participants to do

- *feedback* – the trainer should explain what is expected from participants in feedback and time should be left for open discussion to ensure that the aim of the exercise has been achieved.

In some exercises there is additional guidance for the trainer under 'Note for trainer'.

Case examples and case studies

Case examples are used in the text to illustrate points in the discussion. Some trainers may wish to use them in a similar way in training sessions; especially if they lack direct experience of cases themselves. The case studies have a different objective; they should be used to facilitate participation and can be used to check out whether workers have understood the subject matter under consideration. They can be used either for study in small groups or be given to a worker to work on in between training or supervision sessions. I have not put questions at the bottom of the case studies because I know trainers will want to use them in different ways. Consequently, I have developed a list of possible questions which may be a help in developing group or individual work.

 Handout 1.2, p.23

The case studies should inform general readers further about the types of cases they could come across in their own practice.

Role play

As a trainer I know a lot of people hate role play. It *can* be a useful way to rehearse and learn but only if it is done in a safe environment. Trainers should be honest about role play and not cover it up in terms like 'simulation'. Participants need reassurance that they can learn by their mistakes. I think it is pointless doing role play if people are terrified. I do not think anyone should be made to do something which is not necessary. I propose that role play should be done in a certain way which is explained in Chapter 5.

References and suggested reading lists

Sources which are mentioned in the text are referenced at the end of the manual. The 'Suggested reading' section at the end of each chapter is primarily for workers. The suggestions have been kept to a minimum, because I know that workers have little time to read. I have therefore included in the section what I consider to be the most relevant and useful reading material related to the subject of the chapter. Trainers may want to refer more to the references section in order to read around more texts in preparation for training sessions.

Useful organisations

In Appendix 4 I have listed organisations which could be a useful source of information for workers with the contact address, telephone/fax numbers, e-mail addresses and website (when available). I have used these organisations and have read their information myself. I have only made recommendations where I think it would be worthwhile for workers to take the time to contact these organisations or use their websites.

Guidance for trainers

Abuse is a very emotive issue and trainers should be aware that some participants can become very upset during a training course. This can be for any number of reasons but commonly a participant may just find the subject matter extremely hard-going or he or she may have experienced abuse in childhood or adulthood. The trainer needs to be sensitive to these situations and be aware that it may not be appropriate in some cases for the participant to continue with the training at this point in time. These issues are discussed more fully in Chapter 6, 'Difficult issues for the trainer', in *Becoming a Trainer in Adult Abuse Work* (Pritchard 2001a).

Getting started

Everyone is under time pressures and people who have to train on top of their usual job activities can feel really pressurised. Nevertheless, it is imperative that time is put aside to prepare. Some basic questions which need to be asked and answered are:

- How long will the training course be?

- How many participants will there be?

- What are the aims and objectives?

- What are the learning outcomes?

- Which handouts are needed?

- What equipment will be used?

- Will a certificate of attendance be needed?

The best training needs to be participative. Few people like to be 'lectured at'. If a large number of people need to be trained in a session (i.e. 20 or more) then it becomes more of an information-giving than a training session. Groups of between 8 and 16 participants are ideal.

It is important that a trainer ensures that he or she has organised all the equipment they need before the course begins (see Handout 1.1).

Participants should know what they are going to be trained on and therefore it is essential to design an information sheet or flyer. Handout 1.3 is a typical example.

 Handout 1.3, p.25

Some participants may also require a certificate of attendance and an example is given in Handout 1.4.

 Handout 1.4, p.26

I have also designed a list of terms used in adult protection work which can be introduced at the beginning of any course:

- adult abuse
- elder abuse
- adult protection
- safeguarding adults
- vulnerable adult
- victim
- survivor
- abuser
- perpetrator
- alerter
- referral

- strategy meeting
- investigation
- investigating officer
- supporter
- intermediary
- appropriate adult
- risk assessment
- public protection
- case conference
- protection plan.

Handout 1.5, p.27

Documents

It is good if participants have the opportunity to look at books and documents during a training course. It is helpful if a trainer can provide:

- the local multi-agency policy on vulnerable adults/adult abuse

- any leaflets which may be available locally

- Department of Health guidance *No Secrets* (Department of Health 2000a) or National Assembly for Wales *In Safe Hands* (2000)

- a selection of relevant books/pamphlets.

EQUIPMENT NEEDED FOR EXERCISES

- TV/DVD/Video Combi (optional)

- Flipchart stand

- Flipchart paper

- Flipchart pens/markers

- Pads of A4 paper

- Pens

- Adhesive notes

- Blu Tack

- Adhesive tape

- Scissors

 © Jacki Pritchard 2007

USEFUL QUESTIONS FOR EXERCISES OR GROUP/INDIVIDUAL WORK

These questions can be used as and when needed by a trainer for different purposes.

- What concerns/worries you about this case?

- What is your initial reaction having read this case study?

- What thoughts are going through your mind at this very moment?

- How do you think you would react if you had to deal with this situation?

- How would you feel emotionally?

- What would you struggle with?

- What would you actually say if you were the worker in this situation? (Give the actual words.)

- What more do you want to know?

- Is this a case of abuse? If so, which category of abuse?

- If you were the worker in this case, would you alert your manager?

- Do you think an adult abuse investigation should take place?

- Are there any signs/indicators of abuse?

© Jacki Pritchard 2007

USEFUL QUESTIONS FOR EXERCISES OR GROUP/INDIVIDUAL WORK

- Could they be signs/indicators of other things? If so, what?

- What should happen next?

- What are the main difficulties in dealing with this case?

- What are the professional dilemmas?

- What would you do?

- If you were appointed investigating officer:

  (a) What other information would you like to have access to or gather yourself?

  (b) What questions would you want to ask the alleged victim?

- Before the investigation begins, are any special assessments needed? If so, in regard to what exactly?

- Should any action have been taken before this incident/situation was reached? If yes, what should have happened?

- What are the hazards and dangers in this case?

- What do you think is the level of risk in this case?

- What resources might be used in this case and written into a protection plan?

© Jacki Pritchard 2007

ADULT ABUSE: BASIC AWARENESS TRAINING
(1 day course – 6 training hours)

Trainer
Jacki Pritchard – independent trainer, consultant, researcher.
Author and editor of *Good Practice in Health, Social Care and Criminal Justice* series and *Violence and Abuse* series, both published by Jessica Kingsley Publishers.
Founder of Beyond Existing, Support Groups For Adults Who Have Been Abused.

Objectives
The aim of the course is to raise awareness about adult abuse, that is, to be clear that abuse of a vulnerable adult is an important issue which needs to be confronted by all workers. This course will help participants to:

→consider what constitutes abuse (both in the community and institutional settings)
→develop skills in recognising abuse
→know what to do when abuse is suspected/identified.

Participation
There have been many developments in working with adult abuse since 2000 with the introduction of *No Secrets*. Participants will be informed about national and local developments and practices. This course is timely as the new North Wales Policy is soon to be launched.

Please note
This is a very practice-based course so participants will be expected to engage in group discussion and practical exercises (to be carried out in pairs and small groups).

Abuse is a very emotive issue and some participants may find the subject matter difficult. Ground rules will be set to help participants feel safe.

Learning outcomes
By the end of the course participants will have:

→raised their awareness on the whole issue of adult abuse
→examined values and attitudes in regard to working with adult abuse
→a clear understanding of definitions and categories of abuse
→learnt about signs and symptoms of abuse
→become familiar with local policy and procedures
→a good working knowledge of what constitutes good practice.

Jacki Pritchard Ltd
Training & Consultancy in Social Care
© Jacki Pritchard Ltd: 2007

Tel: 0114 270 1782

Fax: 0114 270 6019

Email: jacki.pritchard@btconnect.com

Jacki Pritchard Ltd

Training & Consultancy in Social Care

Certificate of Attendance

This is to certify that

_____

attended a one-day training course

Adult Abuse: Basic Awareness
(6 training hours)

Held at

The Study Centre, Churchtown
on 20th March 2007

Learning outcomes

By the end of the course the participants will have:

➜ raised their awareness on the whole issue of adult abuse

➜ examined values and attitudes in regard to working with adult abuse

➜ a clear understanding of definitions and categories of abuse

➜ learnt about signs and symptoms of abuse

➜ become familiar with local policy and procedures

➜ a good working knowledge of what constitutes good practice.

Signed	Date

JACKI PRITCHARD BA (Hons) in Economics, MA in Applied Social
Studies CQSW CCETSW Practice Teaching Award

The Globe Business Centre, Penistone Road, Shefield S6 3AE
Tel: +44 (0) 114 270 1782 Fax: +44 (0) 114 270 6019 Mobile: 07850 045929
E-mail: jacki.pritchard@btconnect.com Web Site: www.jacki-pritchard.co.uk

Registered in England No: 4964456
VAT Registration Number: 738 0405 43

© Jacki Pritchard 2007

TERMS IN ADULT PROTECTION WORK

- Adult abuse
- Elder abuse
- Adult protection
- Safeguarding adults
- Vulnerable adult
- Victim
- Survivor
- Abuser
- Perpetrator
- Alerter
- Alert

- Referral
- Strategy meeting
- Investigation
- Investigating officer
- Supporter
- Intermediary
- Appropriate adult
- Risk assessment
- Public protection
- Case conference
- Protection plan

© Jacki Pritchard 2007

Chapter 2

History, Current Guidance and Principles

In any situation it is important to understand how we have reached somewhere and consider the lessons we have learnt along that journey. That is how I have always practised social work and I tend to adopt the same approach when I am delivering training. In any training course it is important for practitioners to know about national guidance and local policies which they should be following. I hear constantly groans from course participants when I bring this up followed by comments regarding 'lack of time' and 'too much paperwork'. I constantly talk about good practice and in order to achieve best practice workers have to keep up to date. Also, I am not into scaremongering but it is a sad fact that we are working in an age when everyone has to cover their own backs. Litigation is rife and workers need to be very careful about how they do their job and also to be able to explain under what statutes and guidance they are doing it.

I feel it is very important for all workers to be proactive in making sure they know what they should be doing and they need to seek out information. Obviously organisations and trainers have a responsibility to teach them and point them in the right direction to access what they need. Experience is a wonderful thing and there is nothing better than learning on the job but the bottom line is workers do need to read! Workers need to know about:

- national guidance
- national standards
- statutes
- local policy and procedures.

This chapter will give a very brief (and I do mean brief) historical overview of developments in adult abuse guidance and then consider which documents are relevant and important for workers now.

The importance of history

Some people are not interested in history and that is fair enough, but it is important that workers understand how we have progressed in the past 30 years and how the terminology has changed and continues to change. What still rages is the debate about the work we actually do and what it should be called. My own personal view is that abuse is abuse and no one should shy away from that fact. Abuse is a horrible subject to have to think about, but the reality is that both children and adults suffer abuse in our society. We should not be using 'softer' terms just to make people feel more comfortable about it.

It has to be acknowledged that abuse is not a new phenomenon developed in the twentieth century. Abuse has been inflicted on human beings for thousands of years! Handouts 2.1 and 2.2 can be used as triggers for discussion and also are a good starting point for any course. Handout 2.1 summarises terms we have used in adult abuse work since the 1970s:

- granny bashing/battering
- old age abuse
- elder abuse
- mistreatment and neglect
- adult abuse
- adult protection
- protection of vulnerable adults (POVA)
- safeguarding adults.

 Handout 2.1, p.38

Handout 2.2 gives a list of documents/guidance with which workers should become familiar:

- *No Longer Afraid* (Department of Health 1993)
- *Action for Justice* (Home Office 1999; revised in 2002)
- *No Secrets* (Department of Health 2000a) or *In Safe Hands* (National Assembly for Wales 2000)
- *Achieving Best Evidence in Criminal Proceedings* (Home Office 2002)
- *Protection of Vulnerable Adults Scheme in England* (Department of Health 2004; revised in 2006) – Department of Health 2006b
- *Safeguarding Adults* (ADSS 2005)
- local multi-agency abuse policy and procedures (current).

 Handout 2.2, p.39

Recent history

It is a sad fact that society has taken a very long time to recognise that all sorts of people are victims of abuse and violence. People failed to be aware for years that both child abuse and domestic violence were rife in our society. Adult abuse has faced the same lack of recognition. People have got excited in recent years that things are moving on, especially since the year 2000. In 2005 people were pleased that BBC Television put on the drama *Dad* as part of the Comic Relief Campaign. I personally felt less enthused about this because I believe such a drama could and should have been made 30 years ago, the reason being that the abuse of older people was being highlighted by two geriatricians in the 1970s (Baker 1975; Burston 1975 and 1977). It was at this time that the terms 'granny battering' and 'granny bashing' were being used. So why has it taken us so long to move on? Part of it is probably because adults are just not seen to be as emotive as babies and children. Society thinks that adults can fend for themselves and children cannot.

In February 2006 the Department of Health, in conjunction with Comic Relief, did launch a major study:

> The £600,000 project aims to highlight the extent of elder abuse and neglect in both private households and sheltered housing, and establish what can be done to prevent it. The project is the result of a Health Select Committee report that called for more research into the issue... Two of the UK's leading research institutions, the National Centre for Social Research and the Institute of Gerontology at King's College London, have been commissioned to carry out the nationwide study... Speaking on the launch of the project, Care Services Minister Liam Byrne said, 'All abuse of vulnerable people is unacceptable. I am determined to ensure that all our older people are treated safely, effectively and with respect for their dignity.' (Department of Health 2006a)

So we are moving on slowly but surely. But when did workers first get any guidance?

Elder abuse policies and procedures

Even though the geriatricians were highlighting the fact that older people were being abused by their carers in the 1970s there was no guidance on how to deal with this issue. In 1987 Kent County Council was the first authority to produce guidance for practitioners regarding elder abuse. Some other authorities followed suit, but many social services departments kept guidance in draft form, so the guidance never became policies and workers were unsure about whether they should be implementing it. In 1991, out of 115 social services departments in England and Wales, 11 had published guidelines, 26 had draft guidelines and 12 had working parties (Hildrew 1991). This lack of direction continued until well into the late 1990s.

Department of Health research and guidance

The Department of Health was active in looking at elder abuse in the early 1990s. The Social Services Inspectorate undertook research in two London boroughs during 1990 in order to consider how social services departments managed cases of elder abuse in domestic settings. The findings were presented in a report, *Confronting Elder Abuse*, which suggested 'ways in which practice might be improved, principally through clearer policies and guidelines' (Department of

Health 1992, p.i). As a result of that research, practice guidelines were produced in the following year, entitled *No Longer Afraid: The Safeguard of Older People in Domestic Settings* (Department of Health 1993). The definition of 'elder abuse' was set broadly enough to include neglect and sexual abuse, neither of which had been given much attention previously because of the assumption of their low incidence: 'Abuse may be described as physical, sexual, psychological, or financial. It may be intentional or unintentional, or the result of neglect. It causes harm to the older person, either temporarily or over a period of time' (Department of Health 1993, p.3).

It took another seven years before the turning point really came in March 2000 when the Department of Health produced *No Secrets* (Department of Health 2000a) and in Wales the National Assembly for Wales published *In Safe Hands* (National Assembly for Wales 2000). In March 2000, *No Secrets: Guidance on Developing and Implementing Multi-Agency Policies and Procedures to Protect Vulnerable Adults from Abuse* (Department of Health 2000a) was launched by the Minister of Health, John Hutton, at a national conference organised jointly by Action on Elder Abuse, UK Voice and the Ann Craft Trust.

People often say that we are not effective in dealing with adult abuse because it is not statutory work. Workers should be reminded that *No Secrets* was introduced under Section 7 of the Local Authority and Social Services Act 1970 which means that social services departments are required to act under the general guidance of the Secretary of State. At the time of the launch a circular issued from the Department of Health stated: 'Directors of Social Services will be expected to ensure that the local multi-agency codes of practice are developed and implemented by 31st October 2001' (Department of Health 2000b, p.2). Not every authority did meet the deadline. It is also necessary to point out that working with abuse is not only about paperwork. Obviously it is vital to have policies and procedures in place, but organisations have to provide comprehensive training in order to implement the policies effectively. Unlike the implementation of the Children Act 1989, there has been no direct funding from the government for the development of training. Organisations have to find funding from their own budgets and many apply for grants to train their staff. If we are to work with adult abuse effectively there are huge cost implications.

In July 2004 the Protection of Vulnerable Adults (POVA) Scheme was launched and many people now talk about the POVA list. The term 'POVA' is also used to refer to abuse policies. Stephen Ladyman said in his Foreword that the scheme:

> will act as a workforce ban on those professionals who have harmed vulnerable adults in their care. It will add an extra layer of protection to the pre-employment processes, including Criminal Records Bureau checks... Along with initiatives such as 'No Secrets' and 'In Safe Hands' and other specific measures to prevent and tackle adult abuse, it will complement the Government's drive to raise standards across health and social care. (Department of Health 2006b, p.4)

After the scheme had been in place exactly one year there had been 2124 referrals (approximately 175 per month), 155 people had been permanently barred from working with vulnerable adults in the future and 559 people were provisionally on the list pending clarification of their cases. (Department of Health 2005).

Home Office guidance

The Home Office does liaise with the Department of Health and much guidance is produced jointly. Back in the 1990s a working party was set up to look at how a vulnerable adult could be helped through the criminal justice system; that is, how he or she could be a good witness. A report was produced by the Home Office in 1998 called *Speaking Up for Justice* which made 78 recommendations to the government. These were duly accepted and an implementation programme, *Action for Justice*, was launched (Home Office 1999). It was revised in 2002 at the time the critical guidance *Achieving Best Evidence in Criminal Proceedings* was launched (Home Office 2002). This guidance is discussed in full in Chapter 6. The important message is that no one should have the attitude that a vulnerable adult is not going to be a credible witness and that therefore it is pointless trying to get evidence. If someone does have communication difficulties then professionals have to try to get the *best evidence* they can.

Safeguarding adults

In many areas people are now using the term 'safeguarding adults' rather than 'adult protection work'. Some Adult Protection Committees have become Safeguarding Adults Boards. Consequently, there has been a lot of confusion about what is the correct term to use. Let us not get too hung up on this but let us also be clear. The document *Safeguarding Adults*, which was launched in October 2005 at the Association of Directors of Social Services (ADSS) Annual Conference, is a national framework of standards for good practice and outcomes in adult protection work (ADSS 2005). It was the result of work and consultation carried out by the Safeguarding Adults Network which was ADSS led. It is an extremely useful tool, but it needs to be stressed that it does *not* replace *No Secrets*. In the section on context and definition it is said:

> Since 'No Secrets' was published, there have been some significant legal and policy changes relating to adult social and health care, together with a refocusing of its language and philosophy...the emphasis is now on supporting adults to access services of their own choosing, rather than 'stepping in' to provide protection...in recognition of the changing context, previous references to the protection of '*vulnerable adults*' and '*adult protection*' work are now replaced by the new term: '**Safeguarding Adults**'. (ADSS 2005, p.5)

At the time of writing this manual, several Adult Protection Committees have taken the decision *not* to adopt this terminology, while acknowledging the framework itself is useful. My own view is we should not get too entrenched in debating about jargon (because that is what it is); the important thing is *how* we work together to offer help to any adult who is being abused.

Protection of Vulnerable Adults (POVA) Scheme

It is important to say something at this point about the Protection of Vulnerable Adults Scheme which was launched on the 26 July 2004. It took a long time for people to realise just how many abusers deliberately went to work in places which gave them easy access to vulnerable people (this applies to both children and adults). For many years workers in the adult sector (residential/day care workers, home carers etc.) never underwent police checks. Within the Care Standards Act

2000 provision was made for a scheme to be set up which allows for workers to undergo checks for criminal records via the Criminal Records Bureau (CRB). This scheme eventually came into being in 2004 and is known as the POVA Scheme; and people tend to refer to 'the POVA list'.

The scheme is a way of safeguarding adults. People do fall through the net, but one hopes that by doing CRB checks the risk of an offender working with a vulnerable adult will be reduced. Some workers who have not got a criminal record will abuse adults and if this is proven then they will be put on the list and banned from working with a vulnerable adult again. However, there are loopholes. The scheme applies to adult placement, schemes, domiciliary care agencies and care homes; there will be workers who fall outside its remit. Another problem is getting enough evidence to prove that a worker has harmed a vulnerable adult.

The guidance states clearly the position of the scheme in relation to other guidance mentioned above:

> Local councils and partner agencies are reminded that their local multi-agency policies and procedures to protect vulnerable adults from abuse based on 'No Secrets' and 'In Safe Hands' should continue to provide the bedrock of local approaches to adult abuse. The POVA scheme, in both this context and the context of rigorous pre-employment checks including CRB Disclosures, significantly adds to the means by which local councils and other providers of care can protect vulnerable adults from harm. While councils and other stakeholders should ensure that they comply with the requirements of the POVA scheme, they should not lessen their efforts, through local codes based on 'No Secrets' and 'In Safe Hands', to prevent and tackle abuse. (Department of Health 2006b, p.9)

The law

One of my major hobby horses that I go on about nearly every day of my working life is that workers in health and social care just are not trained enough on the law. I think workers within mental health are at some advantage in that they seem to be offered more courses related to the law, but other specialisms rarely get half or full days' training on legal issues. It is imperative to provide this as there are so many new bits of legislation being introduced which are key to promoting good practice. It also goes back to the point made before that workers need to be wary of litigation and therefore must know what statutes and guidance they are functioning under (e.g. NHS and Community Care Act 1990; Mental Health Act 1983; Care Standards Act 2000).

It would be impossible to list here every statute that might be relevant to adult abuse work and explain their implications. People who work with vulnerable adults need to have some understanding of the criminal justice system and what constitutes a criminal offence; that is, which abusive acts constitute a criminal offence and what an abuser can be charged with. Lawyers and the police can offer really good training days on this.

As well as thinking about crime, workers must also have knowledge of the law in regard to key issues like capacity and consent (Mental Capacity Act 2005) and sharing of information (e.g. Data Protection Act 1998; Freedom of Information Act 2000). Key statutes and guidance will be mentioned in each chapter of this manual and listed in the references at the end.

Principles underpinning adult protection work

It is important to give some consideration to the principles which underpin adult protection work because many dilemmas can arise for workers when undertaking an adult abuse investigation. Adult protection work is very different to child protection because there is no equivalent to the Children Act 1989. An assumption which is made is that an adult can make decisions about how to live his or her life. Obviously, some vulnerable adults will lack capacity but that has to be proven. Adults can live their life as they wish as long as it is not going to harm anyone else (that is, it is not a public protection issue). So risk assessment is an ongoing consideration and task for all workers.

Workers have to become familiar with the Human Rights Act 1998 because this underpins all actions. A human being has the right to live their life as they wish and this will include an element of risk-taking. If workers have not been trained on the Human Rights Act the Home Office have produced two very useful study guides (2001a and 2001b).

Most vulnerable adult/adult abuse policies will make statements about the principles underpinning adult protection work; these can be written and discussed under different headings, which are often linked. Very broadly the fundamental principles are:

- equal opportunities
- human rights
- service-user focus
- self-determination
- independence
- choice
- confidentiality
- legal responsibilities
- shared information, accountability and decision-making
- staff support and training.

 Handout 2.3, p.40

Equal opportunities

All adults should be treated equally. Just because someone is deemed to be vulnerable does not mean they should be treated any differently. Sometimes allegations from vulnerable adults are not taken seriously because they are thought to be 'unreliable', 'a storyteller'.

Case Example

Joyce was 77 years old and had Alzheimer's disease. She lived in a care home. She regularly told care workers a man came into her room at night and had intercourse with her. No one believed her and no action was taken. A year later another service user disclosed a male service user, John, had tried to rape her. An investigation did take place and it was found that John had been sexually abusing Joyce and two other service users for a long time.

When an investigation does take place, the investigating officers must be sensitive to differences which may exist (due to age, gender, race, religion, culture, disability, sexuality) and provide appropriate help and services when necessary.

Human rights

Every vulnerable adult has the right to live their life as they wish. They have the right to live their life free from fear, violence, abuse and neglect. They also have the right to be protected from harm and exploitation.

Service-user focus

The service user who may be a victim or perpetrator of abuse must be the primary focus of any investigation or intervention under the vulnerable adult/adult abuse policy. Workers should not get side-tracked or lost on focusing solely on other people's needs (e.g. family members – although obviously these must be considered). Workers must strive to provide facilities so that victims can explain what has happened to them and give their best evidence in order that they can be protected from harm in the future. In cases where vulnerable adults are abusers similarly help must be provided.

Self-determination

Many victims choose to remain in an abusive situation for all sorts of reasons. A very common reason is that they have strong feelings for the abuser – especially if the abuser is a partner, family member, and so on. Workers often find it difficult when a person decides to remain with the abuser because there can be an overriding feeling of wanting to protect a vulnerable person. However, workers have to remind themselves that they must not get into the 'rescuing' syndrome. Action must be taken if another person is likely to be harmed. Public protection is a key consideration.

Case Example

Linda had learning disabilities. She had married Jake when she was 20 years old and absolutely adored him. However, Jake physically and emotionally abused Linda and their baby daughter, Kylie, on a regular basis. Linda had received help from workers after the birth of Kylie. Linda talked about the violence she experienced but was clear she wanted to stay with Jake. The workers had to report the abuse both to the learning disabilities team and also to the children and families team.

Sometimes cases are complex because there are doubts surrounding the victim's mental capacity and ability to make informed decisions. In these circumstances, proper assessments of mental capacity must be undertaken.

Independence

Any intervention or support should always consider how to best promote a vulnerable adult's independence.

Choice

Victims should be offered choices. Unfortunately, many of them do not know what help is available to them and feel that they have to remain where they are. Workers are often under enormous work pressures so they may not spend enough time explaining options. In the world in which we work now, we tend to do crisis intervention rather than preventative work. Workers undertaking an abuse investigation will feel under pressure to get the investigation done and present the findings to a case conference. Obviously, it is important to find out whether abuse has happened but it is equally important to focus on the long-term work.

Case Example

Nettie had been abused by her husband for 50 years. When she was 75 years old home care services were put in to help Nettie and her husband. The home carers picked up very quickly that Nettie was being physically abused regularly. An investigation was started. The social worker spent a considerable amount of time talking to Nettie about the abuse she had experienced and offered her a place of safety, which she refused. However, Nettie started attending a group for adults who had been abused and after a year she decided to leave her husband. She went to live in sheltered accommodation.

Confidentiality

Workers should always discuss confidentiality at the beginning of their involvement with a service user. It needs to be made very clear that any information given to a worker belongs to the agency they work for, not to the individual worker. Workers sometimes do not give sufficient explanation regarding the fact that there will be particular circumstances in which confidentiality has to be broken and information shared (e.g. someone is at risk of harm; it is a public protection issue; a crime has been committed).

Legal responsibilities

All workers have to function within a legal framework; they will have statutory responsibilities under different bits of legislation (e.g. NHS and Community Care Act 1990; Mental Health Act 1983). Most policies state clearly that if a crime has been committed then the police must be informed.

Shared information, accountability and decision-making

The Department of Health guidance *No Secrets* stresses the importance of working together and of joint investigations. In order to achieve this agencies will have to share information and this should be done under local sharing information protocols. Workers are accountable to their managers and employers; no worker should be making decisions in isolation – a point which leads to the following principle regarding support and training.

Staff support and training

All organisations should be committed to supporting and training their workers. Once a policy has been developed, training should be provided in order to launch and implement it successfully. Workers need to be aware of what they should do in certain situations (e.g. how to report abuse) and what will happen afterwards (what the investigation process involves). It needs to be made very clear to workers exactly what their roles and responsibilities are in adult protection work. They also need to be confident that they will receive support from managers and colleagues within their own organisation when working with abuse cases. It must be acknowledged that adult protection work can be just as demanding and stressful as child protection work.

Suggested reading

Workers should become familiar with *all* the guidance mentioned in this chapter.

KEY TERMS USED NOW AND IN THE PAST

- Granny bashing/battering

- Old age abuse

- Elder abuse

- Mistreatment and neglect

- Adult abuse

- Adult protection

- Protection of vulnerable adults (POVA)

- Safeguarding adults

 © Jacki Pritchard 2007

KEY DOCUMENTS

- *No Longer Afraid* (Department of Health 1993)

- *Action for Justice* (Home Office 1999; revised in 2002)

- *No Secrets* (Department of Health 2000) or *In Safe Hands* (National Assembly for Wales 2000)

- *Achieving Best Evidence in Criminal Proceedings* (Home Office 2002)

- *Protection of Vulnerable Adults Scheme in England* (Department of Health 2004; revised in 2006)

- *Safeguarding Adults* (ADSS 2005)

- *Local multi-agency abuse policy and procedures* (current)

© Jacki Pritchard 2007

PRINCIPLES UNDERPINNING ADULT PROTECTION WORK

- Equal opportunities

- Human rights

- Service-user focus

- Self-determination

- Independence

- Choice

- Confidentiality

- Legal responsibilities

- Shared information, accountability and decision-making

- Staff support and training

 © Jacki Pritchard 2007

Chapter 3

What is Adult Abuse?

We have to begin by thinking about what constitutes abuse. It is vital in any training session that the trainer encourages participants to talk about their own perceptions and attitudes towards the subject of abuse. By the end of the session participants should be clear about national and local definitions. Before more attention is given to the definitions of abuse, it is necessary to think about the term *vulnerable adult*.

Who is a vulnerable adult?

It has already been said that it is important for a worker to become familiar with certain terms in the field of adult protection. The term 'vulnerable adult' is one such term and is used frequently in relation to this subject area.

> ## KEY QUESTION
>
> Who do you think could be a vulnerable adult?

Many years ago the Association of Directors of Social Services (ADSS) defined a vulnerable adult in terms of service user groups:

1. the elderly and very frail
2. those who suffer from mental illness including dementia
3. those who have a sensory or physical disability
4. those who have a learning disability
5. those who suffer from severe physical illness.

(ADSS 1991)

However, the current definition which should be used is quoted in *No Secrets*; it is a person:

> who is or may be in need of community care services by reason of mental or other disability, age or illness; and who is or may be unable to take care of him or herself, or unable to protect him or herself against significant harm or exploitation. (Lord Chancellor's Department 1997, p.68)

 Handout 3.1, p.73

Although organisations may screen referrals regarding abuse in order to clarify whether someone is a vulnerable adult, it is important to remember that *all* human beings can become vulnerable at different points in their life. Workers can also be vulnerable and the abuse of workers is a subject area which should not be ignored. Exercises 3.1 and 3.2 will help participants think about what 'vulnerability' means.

 Exercise 3.1, p.64, and Handout 3.1, p.73

Exercise 3.2, p.65, and Handout 3.2, p.74

KEY QUESTIONS

Do you know any vulnerable adults in your personal life?

Do you work with any vulnerable adults?

What makes these people vulnerable?

Definitions of abuse

Workers do not want to get bogged down with too much theory on a basic awareness course – especially if the training they are receiving is time-limited. Participants on a training course often feel that there is too much information to take in about a very complex subject. Therefore it is important to keep to the key points. However, a worker must realise that having knowledge about the definitions and categories of abuse is imperative as any written records must relate to the definitions stated in local policies and procedures.

KEY QUESTIONS

What does the word 'abuse' mean to you?

Can you think of three things which you think
might be abusive behaviour?

Sometimes giving a little bit of history can be helpful in explaining how definitions have come into being and illustrates how we are moving on – slowly but surely – in recognising that adult abuse is a very important subject. Back in the 1980s, there were just three main categories of abuse –

physical, emotional and *financial* – and most people quoted Eastman's definition of *old age abuse*: 'The systematic maltreatment, physical, emotional, or financial, of an elderly person…this may take the form of physical assault, threatening behaviour, neglect and abandonment or sexual assault' (Eastman 1984, p.3).

In 1993, the Department of Health broadened the definition to include two more categories – *neglect* and *sexual*: 'Abuse may be described as physical, sexual, psychological, or financial. It may be intentional or unintentional, or the result of neglect. It causes harm to the older person, either temporarily or over a period of time' (Department of Health 1993, p.3). This definition moved us on in the sense that it acknowledged the fact that some abuse can be inflicted unintentionally; that is, a person can do something which is abusive but this is because of lack of knowledge, understanding, education or training. However, the important point is that even if the behaviour/act is unintentional it cannot be ignored – it has to be investigated. Another point which needs to be stressed about this useful definition is that it acknowledges by using the word 'temporarily' that abuse does not have to be 'systematic' as defined by Eastman; it can be a one-off incident.

So by the early 1990s there were five categories of abuse and much of the literature was focusing on older people. It was after 1993 that greater emphasis was placed on vulnerable adults; that is, anyone over the age of 18. It took another seven years before the important guidance *No Secrets* (Department of Health 2000a) was implemented. There are two key definitions of abuse in the guidance. The shorter definition states that abuse is: 'a violation of an individual's human and civil rights by any other person or persons' (Department of Health 2000a, p.9). The longer definition is the one all workers should become very familiar with – especially when suspecting abuse is happening or when witnessing an incident:

> Abuse may consist of a single act or repeated acts. It may be physical, verbal or psychological, it may be an act of neglect or an omission to act, or it may occur when a vulnerable person is persuaded to enter into a financial or sexual transaction to which he or she has not consented, or cannot consent. Abuse can occur in any relationship and may result in significant harm to, or exploitation of, the person subjected to it. (Department of Health 2000a, p.9)

 Handout 3.3, p.75

Again this definition recognises that behaviour/acts do not have to be recurring before we define them as abuse. Handout 3.4 summarises the key definitions of abuse which have been used over time and can be useful to stimulate discussion during a training course or in a supervision session.

 Handout 3.4, p.76

The other important development is the recognition that abuse can happen in 'any relationship'. Much of the previous literature has emphasised that adults are abused by someone they know; for example, a relative, friend, neighbour. Much has also been written about carers' stress; the typical scenario being that the victim is a dependent person causing stress for the carer. What has never been given enough attention is the fact that some vulnerable adults are deliberately targeted and groomed by strangers. *No Secrets* states:

Stranger abuse will warrant a different kind of response from that appropriate to abuse in an ongoing relationship or in a care location. Nevertheless, in some instances it may be appropriate to use the locally agreed inter-agency adult protection procedures to ensure that the vulnerable person receives the services and support that they need. Such procedures may also be used when there is potential for harm to other vulnerable people. (Department of Health 2000a, p.11)

 Handout 3.5, p.77

But it is not just vulnerable people who may be harmed. In adult protection work, a key consideration is *public protection*. Other people (in addition to the vulnerable adult) could be at risk of harm – service users, workers, members of the public. Thought also must be given to the risk of harm to property (see Chapter 8 for full discussion of risk assessment). This leads us to think about the word 'harm'.

KEY QUESTION

How can adults be harmed?

In adult protection work we should be using the term *significant harm*, but measuring harm can be extremely difficult. So a starting point for workers has to be defining what harm in general means. Exercise 3.3 will facilitate this.

 Exercise 3.3, p.66, and Handout 3.6, p.78

Prior to the advent of *No Secrets* people tended to think in terms of physical and emotional harm, but harm can encompass many different aspects of a person's life. Consequently, the term 'significant harm' is being used in adult protection work and is defined as:

> not only ill treatment (including sexual abuse and forms of ill treatment which are not physical), but also the impairment of, or an avoidable deterioration in, physical or mental health; and the impairment of physical, intellectual, emotional, social or behavioural development. (Lord Chancellor's Department 1997, p.68)

 Handout 3.6, p.78

Words are often interchangeable. It can be very useful to have exercises in a training course which focus participants on the meaning of words, so that they use terms correctly in their working practices. Some people shy away from using the word 'abuse' because it is a strong word, which conjures up all sorts of images. I personally feel that abuse is abuse and we should not cover it up by using any other terms. However, other words or phrases can describe abusive acts. The purpose of Exercise 3.4 is to get participants to think about when they or a service user may have been taken advantage of, mistreated or abused. This exercise will prepare participants to go on to think about the categories of abuse.

 Exercise 3.4, p.67

A trainer needs to give a lot of thought to how he or she is going to address this with participants. No matter what job workers might be doing, they need to be absolutely clear about what constitutes abuse and they cannot shy away from the horrors of abuse. There will always be 'grey' areas, but it is vital that workers become familiar with how the categories are defined in their local policy. What workers learn on a training course needs to be very closely linked to the definitions in the local multi-agency policy and procedure on abuse. By the end of any training session workers should be very familiar with the categories of abuse. They need to have explored all forms of abuse so that if they witness an incident or suspect that abuse is going on, they can produce a written record which links closely to the local policy.

Categories

It is good for workers to be given time for their own thoughts before they are bombarded with information about the various categories of abuse.

> ### KEY QUESTIONS
>
> How many categories of abuse do you think there are?
>
> What might the categories be?

Exercises 3.5 and 3.6 can be used to help workers put forms of abuse into categories and to get into some discussion about whether certain behaviours/actions are abusive.

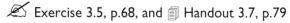 Exercise 3.5, p.68, and Handout 3.7, p.79

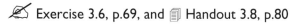 Exercise 3.6, p.69, and Handout 3.8, p.80

Through considering the categories of abuse, a worker should become more aware of what constitutes abuse. Some agencies and organisations may put emphasis on particular types of abuse by highlighting them as a separate category within their policy – for example chemical or medication abuse. However, the main categories as defined in *No Secrets* are:

- physical
- sexual
- emotional/psychological
- financial/material
- neglect/acts of omission
- discriminatory.

(Department of Health 2000a, p.9)

 Handouts 3.9 and 3.10, pp.81–82

It is important to get workers to think creatively around the subject of categories of abuse and it is helpful if the trainer can give some real case examples as well as encouraging participants to give their own practice examples; some case examples will be given below which can be used by a trainer.

It is wrong to compare types of abuse, saying something is only minor compared to more serious forms of abuse. The starting point should always be the question 'How does the victim feel about this?' *All* forms of abuse have to be taken seriously; no form of abuse is acceptable.

Physical abuse

Physical abuse can be inflicted in many different ways and does not always result in injuries. People tend to think of physical violence involving the use of hands, feet or implements in actions like kicking, slapping, punching, pushing, pinching, scratching or hair pulling. These actions could be deemed to be forms of assault, but there are other actions which could also be assault – force-feeding or restraining someone.

Case Examples

- Andrea has learning disabilities and when she was admitted to hospital she needed help with eating her meals. She said she did not like vegetables. A nurse put carrots into Andrea's mouth; when she spat them out the nurse put them into her mouth again.

- Ethel has dementia and does not like anyone helping her with personal care tasks. One care worker held Ethel's arms while another worker brushed her teeth.

There are different forms of medication abuse and sometimes there is a close link with financial abuse. A person can be over-medicated because the abuser wants to calm him or her down to be 'more manageable'. However, victims can be drugged up to the point where they are very drowsy but they can still sign documents or make their mark on a blank cheque or at the bottom of a letter to a bank or building society. A good example of premeditated abuse is medication being withdrawn in order to cause a crisis; that is, the victim ends up in hospital (and hence is out of the way – the 'problem' has been removed).

Some vulnerable adults may refuse to take medication and workers should not make a decision to hide it in food or drink or force its administration. This is where it is vital to undertake proper risk assessments and take advice from a medical practitioner on how to administer medication. In cases where the adult has mental capacity, dilemmas arise about making choices. Finally, it is an abuse if medication is not reviewed regularly.

Case Examples

- A manager in a supported accommodation project asked a GP if two service users could be prescribed largactyl to quiet them down because they were always fighting with each other. She said it would help the staff.

- Terry gave his aunt too much medication so that she was drowsy most of the day. When she was almost asleep he would get her to sign blank cheques and then he paid them into his own bank account.

- Harry is in his early fifties and has suffered with depression for many years, but has not seen his GP for over a year. Harry's wife rings the surgery for repeat prescriptions every two months. Harry takes anti-depressants and sleeping tablets.

Many forms of abuse can fall under two or more categories; malnutrition and dehydration are good examples. They could be the result of physical abuse but also neglect. Again there can be a close link with financial abuse. Sometimes people have a poor diet because their money is going elsewhere.

Case Examples

- Barbara is physically disabled. Her daughter, Val, visits every day and is the primary carer; she insists on managing everything in Barbara's life. This includes her finances, doing the shopping, arranging meals and so on. When Barbara complains that she is not getting enough to eat, Val says that she must eat healthily by just having one meal at midday and limiting her intake of tea and coffee.

- Service users in a care home became dehydrated one summer when there was a hot spell because they were only allowed drinks at certain times of the day.

Bullying is something people tend to associate with children, but adults can be bullied in exactly the same way – especially vulnerable adults. Bullying is a form of abuse which can fall into the physical category but also the emotional category.

Case Examples

- Three service users in a day centre made another service user, Maxine, who is African Caribbean, do things for them; for example, steal from other service users and staff.

- A home care manager was always telling one of her workers that she was 'useless'. Every week she queried her time sheet and accused her of not doing her job properly.

To summarise, physical abuse can be:

- the use of hands and feet to, for example, kick, slap, punch, push, pinch, scratch or pull hair

- using an implement; throwing things

- inappropriate/rough handling

- assaults

- force feeding

- restraint

- medication
    - over-medicating
    - withdrawing medication
    - hiding medication
    - administering another person's medication
    - not reviewing medication regularly

- malnutrition/dehydration

- bullying.

 Handout 3.11, p.83

Sexual abuse

When the word 'abuse' is used people tend to think in terms of physical and sexual violence. Workers can often feel very uncomfortable talking about sexual abuse, but they need to be clear what it might involve and be able to respond appropriately if a victim discloses to them what has been done to them. Workers can feel very embarrassed when having to think about what acts might be involved.

Sexual abuse is not just about full-blown sexual intercourse. Many things can be done to a victim which would be deemed to be sexual abuse. The crucial point is whether the victim has consented to the act. A key dilemma for many workers is knowing whether the vulnerable adult has the capacity to consent.

Again it is important to remember that one should not compare different types of abuse. For example, talking in a sexualised manner should not be seen as 'trivial' or 'minor' compared to rape. Sexual abuse can involve touching or penetration.

Case Examples

- Eddie told his key worker that he found it embarrassing when another male worker talked about his sex life to him.

- Chloe was sexually abused when she was a child and now has mental health problems. She does not like it when some nurses in the hospital are tactile towards her.

- Paul and Katy have learning disabilities and both attend a day centre. Paul used to regularly touch Katy's breasts, then one day he put his finger in her vagina. When he did this Katy told one of the day care workers Paul had 'hurt' her.

An abuser can force a victim to do things and then enjoy watching the activity (for example, masturbation or having sex with someone else), which is called *voyeurism*. Alternatively, the victim can be forced to look at or watch things. Vulnerable adults can be exploited sexually in all sorts of ways; for example, being forced into prostitution.

Case Examples

- Mr Hughes made his wife watch pornographic videos before they had sex. If she refused to watch he abused her physically.

- A support worker finds a colleague showing his penis to a group of female service users who have profound learning disabilities.

Then there are the forms of sexual abuse which have caused a great deal of discussion and debate over the years – satanic and ritual abuse. Workers should keep an open mind and read around some of the literature which has been written on this subject (Sinason 1994). All allegations of abuse have to be taken seriously. None of us like to think about horrible things but again workers need to be aware of the fact that bestiality (sexual intercourse with animals) does happen.

To summarise, sexual abuse can be:

- forcing someone into sexual activity without his or her consent
- sexualised language/conversation
- sexual harassment
- inappropriate touching
- kissing
- fondling
- exposure
- voyeurism

- masturbation
- inflicting pornography on someone
- indecent assault
- penetrating someone's mouth/anus/vagina (with finger, penis or other object)
- rape
- exploitation/prostitution
- satanic/ritual abuse
- bestiality.

 Handout 3.12, p.84

Emotional/psychological abuse

It could be argued that anyone who is abused is likely to be emotionally harmed because of what they have experienced. However, it is important to consider what emotional abuse might involve. It is not uncommon for women who have been victims of domestic violence to say that the emotional abuse was worse than the physical abuse. Emotional abuse is often carried out in very subtle ways, so it is extremely hard to identify and quantify. The abuser will often play on the victim's vulnerability, knowing how to humiliate, ridicule, intimidate, degrade.

Case Examples

- Mrs Brown had been a victim of domestic violence all through her marriage. After her husband had a stroke and was physically disabled, Mrs Brown emotionally abused Mr Brown by making fun of her husband's condition: 'You used to think you were the strong man. Look at you now. You can't do anything for yourself. You're a weakling.'

- Service user to another service user: 'Who's a scaredy cat then? You have to sleep with the light on.'

A common trait is for abusers to threaten their victims. Some of the threats may be very bizarre but a vulnerable adult may truly believe the threat will be carried out and therefore will not disclose to anyone. We also need to consider emotional blackmail. Some people argue that 'blackmail' is a word which is not politically correct; however, blackmail for financial gain is an offence. A vulnerable adult may be very lonely and may depend on someone or a group of people for company; they would rather put up with abuse rather than losing the company of the abuser(s).

Case Example

Ella was in her seventies and had been a widow for many years; she had never had any children. When her husband died she had started to drink heavily and eventually her close friends stopped visiting her. She met three boys in the off-licence one evening and they came back to her house. From then on they started to visit her most evenings. She enjoyed their company and missed them if they did not visit. When she complained she had not seen them they said they would only visit if she bought them alcohol and gave them money.

Stranger abuse was mentioned before and it is important to think about how strangers can harass vulnerable adults, who live alone or where vulnerable adults live together (e.g. in supported or sheltered accommodation). The Protection from Harassment Act 1997 is a very useful bit of legislation which can be used to address this form of abuse. Verbal abuse can involve making inappropriate comments, shouting, swearing or misusing names (e.g. name calling, using nicknames, using the wrong name).

Case Examples

- Harriet's garden backs onto a small patch of waste land, where a gang of teenagers play after school every day. They continuously kick the football against the garden fence. Harriet has mental health problems and cannot stand repetitive noise. She asks the boys to play football elsewhere and gets very agitated when they refuse. The boys laugh at Harriet and torment her even more when she gets angry and upset.

- Mrs Pampo is an African Caribbean woman in her nineties. She is admitted to hospital with pneumonia. On admission the nurses call her Eleanora. Mrs Pampo says she wants to be called Mrs Pampo.

- A Muslim man was offended when a worker confused his family and religious names.

Every person has human rights and workers do need to have some basic knowledge about the Human Rights Act 1998; some useful study guides were originally produced by the Home Office (Home Office 2001a and 2001b), but updated study guides are now available on the internet. If a person is denied his or her rights it could be argued that he or she is being emotionally abused or neglected. Sometimes an adult wants to do things which may be deemed to be 'too risky' by others. Carers, for example, can be over-protective – not allowing someone to make their own choices about how they live their life. Also, every adult should be treated equally, and again if they are denied access to services then they may be emotionally abused, but this may also be discriminatory abuse which will be discussed below.

Isolation can be a form of emotional abuse but, depending on the circumstances, could also be physical abuse or neglect. Adults can be physically locked away in confined areas (that is, imprisoned). Very simple actions can cause emotional abuse to someone, and ignoring someone or not including him or her in activities can cause emotional hurt and harm. Some adults are abandoned when friends or family no longer wish to help them. The Case Examples illustrate both the extreme and the more subtle forms of this type of abuse.

 Case Examples

- Jenny likes to go to the toilet a lot and the care staff get fed up having to take her. So they respond by saying to Jenny: 'I'll be back in a minute', but they do not come back.

- All the service users in the house go shopping on a Friday afternoon for the weekend. The support worker tells Ellie she can never go because she is 'too slow and holds everyone up'.

- Mrs Collins was kept in her bedroom for 25 years. Her son had told everyone she was dead.

To summarise, emotional/psychological abuse can be:

- humiliation

- intimidation

- ridicule

- verbal abuse – shouting, swearing, misuse of names, name calling, using nicknames

- harassment

- threats
- causing fear/anxiety/mental anguish
- emotional blackmail
- being over-protective
- withholding social contact
- isolation
- imprisonment

- bullying
- denial of human rights
- denying access to services
- ignoring
- excluding
- abandoning.

 Handout 3.13, p.85

Financial/material abuse

Financial abuse is probably the most common form of adult abuse, because it is just so easy to take advantage of someone who has to rely on someone else to help them with their finances or because they do not understand about financial matters. Financial abuse is basically the mismanagement of money/assets. Many difficult cases present themselves when family members manage a vulnerable adult's finances but will not purchase things they want or will not let them spend money on things they would like to do.

Financial abuse includes theft and fraud, but in reality there are just so many different ways to financially abuse someone. Abusers can persuade a vulnerable adult to put bank or building society accounts into joint names or to obtain a cash or credit card and then use it themselves.

Abusers may appear kind in offering to pay bills or do the shopping, but they actually keep money for themselves. People may obtain the right to access or manage a person's money (e.g. being an appointee through the Benefits Agency or having registered a power of attorney through the Court of Protection) but again they keep money for themselves or mismanage it.

Most organisations have strict policies and guidance regarding financial matters for workers. However, it still happens that workers accept gifts from service users or they are put in someone's will. Another very common scenario is workers shopping for service users and using their own (not the service users') rewards points cards in a supermarket.

But it not just money that can be involved in financial abuse cases. We have to think on a broader level about assets. Vulnerable adults may have possessions (e.g. jewellery, antiques) which they do not realise are valuable. They can be coerced into handing things over. Yet another form of abuse is when a person is charged for services which should be included in a fee.

Case Examples

- While Sally was in hospital she got to know the son of the woman who was in the next bed to her. Sally talked about having savings and not knowing how to invest wisely. The son persuaded Sally to put money into his business. Sally never received any dividends, which she had been promised.

- A home carer saw Jim's PIN number for his cash card lying on the table. She noted it down and then took Jim's card when she went to do the shopping.

- When Mr Andrews went in the care home he was told he would have to pay £5 a week to have his clothing washed.

To summarise, financial abuse can be:

- taking/spending money without consent

- taking pension/benefit

- taking/selling possessions

- theft

- fraud

- acting as appointee, attorney or receiver and then misusing money/assets

- charging for services which should be inclusive in fees

- adding points to one's own reward points card and not the service user's when shopping

- putting bank/building society accounts into joint names and withdrawing large amounts of money

- obtaining a credit card in someone else's name

- using a cash card without consent

- forcing changes to bank accounts, wills, and so on

- saying bills are being paid when they are not

- saying shopping cost more than it did

- denying access to money/assets

- persuading someone to hand over something which is valuable.

 Handout 3.14, p.86

Neglect/acts of omission

Neglect is probably one of the most difficult forms of abuse to prove in a court of law. This is partially due to the fact that we are not very good at monitoring adults' health: we do not monitor adults in the same way we monitor children. A simple way of thinking about neglect is to think about *needs*. It could be argued that if a person's needs are not being met then they are being neglected.

Each individual will have a wide range of needs:

- physical
- emotional
- health
- social
- sexual
- financial
- transport

- accommodation
- food/drink
- warmth
- lighting
- cultural
- spiritual/religious.

Neglect can be physical or emotional. We have already seen above that some forms of abuse which fit into the physical or emotional categories could also come under neglect. Neglect can also be *an act of omission*; that is, failing to do something – not washing, dressing or toileting; failing to get medical attention, and so on.

It can be incredibly difficult to prove neglect because it can be inflicted in very subtle ways; for example, by consistently leaving a zimmer frame out of reach. Rarely are people seen every moment of the day, so it might be difficult to pick up the fact that someone is not being stimulated. Failure to stimulate can occur at varying levels; for example, ignoring someone or not encouraging them to pursue leisure, education or employment interests.

Every human being needs some form of social contact, otherwise he or she will become isolated. If someone is not allowed out or is kept in a confined area it may feel like imprisonment. Other vulnerable adults can be abandoned when carers have had enough so they no longer visit them, or dump them in a casualty department. Finally, we must not forget that spiritual, religious and cultural needs must be met.

In discussing forms of neglect it is also necessary to think about the concept of systemic abuse; that is, where it is the system rather than a person that abuses. It is not uncommon for people to be unable to access services or resources (and hence experience a form of neglect) because of a lack of money/budgets/staff.

Case Examples

- Gertie was doubly incontinent. Her son used to leave her to sit in her own urine and faeces for hours.

- Mr and Mrs Jackson became concerned about the care of their daughter, Linda, who had learning disabilities when she attended a day centre. They started marking her continence pads and proved that they were never changed during the day.

- Mrs Rashid was told that there were not enough staff on duty so no one could take her to the mosque.

- Ken had to wait 24 hours before he got a new battery for his hearing aid. He had asked care workers four times for a new battery.

- Joy was in hospital. She was very hungry, because she could not feed herself and the nursing staff did not help her to eat.

- Mrs Evers, aged 80, lived in a very rural area. All her family and friends were dead so she had become very isolated. She welcomed the idea of going to a day centre to get out and about. However, transport could not be arranged because Mrs Evers 'lives out in the sticks. The transport does not pick up out there and there is no money for taxis.'

To summarise, neglect can be:

- an act of omission

- not meeting someone's needs

- not washing, dressing, toileting someone

- a lack of food/drink

- not providing an adequate/appropriate diet

- a lack of heating/light

- leaving someone to sit/lie in urine/faeces

- failure to change continence pads regularly

- the absence of mobility aids

- not meeting cultural, spiritual or religious needs

- not meeting employment or education needs

- a lack of stimulation

- isolation

- imprisonment

- ignoring

- exclusion

- denying access to medical/health services

- abandoning someone

- not aiding communication
- not providing transport
- providing only communal clothing
- providing no access.

 Handout 3.15, p.87

Discriminatory abuse

Discriminatory abuse is a 'new' category of abuse in that it became the sixth category of abuse when *No Secrets* came into being in the year 2000. Formerly, many abuse policies had statements about principles underpinning adult protection work and this usually included something about equal opportunities and anti-discriminatory practice. Having discriminatory abuse as a category in its own right gives more recognition to the issue. However, many policies are not detailed enough about this type of abuse. Many state the obvious that no person should be discriminated on the grounds of:

- age
- gender
- race
- culture
- religion
- sexuality
- disability.

 Handout 3.16, p.88

 Case Examples

- Gillian has Down's syndrome. Her support worker had made an appointment to have her hair cut at the new hairdresser's in town. When the hairdresser saw Gillian she said there must have been a mistake because they were fully booked. No one was in the salon.

- Oliver had been attending the mental health day centre for nine years. Just before his 65th birthday his community psychiatric nurse told him he would have to move to a day centre for older people.

- A group of adults with learning disabilities were asked to sit 'out of the way' and were put in the snug room of the pub so that they would 'not put customers off their meals'.

- A police video suite does not have disabled access.

However, few policies go into depth and give practice examples of what constitutes discriminatory abuse. It is an issue which is not being given enough attention. Workers often say to me that discrimination can be dealt with in other ways without having to use the abuse procedures.

To summarise, discriminatory abuse can be:

- derogatory comments

- harassment

- being made to move to a different resource/service based on age

- being denied medical treatment on grounds of age or mental health

- not providing access.

 Handout 3.17, p.89

The following questions can be used in group work after participants have been taken through the categories of abuse. Some of the questions will encourage participants to vent their feelings: they may be feeling a whole gamut of emotions because of what they now realise constitutes abuse.

QUESTIONS FOR GROUP WORK

1. Which categories/forms of abuse had you not thought about before?
2. How did you feel when you were learning about the categories of abuse?
3. How do you feel now?
4. Have you seen something in the past and now realise it is abuse?
5. Do you think you have unintentionally abused someone?
6. Do you think you have been prejudiced or discriminated against someone?

Workers can also feel guilty because they realise they may have abused a service user (unintentionally) in the past or they know colleagues are abusing currently.

Institutional abuse

All the categories of abuse discussed in the previous section could occur in an institution (some examples have been cited in the case examples); it is also necessary to consider the concept of institutional abuse. This is a huge topic in itself but needs to be addressed in basic awareness training. We must focus on what constitutes institutional abuse when thinking about 'What is Adult Abuse?'.

What is an institution?

The word 'institution' conjures up all sorts of different images for people – usually images from the past where bad things may have happened; for example, the workhouse, mental hospitals. An institution is a place where rules and regulations exist. Just a few examples are:

- a care or nursing home

- a day centre or day hospital

- a hospital ward

- supported accommodation

- an educational establishment, for example a school, college, training centre

- prison.

 Handout 3.18, p.90

I just want to point out at this point that there are many vulnerable adults in the prison system and *No Secrets* does acknowledge this. It is an issue agencies should be addressing. It is hard to access exact figures regarding prisoners with mental health problems and learning disabilities, but statistics for older people (aged 60 or above) are available. In 1994 older people constituted 1 per cent of the prison population. By the following year this had increased to 2 per cent and to 3 per cent in 2004. Eighty per cent of those prisoners were chronically sick and disabled (Home Office 2005).

Staff can work in certain environments and not consider them to be institutions because they are striving to ensure that service users feel that the place is their home (e.g. support workers in supported accommodation). However, regimes can develop which become oppressive. Service users can be treated as a homogeneous group which can lead to individuals losing their identity.

 Case Examples

- Service users are told they have to be in bed by 10.00 p.m.

- There is a set menu for each mealtime; there is no choice or alternatives.

- A local entertainer has come into the home every Thursday night for the past five years. Services users are not asked about what entertainment they might like to have in the evenings.

With stricter regulations being introduced under the Care Standards Act 2000, it is to be hoped that such regimes are not so prevalent as they have been in the past.

How much abuse is there?

Abuse is always hard to quantify and the underlying problem is that much of it remains well hidden, so we shall never get a true picture. People are often afraid to speak out, especially if they are dependent on certain people for their care. If staff are abusing service users then the victims may be fearful of the consequences if they do speak out. Another problem is that many vulnerable adults literally cannot speak out because they have communication difficulties. Other adults may have no one to whom they can turn other than staff because they have no family, friends or visitors.

Abuse in institutions is not a new phenomenon. There have been many scandals over the years where adults have been abused in institutions but they are quickly forgotten – primarily because vulnerable adults are not as emotive as children. It is useful to read back over early reports, for example from the Independent Review of Residential Care chaired by Gillian Wagner (Sinclair 1988; Wagner Committee 1988). The Beech House Inquiry was concerned with the mistreatment of patients residing at Beech House, St Pancras Hospital, between 1993 and 1996 (Camden and Islington NHS Trust 1999). The Longcare Inquiry was another tragedy, yet few people have heard about the abuse which took place in two homes for adults with learning disabilities in Buckinghamshire (Burgner 1998).

When scandals do hit the press they are often presented in a very sensationalised way; as are documentaries concerned with exposing abuse and violence. It is important for workers to realise that abuse in extreme forms does happen, but it is equally important to stress that the more subtle forms of abuse are just as important and can also harm a victim: for example, putting a tray across the victim's lap so he or she cannot get out of a chair. When discussion in training focuses on such actions some workers may start to feel guilty because they may have engaged in what may be perceived as abusive practice. A great deal of sensitivity and understanding is needed when this type of discussion takes place.

Being institutionalised

KEY QUESTION

When and how have you been institutionalised?

Nearly every one of us will have been in an institution at some point in our lives. Probably without realising it we have become institutionalised; that is, the way things are run becomes the norm. Exercise 3.7 will help workers to think about when they have become institutionalised themselves and this should lead them on to think about how the same process can happen to service users.

✍ Exercise 3.7, p.70

Abuse or just bad practice?

The following is a crucial question when considering abuse in institutions:

KEY QUESTION

When does bad practice cross that fine line and become abuse?

Some people may argue that bad practice is abuse. However, workers can hide behind the excuse that 'it is only bad practice'. Exercise 3.8 may be a very good way of getting workers to think around these issues before the trainer introduces the current definitions of institutional abuse.

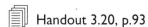 Exercise 3.8, p.71, and 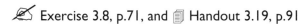 Handout 3.19, p.91

In training sessions, no matter what subject is being studied, there will be a great emphasis on values. The general principles of care we use nowadays were developed from the original values which were written in a Social Services Inspectorate tool in 1989, *Homes Are For Living In* (Department of Health 1989), namely:

- privacy
- dignity
- independence

- choice
- rights
- fulfilment.

 Handout 3.20, p.93

Even though *Homes Are For Living In* was written many years ago I think workers today can still learn a great deal from it as it was a model for evaluating the quality of care provided, and quality of life experienced, in residential care homes for older people. The intention was that the model, which was: 'devised for managers and inspectors as an aid to inspection, would also be suitable for use by residential staff as a focus for self-evaluation and development, and by agencies charged with training those members of staff' (Department of Health 1989, p.6).

The TOPSS Induction Standard 1 states that care workers should understand the importance of promoting the following values at all times:

- individuality and identity
- rights
- choice
- privacy

- independence
- dignity
- respect
- partnership.

(TOPSS 2001, p.14)

Handout 3.21, p.94

Exercise 3.9 can be used to facilitate a session on thinking about values which should exist in all institutions.

 Exercise 3.9, p.72, and Handouts 3.20 and 3.21, pp.93–94

Once the trainer has got workers to think about values and the quality of care which should be offered, the definition of institutional abuse needs to be introduced. *No Secrets* states:

> Neglect and poor professional practice also need to be taken into account. This may take the form of isolated incidents of poor or unsatisfactory professional practice, at one end of the spectrum, through to pervasive ill treatment or gross misconduct at the other. Repeated instances of poor care may be an indication of more serious problems and this is sometimes referred to as *institutional abuse*. (Department of Health 2000a, p.10)

Handouts 3.22 and 3.23, p.95–96

Many workers will have worked in care settings previously. It is always good to get people to think about what they have seen or what they actually did themselves many years ago. It is important for a trainer to emphasise that practice across the sectors and disciplines does change over time. Practices that were acceptable years ago may not be deemed to be good practice now. This is why it is imperative for staff to attend training sessions regularly and be updated. It is no good saying 'I have done care for years'.

KEY QUESTIONS

What have you seen in the past or more recently that might be considered to be institutional abuse?

At the time did you think it was abuse?

Did you report it?

Would you report it now?

Key learning points from this chapter

- Workers must become familiar with the guidance in *No Secrets* or *In Safe Hands* and learn the definitions of vulnerable adult, abuse, significant harm and the categories of abuse.

- There are six categories of abuse: physical; sexual; emotional/psychological; financial/material; neglect/acts of omission; discriminatory. Forms of institutional and systemic abuse must also be considered.

- Abuse can take many forms.

- Abuse can be a single act; that is, be a one-off incident.

- Abuse can be a failure to act.

- Abuse can be unintentional but it can also be deliberate.

- Vulnerable adults can be targeted and groomed by their abusers.

- A person can be abused in any relationship and by strangers.

- Abuse can happen anywhere (i.e. in the community or in communal settings).

- Thought must be given to the question – when does bad practice cross that fine line and become abuse?

- Abuse is not always obvious; it can be inflicted in very subtle ways.

- Do not compare types of abuse; all abuse is serious.

- Public protection must be a consideration in adult protection work.

Suggested reading

Department of Health (2000) *No Secrets: Guidance on Developing and Implementing Multi-Agency Policies and Procedures to Protect Vulnerable Adults from Abuse.* London: Department of Health.

Issue focussed on financial abuse (2003) *Journal of Adult Protection 5*, 2.

National Assembly for Wales (2000) *In Safe Hands.* Cardiff: National Assembly for Wales.

Local policy and procedures on vulnerable adults/adult abuse.

Video

WAA1: What is Adult Abuse?

This video can be used to introduce workers to the subject of adult abuse. It contains case studies covering different service user groups.

WHO IS A VULNERABLE ADULT?

Objective

To make participants think about who may be defined as a vulnerable adult in an abuse policy.

Participants

In small groups.

Equipment

Flipchart paper and pens.

Copies of Handout 3.1.

Time

15 minutes.

Task

1. Participants think about people they are currently working with who they think are vulnerable.

2. List the reasons why these people are vulnerable.

Feedback

1. Each group feeds back their lists.

2. General discussion follows as to whether these reasons could be criteria for defining a vulnerable adult in an adult abuse policy.

3. Participants are given the definition of a vulnerable adult (Handout 3.1) for full discussion.

 © Jacki Pritchard 2007

WHEN HAVE I BEEN VULNERABLE?

Objective

To make participants think about times in their life when they have felt vulnerable.

Participants

Individual work then work in pairs.

Equipment

Paper and pens.

Time

5 minutes for individual work; 10 minutes in pairs.

Task

1. Participants are asked to think about times in their life (childhood through to adulthood) when they remember feeling vulnerable.

2. Participants list the situations they were in and what caused them to feel vulnerable.

3. Participants find a partner and they share their experiences.

Feedback

1. Pairs feed back into the large group the common factors which made them feel vulnerable.

2. Participants are given Handout 3.2 to be used as a basis for discussion in a large group.

WHAT DOES HARM MEAN TO YOU?

Objective

Being 'harmed' will mean different things to different people. This exercise will help participants think about what the word means to them.

Participants

In small groups.

Equipment

Flipchart paper and pens.

Time

15 minutes in groups.

Task

1. Participants should think about when they or someone they have worked with has been hurt or harmed in some way.

2. Groups will compile a list of ways adults can be harmed.

Feedback

1. Each group will feed back their lists.

2. The trainer will facilitate a general discussion on the meaning of harm.

3. Participants are given Handout 3.6 and the definition of significant harm will be discussed.

 © Jacki Pritchard 2007

TAKING ADVANTAGE, MISTREATMENT AND ABUSE

Objective

People sometimes use different words to mean the same thing. All workers need to be clear about what abuse means to them.

Participants

Participants will be divided into three groups.

Equipment

Flipchart paper and pens.

The trainer will have prepared the flipchart sheets beforehand. One heading will be at the top of each sheet: 1. Taking Advantage; 2. Mistreatment; 3. Abuse.

Time

15 minutes in groups.

Task

1. Each group will be given a flipchart sheet with one heading on it.

2. Participants are asked to list examples for the subject heading on the sheet.

Feedback

1. Each group will feed back their lists.

2. The lists will be compared and discussion should focus on whether some examples could be moved to other lists.

© Jacki Pritchard 2007

WHAT KIND OF ABUSE IS IT?

Objective

To get participants to think how different forms of abuse could be categorised.

Participants

To work in small groups.

Equipment

Pens.

Time

30 minutes in small groups.

Copies of Handout 3.7.

Task

Having been given Handout 3.7, participants are asked to discuss each scenario and put it in one or more categories of abuse.

Feedback

Trainer takes one scenario at a time and asks each group for their answer. If there is any disagreement, a full discussion will be encouraged by the trainer.

Note for trainer

Some participants may argue that the scenarios do not portray abuse. The trainer should invite participants to explain *why* they do not think this is a case of abuse. A debate should then be encouraged.

© Jacki Pritchard 2007

ABUSE OR NOT ABUSE?

Objective

To make participants think about what constitutes abuse in a variety of settings.

Participants

In small groups.

Equipment

Copies of Handout 3.8.

Time

Groups spend 30 minutes undertaking the exercise.

Task

1. Groups will consider each scenario in turn. They have to reach a consensus regarding whether this is a case of abuse or not.

2. If the consensus of opinion is that it *is* abuse, the group has to decide into which category or categories of abuse they would put the action/behaviour.

Feedback

1. Participants remain sitting in their groups. The trainer takes one scenario at a time and goes around asking each group what their consensus of opinion was.

2. If there was a disagreement *within* the group, the trainer will ask participants to explain what they discussed. Where there are differences *between* the groups, the trainer will ask the groups to debate; that is, put forward their arguments.

Note for trainer

This exercise is suitable for all workers across the disciplines and will help participants think about abuse in a variety of settings.

BEING INSTITUTIONALISED

Objective

To make participants think about institutions they have been in and how their choices may have been restricted at times so that their lives became controlled.

Participants

Small groups.

Equipment

Flipchart paper and pens.

Time

20 minutes.

Task

1. Participants list all the institutions they have visited or been part of throughout their life (i.e. in childhood and adulthood).

2. Participants list any rules, regulations or regimes which existed and restricted what they could do.

Feedback

1. Groups feed back their lists and compare them.

2. The group as a whole discusses whether:

   (a) participants had become institutionalised and if so in what ways

   (b) being institutionalised resulted in any harm

   (c) service users are institutionalised in similar ways.

© Jacki Pritchard 2007

ABUSE OR BAD PRACTICE?

Objective

To make participants think further about what constitutes abuse in an institution.

Participants

In small groups.

Equipment

Copies of Handout 3.19.

Time

Groups spend 30 minutes undertaking the exercise.

Task

1. Groups will consider each scenario in turn. They have to reach a consensus regarding whether this is a case of abuse *or* bad practice.

2. If the consensus of opinion is that it *is* abuse, the group has to decide into which category or categories of abuse they would put the action/behaviour.

Feedback

1. Participants remain sitting in their groups. The trainer takes one scenario at a time and goes around asking each group what their consensus of opinion was.

2. If there was a disagreement *within* the group, the trainer will ask participants to explain what they discussed. Where there are differences *between* the groups, the trainer will ask the groups to debate; that is, put forward their arguments.

Note for trainer

It must be made clear when explaining the purpose of the exercise that the groups cannot say the scenario is both abuse and bad practice. The main purpose of the exercise is to get participants thinking about when bad practice crosses that fine line to become abuse.

VALUES

Objective

To make participants think about the values in their workplace or in institutions they visit.

Participants

In small groups.

Equipment

Flipchart paper and pens.

Copies of Handouts 3.20 and 3.21.

Time

15 minutes.

Task

1. Participants are given a copy of Handout 3.20. If anyone works in an institution they are asked to share their views about whether these values exist and whether they could be improved upon.

2. Participants who have worked in an institution in the past are asked to share their past experiences in relation to these values.

3. Participants are asked to think about the values in relation to places they visit.

4. Key points from the discussions will be written on flipchart sheets.

Feedback

1. Groups feed back the key points from their discussion.
2. Handout 3.21 is discussed in the large group.

© Jacki Pritchard 2007

DEFINITION OF VULNERABLE ADULT

A *vulnerable adult* is a person over 18 years of age:

who is or may be in need of community care services by reason of mental or other disability, age or illness; and who is or may be unable to take care of him or herself, or unable to protect him or herself against significant harm or exploitation.

Originally from Lord Chancellor's Department (1997) *Who Decides? Making Decisions on Behalf of Mentally Incapacitated Adults.* London: The Stationery Office; quoted in Department of Health (2000) *No Secrets: Guidance on Developing and Implementing Multi-Agency Policies and Procedures to Protect Vulnerable Adults from Abuse.* London: Department of Health, pp.8–9.

© Department of Health 2000

DEFINITIONS OF 'VULNERABLE'

- Capable of being physically or emotionally wounded or hurt.

- Open to temptation.

- Exposed to attack or harm.

Associated words from a thesaurus

- Susceptible
- Powerless

- Weak
- Exposed

- Defenceless
- Exposed

- Unprotected
- Sensitive

- Unguarded
- In danger

- Helpless
- At risk

 © Jacki Pritchard 2007

DEFINITION OF ABUSE

Abuse may consist of a single act or repeated acts. It may be physical, verbal or psychological, it may be an act of neglect or an omission to act, or it may occur when a vulnerable person is persuaded to enter into a financial or sexual transaction to which he or she has not consented, or cannot consent. Abuse can occur in any relationship and may result in significant harm to, or exploitation of, the person subjected to it.

From: Department of Health (2000) *No Secrets: Guidance on Developing and Implementing Multi-Agency Policies and Procedures to Protect Vulnerable Adults from Abuse.* London: Department of Health, p.9.

© Department of Health 2000

DEFINITIONS OF ABUSE

The systematic maltreatment, physical, emotional, or financial, of an elderly person…this may take the form of physical assault, threatening behaviour, neglect and abandonment or sexual assault.

From: Eastman, M. (1984) *Old Age Abuse.* London: Age Concern, p.3.

Abuse may be described as physical, sexual, psychological, or financial. It may be intentional or unintentional, or the result of neglect. It causes harm to the older person, either temporarily or over a period of time.

From: Department of Health (1993) *No Longer Afraid: The Safeguard of Older People in Domestic Settings.* London: HMSO, p.3.

[A] violation of an individual's human and civil rights by any other person or persons.

From: Department of Health (2000) *No Secrets: Guidance on Developing and Implementing Multi-Agency Policies and Procedures to Protect Vulnerable Adults from Abuse.* London: Department of Health, p.9.

Abuse may consist of a single act or repeated acts. It may be physical, verbal or psychological, it may be an act of neglect or an omission to act, or it may occur when a vulnerable person is persuaded to enter into a financial or sexual transaction to which he or she has not consented, or cannot consent. Abuse can occur in any relationship and may result in significant harm to, or exploitation of, the person subjected to it.

From: Department of Health (2000) *No Secrets: Guidance on Developing and Implementing Multi-Agency Policies and Procedures to Protect Vulnerable Adults from Abuse.* London: Department of Health, p.9.

A single or repeated act or lack of appropriate action, occurring within any relationship where there is an expectation of trust, which causes harm or distress to an older person.

From: Action on Elder Abuse, 'What is elder abuse?' London, UK. Available at www.elderabuse.org.uk.

© Jacki Pritchard 2007

STRANGER ABUSE

Stranger abuse will warrant a different kind of response from that appropriate to abuse in an ongoing relationship or in a care location. Nevertheless, in some instances it may be appropriate to use the locally agreed inter-agency adult protection procedures to ensure that the vulnerable person receives the services and support that they need. Such procedures may also be used when there is potential for harm to other vulnerable people.

From: Department of Health (2000) *No Secrets: Guidance on Developing and Implementing Multi-Agency Policies and Procedures to Protect Vulnerable Adults from Abuse.* London: Department of Health, p.11.

DEFINITION OF SIGNIFICANT HARM

…not only ill treatment (including sexual abuse and forms of ill treatment which are not physical), but also the impairment of, or an avoidable deterioration in, physical or mental health; and the impairment of physical, intellectual, emotional, social or behavioural development.

From: Lord Chancellor's Department (1997) *Who Decides? Making Decisions on Behalf of Mentally Incapacitated Adults*. London: The Stationery Office, p.68.

 © Crown copyright 1997

WHAT KIND OF ABUSE IS IT?

1. Irene is becoming very confused and asks the same questions all the time; she also gets very agitated. Her daughter often slaps her and gives her too much medication to keep her quiet.

2. Justine has learning disabilities. When staff consider her to be 'kicking off' she is made to sit in a corner facing the wall for 15 minutes and then is not allowed a pudding at the next mealtime.

3. Todd has persuaded his mother to have her pension paid into his bank account. He gives her £40 for her food each week and says she must pay the bills out of that money as well. She has got into arrears and has received notices about disconnecting her gas and electricity supplies.

4. Morgan is 40 years old and well known in the local community; he has schizophrenia. Whenever he goes out a gang of local teenagers shouts comments at him, such as 'nutter', 'schizo', 'Welsh git'. On other occasions they visit him, eat and drink whatever they can find, and take things from the house.

5. Care workers say it is not worth buying Beattie any new clothes because 'she is 102 years old and cannot last much longer'.

6. A nurse has little patience with Zetta who has a dual diagnosis of learning disabilities and mental health problems. Whilst on the ward the nurse rough-handles Zetta when she hurries her to get dressed, washed etc.

7. Lara is in her twenties, physically disabled and lives in a bungalow with her parents and teenage brother. She spends a lot of time in her bedroom as she is not allowed to see anyone who visits the house.

8. Katy has been sectioned and is in hospital. A male nurse regularly pats her on the bottom.

9. A son only lets his mother bath and change her clothes once a week. He threatens that if she complains he will send her into a care home.

10. Oswald has had a sexual relationship with his sister, Colette, since they were in their teens. Colette, who is now in her forties, had an accident at work two years ago and sustained brain injury. Their sexual relationship continues.

11. Wesley is an African Caribbean man with learning disabilities. Support workers and other service users refer to him as 'the Coloured'.

12. Mandy has had an operation and is still very weak a few days later. She cannot feed herself. Meals are left on a tray, which is placed out of reach.

ABUSE OR NOT ABUSE?

1. It is Monday morning. Staff are washing Maggie who has profound learning disabilities. They talk across Maggie about what they have done during their weekend off. They never talk directly to Maggie or include her in their conversation.

2. A husband will not let his wife, who has a continence problem, have a drink after 7.00 p.m. in case she wets the bed in the night.

3. Fred has had one lung removed because of cancer. He returns to the nursing home and staff say he cannot have any cigarettes. Fred wants to continue to smoke.

4. Madeleine has mental health problems and has been in many institutions during her life. She has made allegations of abuse in the past relating to family members and care staff. She is currently in hospital again and says she has been sexually assaulted by another patient. The allegation is not taken seriously.

5. A home carer uses her own reward points card in a supermarket when she goes shopping for service users.

6. Chris lives in supported accommodation for learning disabled people and there is an active support programme in place. In recent weeks he has made it clear he does not want to go swimming. Staff say he has to go.

7. Andrew's mother believes his mental health problems are due to diet. She has changed his way of eating completely and forces him to eat food he does not like.

8. Ethel is 75 years old and blind. Six months ago she met Bert at the day centre she attends. She is planning to go away on holiday with Bert but her son and daughter-in-law say she is too old to have a boyfriend and he is probably only after her money, which is their inheritance.

9. Leanne, who is physically disabled, wants to have a bath at 10.00 p.m. Night staff say 'it is too late for a bath'.

10. After Mrs Patel's husband died, her eldest son and his family moved into her house. Mrs Patel is now forced to live in the attic room and her son manages all her finances.

© Jacki Pritchard 2007

CATEGORIES OF ADULT ABUSE

- Physical

- Sexual

- Emotional/psychological

- Financial/material

- Neglect/acts of omission

- Discriminatory

© Jacki Pritchard 2007

FORMS OF ABUSE

The Department of Health has said a consensus has emerged identifying the following main different forms of abuse:

- *Physical abuse* – including hitting, slapping, pushing, kicking, misuse of medication, restraint, or inappropriate sanctions.

- *Sexual abuse* – including rape and sexual assault or sexual acts to which the vulnerable adult has not consented, or could not consent or was pressured into consenting.

- *Psychological abuse* – including emotional abuse, threats of harm or abandonment, deprivation of contact, humiliation, blaming, controlling, intimidation, coercion, harassment, verbal abuse, isolation or withdrawal from services or supportive networks.

- *Financial or material abuse* – including theft, fraud, exploitation, pressure in connection with wills, property or inheritance or financial transactions, or the misuse or misappropriation of property, possessions or benefits.

- *Neglect and acts of omission* – including ignoring medical or physical care needs, failure to provide access to appropriate health, social care or educational services, the withholding of the necessities of life, such as medication, adequate nutrition and heating.

- *Discriminatory abuse* – including racist or sexist abuse, abuse based on a person's disability, and other forms of harassment, slurs or similar treatment.

(From: Department of Health (2000) *No Secrets: Guidance on Developing and Implementing Multi-Agency Policies and Procedures to Protect Vulnerable Adults from Abuse.* London: Department of Health, p.9.

© Department of Health 2000

PHYSICAL ABUSE

- The use of hands and feet to, for example, kick, slap, punch, push, pinch, scratch or pull hair

- Using an implement; throwing things

- Inappropriate/rough handling

- Assaults

- Force feeding

- Restraint

- Medication:

  (a) over-medicating

  (b) withdrawing medication

  (c) hiding medication

  (d) administering another person's medication

  (e) not reviewing regularly

- Malnutrition/dehydration

- Bullying

© Jacki Pritchard 2007

SEXUAL ABUSE

- Forcing someone into sexual activity without his or her consent

- Sexualised language/conversation

- Sexual harassment

- Inappropriate touching

- Kissing

- Fondling

- Exposure

- Voyeurism

- Masturbation

- Inflicting pornography on someone

- Indecent assault

- Penetrating someone's mouth/anus/vagina (with finger, penis or other object)

- Rape

- Exploitation/prostitution

- Satanic/ritual abuse

- Bestiality

© Jacki Pritchard 2007

EMOTIONAL/PSYCHOLOGICAL ABUSE

- Humiliation

- Intimidation

- Ridicule

- Threats

- Causing fear/anxiety/mental anguish

- Emotional blackmail

- Verbal abuse – shouting, swearing, misuse of names, name calling, using nicknames

- Harassment

- Bullying

- Denial of human rights

- Denying access to services

- Being over-protective

- Withholding social contact

- Isolation

- Imprisonment

- Ignoring

- Excluding

- Abandoning

© Jacki Pritchard 2007

FINANCIAL ABUSE

- Taking/spending money without consent

- Taking pension/benefit

- Taking/selling possessions

- Theft

- Fraud

- Acting as appointee, attorney or receiver and then misusing money/assets

- Charging for services which should be inclusive in fees

- Adding points to one's own reward points card and not the service user's when shopping

- Putting bank/building society accounts into joint names and withdrawing large amounts of money

- Obtaining a credit card in someone else's name

- Using a cash/credit card without consent

- Forcing changes to bank accounts, wills, and so on

- Saying bills are being paid when they are not

- Saying shopping cost more than it did

- Denying access to money/assets

- Persuading someone to hand over something which is valuable

© Jacki Pritchard 2007

NEGLECT

- An act of omission

- Not meeting someone's needs

- Not washing, dressing, toileting someone

- A lack of food/drink

- Not providing an adequate/appropriate diet

- A lack of heating/light

- Leaving someone to sit/lie in urine/faeces

- Failure to change continence pads regularly

- The absence of mobility aids

- Not aiding communication

- Providing only communal clothing

- Not meeting cultural, spiritual or religious needs

- Not meeting employment or education needs

- A lack of stimulation

- Isolation

- Imprisonment

- Ignoring

- Exclusion

- Denying access to medical/health services

- Abandoning someone

- Not providing transport

- Providing no access

ANTI-DISCRIMINATORY PRACTICE

All service users should be treated equally regardless of:

- age

- gender

- race

- culture

- religion

- sexuality

- disability.

© Jacki Pritchard 2007

DISCRIMINATORY ABUSE

- Derogatory comments

- Harassment

- Being made to move to a different resource/service based on age

- Being denied medical treatment on grounds of age or mental health

- Not providing access

© Jacki Pritchard 2007

TYPES OF INSTITUTIONS

- A care or nursing home

- A day centre or day hospital

- A hospital ward

- Supported accommodation

- An educational establishment, for example a school, college, training centre

- Prison

© Jacki Pritchard 2007

ABUSE OR BAD PRACTICE?

- Lionel has mental health problems. He likes to go to sleep in bed wearing his baseball cap. Staff say he has to take it off.

- Every time June talks to a service user she calls them 'love'. She does not distinguish between them.

- Esther is physically disabled and needs help with personal care tasks. She asks to have a bath on Friday morning. She is told she will have to wait until 2.00 p.m. By teatime Esther still has not had her bath.

- Frank has learning disabilities and likes to follow staff around the house. Some staff find this irritating and tell him to 'Stop being a nuisance'.

- Ceris is told that if he does not 'calm down and behave' his parents will be told they cannot visit him at the weekend.

- Service users are not allowed to read their files which are kept in the office filing cabinet.

- Service users are charged for electricity; the manager says it is not included in the fees they pay.

- Jude is a male care worker, who is said to be 'one for the ladies'. Some of the female service users find it embarrassing when he puts a sexual innuendo into the conversation.

© Jacki Pritchard 2007

ABUSE OR BAD PRACTICE?

- A group of female service users make racist comments to Violet, who is African Caribbean. Staff do nothing when they hear the comments.

- Ena, a care worker, kisses service users 'good-bye' just before she goes off duty.

- Alan has always kept goldfish but when he is admitted to care he is told he cannot keep the fish in his room because 'it is not healthy'.

- Service users are not allowed to make themselves a drink between meals.

- Six adults with learning disabilities live together. A support worker says that, as they are short staffed, for activities that day they can either watch TV or go shopping in the supermarket to get food for tea.

- Kelly sells goods from her catalogue to service users. She puts pressure on service users to buy things from her saying she is 'giving them a good deal'.

- The senior staff decide when and where service users go on day trips without consulting the service users.

 © Jacki Pritchard 2007

VALUES (1)

The following values should be present in any home:

- *Privacy* – the right of individuals to be left alone or undisturbed and free from intrusion or public attention into their affairs.

- *Dignity* – a recognition of the intrinsic value of people regardless of circumstances by respecting their uniqueness and their personal needs; treating them with respect.

- *Independence* – opportunities to think and act without reference to another person including a willingness to incur a degree of calculated risk.

- *Choice* – opportunity to select independently from a range of options.

- *Rights* – the maintenance of all entitlements associated with citizenship.

- *Fulfilment* – satisfaction or happiness as a result of fully developing one's abilities or character.

From: Department of Health (1989) *Homes Are For Living In.*
London: Department of Health.

VALUES (2)

- Individuality and identity

- Rights

- Choice

- Privacy

- Independence

- Dignity

- Respect

- Partnership

From: Training Organisation for the Personal Social Services (2001) *The First Six Months:A Registered Manager's Guide to Induction and Foundation Standards.* Leeds: TOPSS, p.14.

 © Jacki Pritchard 2007

INSTITUTIONAL ABUSE

Neglect and poor professional practice also need to be taken into account. This may take the form of isolated incidents of poor or unsatisfactory professional practice, at one end of the spectrum, through to pervasive ill treatment or gross misconduct at the other. Repeated instances of poor care may be an indication of more serious problems and this is sometimes referred to as *institutional abuse*.

From: Department of Health (2000) *No Secrets: Guidance on Developing and Implementing Multi-Agency Policies and Procedures to Protect Vulnerable Adults from Abuse.* London: Department of Health, p.10.

© Department of Health 2000

EXAMPLES OF INSTITUTIONALISATION

- Set times for going to bed, getting up, having meals.

- All service users are toileted before mealtimes.

- No choice is given about meals, activities, clothing.

- Communal clothing only is provided, and communal face cloths, brushes, combs.

- Assumptions are made, for example all older people like to play bingo, watch old films, have a sing-song; younger service users will enjoy walking, swimming.

- Service users sit in the same places every day – in the lounge or at the dinner table.

- Personal possessions of any value have to be put in the office safe.

- The manager decides which daily newspapers should be delivered to the home.

© Jacki Pritchard 2007

Chapter 4

Recognising Adult Abuse

Many workers at the beginning of a training course on adult abuse think or actually say, 'What's the point of this? I'll never come across abuse.' Adult abuse still does not get the attention or high profile it deserves. Since the 1970s society has gradually recognised that women and children are abused, so that cases of child abuse and domestic violence do hit the press regularly now. The general public recognises that abuse and violence is not uncommon. However, if we talk about vulnerable adults, people may not understand to whom we are referring. Therefore, it is important for workers to understand that *all* forms of abuse can happen anywhere.

KEY QUESTION

Where do you think adult abuse could happen?

This question is a good one to raise in order to start a general discussion about where abuse might happen, before going on to considering who might be a victim or abuser.

A trainer needs to get participants to think broadly about abuse occuring:

- in the community
- in institutional/communal settings

and then to go into much more detail, because some workers might be quite naïve. They may not have thought about how quickly (and often in a very subtle way) an abuser can take advantage of a vulnerable person in all sorts of places, for example in a:

- person's home
- public place
- workplace
- day centre

- day hospital

- hospital ward

- education/training establishment

- care home

- prison.

 Handout 4.1, p.124

Exercise 4.1 can be used for group work to start workers thinking about exact locations where abuse can be carried out.

 Exercise 4.1, p.121, and Handout 4.1, p.124

Case Examples

- Lisa, a home carer, took £25 from Mr Elliott's sideboard.

- After he finished cooking in the kitchen, Montgomery would put extra medication in his wife's food to calm her down.

- In a care home a male service user used to go into Betty's bedroom during the night and have sexual intercourse with her. Betty had Alzheimer's disease.

- Eddie used to meet Stephen, who had moderate learning disabilities, outside the post office every Tuesday when Stephen cashed his benefit. Eddie would then take Stephen shopping in the local supermarket and steal money from him.

- Isaiah was African Caribbean and had mental health problems. He was regularly beaten up in prison by other inmates. This usually happened in the shower room or in his cell.

- Teenagers regularly shouted discriminatory comments at the older people when they came out of the sheltered housing complex.

- A nurse always left food out of the reach of Mr Sayers, who could not feed himself.

Stereotyping

Very often people do not want to admit that they stereotype, but we all do it at some time or other. It is very wrong to do so, but sometimes we are conditioned to think in a certain way. We can all remember something that has been said to us in the past that we now know to be false, for example:

'People with their eyebrows too close together are sly.'

'Red-haired people have fiery tempers.'

'You can't trust people with green eyes.'

It is good to get participants to think about how they might have stereotyped people recently or in the past. Exercise 4.2 usually brings out defensive comments and protestations from participants that they have never ever stereotyped anyone; therefore, the trainer may need to give some examples when introducing the exercise.

✍ Exercise 4.2, p.122

This exercise will usually bring out some discussion about gender which will lead the trainer nicely on to give the historical perspective of how victims and abusers have been stereotyped in the past.

Victims and abusers – the past

It has already been said that adult abuse does not have the recognition it deserves. Unfortunately research in this field has been limited and it is only now that more studies are being undertaken. So people often revisit earlier literature – which can lead us down the wrong path.

In the 1980s, research about elder abuse was being undertaken in North America and the UK. Mervyn Eastman said of victims in the UK: 'The majority are female, over 80 and are dependent as a result of physical and mental capacity' (Eastman 1984, p.41). So the image that was created was one of dependency and of stress being caused for the carer.

At the same time, there were many studies in America regarding family violence and again elder abuse was given recognition. Gelles and Cornell said: 'The abuser is typically identified as being female, middle-aged and usually the offspring of the abused' (Gelles and Cornell 1985, p.105). So here the image was of middle-aged women taking on the role of primary carers and, like Eastman, they were suggesting that they lash out when stressed. Obviously this can happen, but in regard to adult abuse we must realise that abuse can happen for all sorts of different reasons which will be discussed in more detail below.

In more recent years people have tended to stereotype the abuser as male, probably due to the fact that domestic violence has been receiving more attention. The typical image of domestic violence has been one of a woman being battered by her husband/partner. Again we have moved on and domestic violence now encompasses many different relationships. It may include other familial relationships, gay men and lesbians.

Many people still find it hard to accept that a female can abuse. Society is well aware of the notorious female offenders like Myra Hindley and Rose West. However, they are thought to be extraordinary females, who are few and far between. This is because people have the image of a woman being of the nurturing kind. However, there has been research which clearly indicates that females can abuse children and adults (Elliot 1993; Saradjian 1996). This leads us back to the point that either a male or female can be a victim. Suzanne Steinmetz as far back as 1978 undertook research and wrote about the 'The Battered Husband Syndrome' (Steinmetz 1978) and other academics also pursued this area of research (Gelles 1997; Straus 1999; Straus and Gelles 1986).

It is very important that workers never take things at face value. It is also important *not* to read things into situations. There has to be a balance. A worker must keep an open mind. It is also hard for a worker to accept the fact that much abuse is premeditated; it is deliberate. The following case examples illustrate different victims and abusers – male, female, younger and older.

Case Examples

- Victoria was 103 years old; she was very frail but perfectly mentally sound. She was kept imprisoned in one room and financially abused by her grandson.

- Joanne, who was in her twenties, attended a day centre for people with mental health problems. She was emotionally bullied by Michaela, a support worker.

- Brian had learning disabilities and lived in supported accommodation. He was sexually abused by another male service user over a 12-month period.

- Tony was severely physically disabled after an accident at work. He returned home to live with his father and stepmother when he knew he would never work again. His stepmother physically hit him and often left him lying in urine and faeces during the day time. She cleaned him up before his father came home.

Why abuse happens

It has already been said that adult abuse is not just about carers' stress. The reasons why abuse happens can be numerous. There are many different theories and it is important workers have a basic knowledge of them. This is often an area which is left out of training sessions – usually because adult abuse courses are given limited time. If theories are not explored, then, again, workers can develop incorrect concepts; for example, 'Abusers are people who have been abused themselves.' The reality is that some perpetrators of adult abuse may have been abused in childhood, but it is a small percentage. There can be many causal factors of abuse and we shall now consider some of them.

KEY QUESTION

Can you think of reasons why abuse might happen?

Workers need to think about the following factors:

- historical
- social
- economic
- environmental
- political.

Handout 4.2 summarises the key things a worker should think about when trying to consider what may have caused abuse to occur. It can be used as a reminder checklist:

- past relationships
- past experience of violence/abuse/neglect
- past problems
- history of offending
- current problems
- addictions
- financial problems
- losses
- physical and mental health problems
- stresses
- dependency (emotional and physical).

 Handout 4.2, p.125

The importance of history

When suspecting or finding abuse it is very important not to focus just on the present situation. 'Social history' is considered to be a very 'old-fashioned' term nowadays, but it is helpful to undertake social histories on both the victim and the abuser. People now undertake assessments under the NHS and Community Care Act 1990 or perhaps the Mental Health Act 1983 and workers often complain that there is not enough time to do them as comprehensively as they would like. By this they mean they cannot spend long periods of time talking to a service user and getting to know about them and their past. A good social history looks back at what has happened in a person's life and should be thorough and in-depth – the theory being that what has happened to a person in the past will affect who they are today and how they behave.

Sometimes the past is the root cause of the current abusive situation, so it is important to find out something about relationships; that is, the relationship between the victim and their abuser and perhaps other significant people. Sometimes a person finds him- or herself in a situation where they are the primary carer for someone they dislike intensely or cannot forgive them for something they did in the past.

History of child abuse

As stated above it should not be assumed that a child who has experienced abuse is going to grow up to be an abuser. However, the history of child abuse in a family may be of relevance in some cases. For example, a child who has been abused by a parent may end up having to be the primary carer for his or her abuser in later life.

The abuser has problems

It has been said above that historically the victim has been stereotyped as someone who is dependent and causing stress for the carer. This has created the image of the victim being 'the problem'. In reality it may be that the abuser has problems, some of the most common being situations where there is a need for money, for example to finance a gambling habit or drug use.

The abuser may have experienced losses in his or her life, which he or she has not been able to come to terms with. This could be a physical loss resulting in a form of disability or a loss of a person or situation. The abuser may blame someone (the victim) for that loss.

There may be a history of offending. It is important to obtain background information about past behaviour in order to predict the risk of harm for the future (see Chapter 8 for full discussion of this point). It will be useful to know whether someone has a history of committing violent or sexual offences, theft or fraud, and so on.

Environment is also important. The abuser may be living in poor conditions or there may be stresses within the family home. For example, the abuser may be part of a multiple-dependency family; there could be young children as well as adults who are dependent in the household. Where people are living in overcrowded conditions, physical and emotional abuse can occur. Or where the family are living on a low income or benefits, there could be a need for money, which can lead to financial abuse. Sometimes there can be a change in circumstances which creates unwelcome alterations in lifestyle, for example loss of employment.

KEY QUESTIONS

How would you find out about a person's history?

Bear in mind issues around confidentiality, but
ideally who would you contact/talk to?

Domestic violence

We often hear the positives of working in specialisms rather than working generically; however, there can be some negatives. People can become very precious about the work they do and perhaps they do not liaise enough with people in other specialisms. Child abuse and adult abuse could be happening within one family – across generations. Likewise, domestic violence could be occurring within a family where other family members are experiencing other forms of abuse. Therefore, it is imperative that people talk to and learn from each other.

Some workers say that domestic violence is 'different' to adult abuse. Domestic violence is a form of adult abuse. Professionals can get into lots of arguments about which policy to follow and who should become involved. Ingram fully explores this and illustrates the debate about policy implementation through a case study (Ingram 2001).

I have heard people say frequently over the years that it is too late for older people to change. Comments like: 'Well she's been battered all her life. Why should we do anything to help now? She won't leave,' or 'She must enjoy it if she's stayed so long.' It is never too late to change. So if domestic violence has persisted and continues into later adulthood, this is not a reason not to implement the adult abuse policy. Many older people have felt unable to speak out in earlier years but in later life may welcome the opportunity to talk about what has happened. Also, many older people had nowhere to run to when they were younger and may be unaware of resources currently available. It is important that they are given options, so that they can make informed choices. I have worked with people in their nineties who have decided to leave an abusive situation and then had some years of happiness before they died.

It is also important to stress again that men can be victims of domestic violence. We have moved on a great deal in recent years so that we must also acknowledge that domestic violence is not just about married heterosexual couples. It is necessary to think about partnerships – including gay men and lesbians.

KEY FACT

A domestic violence incident occurs in the UK every 6–20 seconds.

Role reversal

In some abuse cases we find that a role reversal has taken place. A typical example is where a woman has been a victim of domestic violence all her married life and when her husband becomes incapacitated (either mentally or physically) she gets her own back and abuses him. This probably happens with men who have been victims of domestic violence too, but our knowledge is very limited in this area.

Mutual abuse

A worker can come across cases where it is difficult to know who is the victim and who is the abuser. This is because the people involved are abusing each other. This can happen in all sorts of relationships – husband/wife; carer/dependent person. Just because these cases are so difficult to work with and there is no clear victim or abuser, the abuse procedures should still be followed.

Carers' stress

Throughout this manual, and particularly in this chapter, it has been emphasised that adult abuse is a very complex issue and there may be many reasons why abuse happens other than carers' stress. Nevertheless we must give some attention to this. No one can really understand how hard it is caring for someone 24 hours a day, seven days a week, unless they have been in a similar situation. It is often forgotten that many carers may have problems themselves; for example, they may be older and not be in the best of health. However, even if you are very fit and healthy, having the responsibility of caring for another human being can be an enormous strain. Undoubtedly, there will be times when a carer might lash out in a fit of temper. It is understandable but it cannot be condoned. Some common causal factors are:

- the high dependency levels of the vulnerable adult

- the behaviour traits of the dependent person

- the nature of the tasks which have to be performed on a daily basis

- monotony

- boredom

- frustration

- isolation – little social contact with other people; being stuck in the house all day and night; little meaningful conversation

- little/no support

- lack of services.

 Handout 4.3, p.126

Targeting and grooming

Because there has been so much emphasis over the years on carers' stress leading to abuse, little attention has been given to the fact that complete strangers can deliberately target and groom vulnerable adults in order to abuse them. Vulnerable adults can be befriended by someone who is going to take advantage of them; this can lead to financial and/or sexual exploitation. It has to be recognised that vulnerable adults can be targeted and groomed in exactly the same way that paedophiles groom children.

Institutional abuse

Finally, some attention must be given to why abuse might happen in an institution (e.g. care home, day centre, hospital ward, prison). Service users could experience abuse in all sorts of forms. It could be workers who are abusing service users or the rules and regimes which exist could be oppressive and abusive. Usually the reasons are complex. Here it will suffice to consider some of the more common root causes of institutional abuse:

- the manager
- existing regimes
- lack of education/training
- staff groups/factions
- the environment

- low staffing levels
- low staff morale
- the characteristics of staff
- the characteristics of service users.

 Handout 4.4, p.127

When discussing these causes in more depth I shall use the term 'home' for simplicity's sake but the discussion relates to any setting which could be deemed to be an institution as listed in Handout 4.1.

The manager

Some managers can rule and dominate both staff and service users. It can be very dangerous if a manager has done the same job for many years and has not developed professionally with the changes in practice. This type of manager will make all the decisions and not listen to staff or service users. It is likely that rules and regulations are enforced which regiment the running of the home.

Existing regimes

Obviously there have to be some rules and regulations in a home where a number of people are living, but they should not impede service users; that is, they should be free to live their lives as they wish to do. The principles of care should be maintained:

- privacy
- dignity
- independence
- choice
- rights

- fulfilment
- respect
- partnership
- individuality and identity.

 Handout 4.5, p.128

Lack of education/training

Nowadays workers should be trained to a high standard with the introduction of the Care Standards Act 2000, the TOPSS Induction and Foundation Standards (TOPSS 2001) and the Health and Social Care National Occupational Standards (Skills for Care 2006). However, sometimes training is not as rigorous as it should be. Recruiting workers can be problematic so sometimes a worker will start a job without adequate training because he or she is needed as quickly as possible out on the floor. That worker may do something which is abusive but it is unintentional. This may be a reason for abuse occurring but it is not an excuse. The matter still has to be investigated.

Staff groups/factions

A staff group can become split for many reasons. It can just be down to a clash of personalities – some people just cannot get on with each other. On the other hand there may be some workers who have been working in a home for many years and they resent new workers coming in; they could also feel very superior and exercise what they see to be their power. Consequently, groups of workers can become competitive with each other and the service users do not get the attention and quality of care they deserve.

The environment

Some homes can be very unattractive – dark, dingy, badly decorated, poorly furnished. This can depress both workers and service users who spend many hours in such an environment.

Low staffing levels

Many institutions are not adequately staffed. Staffing ratios may be too low in general but when high dependency levels exist a great deal of stress and strain is placed on workers. Often staffing levels meet the standards required but workers may have a different view. They may feel there are not enough of them to cope with meeting the needs of the service users. This can lead to low staff morale.

Low staff morale

Morale can be low because staff are overworked and tired. Another reason can be that staff are not valued by management. Many workers are not paid enough for the job they do; therefore, it is vital that managers regularly validate the work which is being undertaken and the service provided.

The characteristics of staff

It can be hard to recruit for some jobs which are low paid. It should not happen but it does – the wrong type of person is employed. It can be hard at interview to suss out whether someone genuinely wants to do the job or whether he or she just wants any job. Caring for people is a vocation; not everyone can do it.

At this point it is important to raise the point again about abusers deliberately targeting and grooming people. In the past, offenders may have gone to work in an institution deliberately to get access to vulnerable people. This should happen less now, with workers having to have checks undertaken through the Criminal Records Bureau, but some people still fall through the net.

The characteristics of service users

It has already been said that dependency levels can be very high in some institutions. If staffing levels are low, workers can become very stressed and, like carers in the community, can lash out in a fit of temper.

Indicators of abuse

So far we have considered other important issues which must be understood before a worker goes on to learn about the indicators of abuse. It cannot be emphasised enough just how difficult it is to recognise abuse and workers should never feel guilty if they have 'missed' cases in the past. They will be better equipped in the future after training on abuse. The main problem is that many indicators of abuse can be signs and symptoms of other conditions. Consequently, when undertaking abuse investigations, it is imperative not to jump to conclusions; that is, it is necessary to rule things out before seeing what 'evidence' is left. The other difficulty is that many signs of abuse can be symptomatic of different forms of abuse.

There has been much debate over the years about the use of checklists – especially in the field of child protection. I believe checklists can be a useful starting point. It has already been said it is necessary to rule things out: a checklist can stimulate a worker to consider various things – it is a useful tool. So some checklists are included in the section.

Since much abuse remains hidden, it is imperative to monitor changes in behaviour over time. So anyone who has been working with a vulnerable adult for some time is a key person who might identify abuse. Workers should always be encouraged to monitor and record even the slightest change they notice. Many workers do find recording a chore, but managers must stress the importance of keeping good, informative and relevant written records. These can often be used as evidence in a court of law. This is discussed in depth in Chapter 9. Let us think further about changes in behaviour.

Changes in behaviour

Every human being is unique and will react differently to situations they find themselves in. Similarly, victims will handle being in an abusive situation in their own individual way; that is, they will develop coping strategies. This makes it harder for a worker to realise what is going on. Some typical changes which may occur are as follows:

- withdrawal
- confusion
- aggression
- fearfulness

- resignation, lethargy, depression
- making inappropriate attachments
- denial
- seeking help from numerous sources.

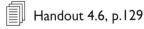 Handout 4.6, p.129

Withdrawal

Victims can become withdrawn in several ways: in the way they communicate or in what they do. It may be if they are verbal and normally very chatty, they will become monosyllabic; it is as though they do not want to talk. The real reason may be that they are scared to speak out – frightened that they may let the cat out of the bag – especially if the abuser has threatened them. Another reason may be that they just feel very depressed and lethargic because of what is happening to them. The withdrawal can also manifest itself in the victim not doing activities which they normally enjoy for the reasons already mentioned.

Confusion

A way of withdrawing is to become confused; often the confused world can be a happier place than the real world. Needless to say so many cases of abuse are missed when working with older people because workers often assume that the confusion is the onset of dementia, Alzheimer's disease, and so on. However, it must be pointed out that confusion can become apparent in younger victims as well.

Aggression

The term 'challenging behaviour' is used a great deal nowadays – and often inappropriately. Some service users tend to get labelled very quickly rather than workers asking 'What has caused this behaviour?', and adults with learning disabilities are often said to be 'challenging'. A reason might be that the person was abused in childhood. Aggression can be a way of venting anger for a victim who cannot vent towards their abuser so they will vent towards someone they trust and whom they know will not retaliate.

Fearfulness

A worker may notice that a service user starts to lose confidence and presents as being fearful when he or she has been very strong before. The victim may become very nervous or jumpy when other people are around. Alternatively the victim may only be different when someone else is around (that is, the abuser).

Resignation, lethargy, depression

If abuse continues for any length of time, the victim will see the situation as the 'norm' and become resigned to it. Over long periods of time victims may become very lethargic because they do not see the point of anything; they cannot see that anything will change – hence they will present as being lethargic and depressed.

Making inappropriate attachments

Many victims crave affection because they have been treated badly by their abusers. Because of their vulnerability, they may cling to anyone who shows them any sign of affection. Abusers can pick up on this vulnerability very easily and hence many victims make inappropriate attachments. This can also lead to a victim being abused by different people through his or her lifetime.

Denial

Many victims are terrified of their abusers or they protect the abuser because he or she is a relative or someone they care for dearly. This may lead to a change in the victim's behaviour – the victim may go 'over the top' by trying to emphasise that 'life has never been better' or emphasising that a certain person is 'absolutely wonderful'. Many victims feel ashamed of the situation they are in and self-blame. Sometimes it is easier for them to deny what is really happening and convince themselves that it is not.

Seeking help from numerous sources

Another overused phrase is 'attention seeking'. Many people labelled as such are deemed to be a nuisance. Again the fundamental starting point should be the question: 'Why is the person acting in this way?' It could be that the victim is hoping that someone will pick up on the fact that something is wrong without having to disclose about the abuse. Or the victim may feel safer when there are people around because the abuser cannot get to harm him or her.

So, when someone's behaviour does change, workers should start to question why this is happening.

KEY QUESTIONS

Why is the person acting in this way?

What could have caused the change(s) in behaviour?

In the following pages you will find handouts relating to indicators for the different categories of abuse. The indicators of emotional abuse could relate to other categories too because most victims will be emotionally harmed whatever form(s) of abuse they are experiencing. So this is a good list with which to start:

- insomnia/deprivation of sleep or need for excessive sleep
- change in appetite
- unusual weight gain/loss
- weepiness/unusual bouts of sobbing/crying

- unexplained paranoia

- low self-esteem

- excessive fear/anxiety

- flinching in the presence of someone

- ambivalence, resignation, passivity.

 Handout 4.7, p.130

Again it has to be stressed that it will be people who know the adult that will notice the changes in his or her behaviour and appearance. Only rarely do workers walk in at the right moment and see someone being ridiculed, humiliated, threatened, verbally abused, and so on. Victims are also good at hiding their emotions; again this is a coping strategy they will have developed. So the indicators listed in Handout 4.7 can be hard to recognise.

Case Examples

- Kay had been a headteacher and well respected by everyone. When she was 70 years of age she started having short-term memory loss. Her son regularly made fun of her and made remarks such as 'You're not so clever now are you?' The home carers began to notice that Kay was crying a lot and wanted to stay in bed most of the day.

- Virginia had mental health problems but had been doing really well. She had got a part-time job helping in an office. When one of the secretaries found out that Virginia had been on a psychiatric ward she started to bully her. Virginia could not sleep at night because she dreaded going to work the next day. She felt sick a lot of the time and could not eat.

Physical abuse

A lot of people think that physical abuse must be the easiest form of abuse to identify, because they think of injuries – cuts, lacerations, bruises, burns, fractures. However, physical abuse can be inflicted in many forms, many of which are not easily identifiable. For example, a slap on the face may not leave an injury but it is an assault. Likewise, in some cases force feeding or physical restraint may not leave any visible effects. When something is not noticeable, one way to pick up on abuse is to monitor changes in behaviour as discussed above.

Medication abuse can be very difficult to prove in a court of law without blood tests, but a worker might notice that someone has become sluggish or is sleeping more. Physical neglect may include malnutrition or dehydration, which may only become obvious over time.

Many vulnerable adults are bullied – either physically or emotionally. This may be done in a very subtle way so that it is never seen by anyone who might do something to intervene. Again there might not be any visible signs, so workers must watch for changes in behaviour – like those listed under 'emotional abuse'.

Case Examples

- Lionel had learning disabilities and lived in supported accommodation. He was regularly brought to casualty with injuries by his key worker, who said he had falls and self-harmed. Nobody in the hospital ever asked Lionel what had happened. On his 12th visit to casualty a doctor questioned whether the injuries were consistent with the story the key worker gave. He then spoke to Lionel without the worker being present. Lionel had been regularly hit and beaten by his key worker.

- Day care workers noticed that Valerie had changed over the past six months. She had always been very lively and wanted to take part in activities. Recently she wanted to sit in a chair and do nothing. Her speech was also very slurred. When social workers investigated it was found that Valerie was being over-medicated by her carers.

Indicators of physical abuse:

- multiple bruising not consistent with a fall

- black eyes

- unexplained marks

- cuts/lacerations

- burns not consistent with scorching by direct heat

- fractures not consistent with falls

- stench of urine/faeces; incontinence

- drowsiness; excessive sleep

- loss of weight

- hunger/thirst

- lack of personal care.

 Handout 4.8, p.131

Sexual abuse

Sexual abuse often remains extremely well hidden and consequently it is particularly hard to identify. Workers often feel very uncomfortable discussing this type of abuse, never mind having to prove it is happening. Workers who are involved in helping with personal care tasks are the ones who are most likely to identify sexual abuse.

Again it is about monitoring any changes. A worker might suddenly notice a female service user is getting a lot of infections/nasty discharges. It is important to seek medical advice if the service user is willing. Sometimes the infections can turn out to be sexually transmitted infections.

Sexual abuse victims can be damaged internally during the abusive acts. This can cause bleeding (from the vagina or anus). If implements have been inserted the victim may be damaged to such a degree that they find sitting or walking extremely painful. Changes might be that they fidget and cannot get comfortable when sitting; or they may walk slower than they usually do. Bruising can also be caused during the sexual acts – a common area is on the inner thighs; but a victim can be held down and hence finger tip bruising may be visible on the arms.

A good indicator of sexual abuse is the sudden onset of confusion, which is quite dramatic. It is essential that other causal factors are ruled out – for example chest infection, urinary tract infections, change in medication. Victims who lack capacity may try to protect themselves by wearing extra layers of clothing or putting things (like newspapers) in their underwear.

If the sexual abuse continues for a long time, a victim may become depressed. Victims can have nightmares about the sexual acts and may want to talk about their nightmares to a worker in abstract terms. Victims can also have flashbacks about what has been done to them. A victim may have no idea what has triggered the memory – it could be a smell, noise, song, seeing a person who resembles the abuser.

Using touch appropriately is very difficult for a worker because a very simple action (like putting a hand on a person's arm) could trigger a memory if this is what the abuser did. Many victims do not like any form of touch. A change in behaviour may be that a service user has previously not had a problem with accepting help with personal care tasks, but suddenly does not want anyone near his or her body (to wash, bath, dress, etc.). Victims are also unlikely to want a medical examination of any kind, even if it is just looking in their mouth if they have a sore throat.

Finally, some victims will start talking overtly about sexual matters, which they have never done before. Again this can be so difficult for workers who support older people because this could also be an indicator of the onset of Alzheimer's disease.

Case Examples

- Loretta had Alzheimer's disease and lived in a care home. She regularly told staff that a man came into her room at night. No one believed her. One day Loretta was bleeding very badly from her vagina and she also had bruising on different parts of her body. When examined it was proven she had been sexually abused.

- Tara had learning disabilities and lived with her family. She always presented as a very happy, easy-going person. She started to attend some classes at a local college. Her parents noticed a sudden change in her. She started using very sexualised language and was aggressive to family members. Months later she regularly had nightmares and woke up other members of the family with her screaming. Tara finally disclosed that she was being forced into sexual activity by an older man at college.

Indicators of sexual abuse:

- genital or urinary irritation
- frequent infections
- pain/itching in genital/anal area
- bleeding from vagina or anus
- sexually transmitted infections
- stains on underwear, nightwear
- wetting/soiling
- bruising on inner thighs/upper arms
- difficulty in walking/sitting
- sudden onset of confusion
- wearing extra layers of clothes
- depression
- nightmares/flashbacks
- severe upset or agitation when there is personal contact
- conversation regularly becomes of a sexual nature.

 Handout 4.9, p.132

Financial/material abuse

Financial abuse is the most common form of adult abuse and it is also very hard to prove. It is very easy to con a vulnerable person if they lack understanding or capacity. For example, a person with learning disabilities may get confused with different coins or notes. Other adults who have to be dependent on someone to help them with their finances (perhaps because they are housebound) may not realise how their money is being mismanaged because they trust their abuser.

Case Examples

- Helen had not been out of the house for years. Her neighbour, Mrs Grimes, used to do the shopping but never gave Helen the receipts. She always said things were much dearer than they were; for example, Helen thought a loaf of bread was 95p when it was 55p. The amount spent on shopping increased so much Helen could not pay her bills.

- John, a befriender, always took Sam, who had learning disabilities, to the cinema on a Saturday afternoon. Sam would always give John a £20 note to buy the tickets, which cost £4 each. John gave Sam £2 change. John then started asking Sam if he could borrow money; at first Sam was happy to help out. However, John wanted more and more. Sam became afraid to say 'no'. He became very withdrawn and did not want to go to the cinema any more.

It will be someone who knows the person well who may pick up that there have been changes. For example, a person is very obviously being cautious about spending money when this has never been a problem before. Or suddenly there is an inability to pay bills or buy essential things. Other indicators of financial abuse are:

- the vulnerable adult lacks money

- the person does not manage his or her own finances although he or she is capable

- a power of attorney has been obtained when the adult cannot comprehend

- the person is reluctant/refuses to buy things which are necessary when finances should not be a problem

- the person is unable to pay bills or buy food or other essential things

- there are unexplained or sudden withdrawals of money from the vulnerable adult's post office/bank/building society accounts

- there is a disparity between the person's income/assets and satisfactory living conditions

- there is extraordinary interest by family members or other people in the vulnerable adult's assets/will.

 Handout 4.10, p.133

Neglect

Neglect is incredibly difficult to prove. It is necessary to remember that neglect can be physical or emotional; therefore, many of the indicators for physical and emotional abuse will be applicable to neglect. Neglect can also be an act of omission so it might take time to see the effects of that.

I do not think we are very good at monitoring adults' health in general; they are never monitored in the same way as children. Obviously it is thought that most adults can look after themselves, but some adults cannot. Gross neglect can be obvious, but there will always be the question – is the person self-neglecting?

Workers need to think about a person's health and physical condition; for example, the state of their:

- skin

- hair

- eyes

- weight.

As with other forms of abuse, neglect can be inflicted in very subtle ways, so a worker may not be able to pick up on the fact that a person is not allowed social contact (e.g. visitors, telephone calls) or that medical help was not obtained when needed. A worker cannot be with a person 24/7 and the abuser will be making every effort to be careful to ensure that everything seems fine on the surface. Consequently, monitoring a vulnerable adult is crucial in order to identify that abuse is happening.

We must not forget that a person's cultural, religious and spiritual needs might not be met and that this can be a form of neglect.

Case Examples

- Sam was physically disabled and slightly confused. His wife considered him to be 'an embarrassment' so she told him he must stay in his bedroom upstairs if she was to care for him.

- Home carers started to work with twins, Mitchell and Wilbur, who were in their seventies, when their niece was suddenly admitted to hospital. The brothers, who were both disabled after having strokes, were living in the most appalling, squalid conditions. The niece had managed all their affairs, including finances; nobody else visited the house.

- At her annual review the social worker noticed that Shahida had lost a lot of weight. She told the social worker that she was very worried that she had not been to the mosque for a year and felt guilty about this. The fact was that staff had refused to take her. Also she was not given halal meat. She was given the same meals as the other service users, so she just ate vegetables.

- Lorna had a brain injury. She lived with her son who was agoraphobic. Nobody visited them. One day neighbours called the police when they heard shouting and screaming. The smell in the house was putrid. They found Lorna sitting in urine and faeces; her clothes were thoroughly soiled and her hair matted with faeces.

- An African Caribbean man, Errol, was never asked if he wanted to join in the activities in the care home. When family members visited they noticed that Errol had become very quiet and did not want to speak to them.

Indicators of neglect:

- inadequate heating, lighting
- accommodation, environment in general is poor
- ulcers, pressure sores
- smell of urine/faeces
- weight loss
- malnutrition
- dehydration
- unkempt, for example clothing in poor condition; wears same clothes; soiled clothing
- absence of mobility aids, hearing aid, glasses
- objects used to restrict movement
- difficulty in gaining entry/access to adult
- reluctance/failure/prohibition to access services.

 Handout 4.11, p.134

Discriminatory abuse

Many of the indicators discussed above will be relevant to discriminatory abuse. However, workers must remember that some vulnerable adults may not realise that they are victims of discrimination. This may be because they lack capacity or they have accepted actions/behaviours as the 'norm' or 'way of life'.

Case Examples

- Nicholas had been known to the mental health services for over 25 years. He had attended the same mental health day centre for a long time and loved it. As he was approaching 65 years of age he was told that he would have to move to a centre for older people after his birthday. Nicholas became very depressed and agitated because he did not want the change in his life.

- Joseph was homosexual and had been placed in a care home. He was told his partner could not go into his bedroom. As the months went on Joseph became very angry with staff, but also very sad and depressed. He spent a lot of time in his room and only came out when his partner visited. They had to sit in one of the lounges.

Handout 4.12 lists some particular signs which may indicate that discriminatory abuse is taking place:

- reluctance to go out
- refusal to attend places previously visited frequently
- general withdrawal
- crying
- fear
- anxiety
- depression
- anger
- questioning of self.

 Handout 4.12, p.135

General indicators

Finally, Handout 4.13 is a checklist of things which may indicate that abuse may be occurring. It is important to emphasise that if one or more of these things is happening it is *not* conclusive that abuse is occurring, but a worker should start questioning whether there is a possibility that abuse is happening:

- changes in behaviour

- changes in appearance

- change in usual routine/lifestyle

- victim becomes over-protective/defensive

- someone shows extraordinary interest in the vulnerable adult

- repeated requests for GP (or other professional/worker) to visit

- frequent visits to casualty

- regular admissions to hospital

- repeated falls, injuries

- carer has negative perception of vulnerable adult

- carer goes to see GP regularly.

 Handout 4.13, p.136

Some of the indicators listed do not need explanation; however, some do. A victim may repeatedly contact the GP or other professional or worker in the hope that someone will pick up on the fact that they are being abused. Victims will feel less guilty if someone else identifies abuse without them having to disclose. Also, carers may feel guilty that they do not really want to be in the role of carer but feel it is their duty to do so. They may psyche themselves to tell the GP that they do not want to be doing this or they need more help, but when they get into the surgery they cannot say anything about the true situation.

Recognising abuse in institutions

All the checklists and indicators discussed above could apply to service users living in or attending an institution. It is important to talk to service users in order to give them an opportunity to speak out if something is wrong. Also, professionals and workers going into an institution should be observant. Going in at unexpected times of day can be very enlightening. However, it is important to be aware of other things which may happen and question why this is so; for example, high turnover of staff, frequent absences due to sickness. Other indicators may be:

- service users have no choice about when and how to do things

- set times for getting up, going to bed, toileting, meals, and so on

- no menu or choice of alternative meals

- no opportunity for getting drinks and snacks when required

- lack of organised activities

- minimal interaction between workers and service users

- lack of personal possessions

- service users appear unkempt

- smell of urine/faeces

- poor standard of cleanliness in the surrounding environment

- complaints not followed through.

 Handout 4.14, p.137

Exercises and using case studies

It can be quite heavy going through the indicators of abuse and a trainer needs to be creative in the way a course is delivered to cover this. Exercise 4.3 can be used to get workers to realise that they may have missed indicators of abuse but also to reiterate the point that some indicators of abuse can be a symptom of some other condition or situation.

 Exercise 4.3, p.123

Trainers should always allow enough time on a course for participants to undertake case studies which will test out whether participants have learnt the indictors of abuse. Chapters 10, 11 and 12 include a variety of additional materials which can be used for this purpose. In addition there are 20 case studies provided in *Becoming a Trainer in Adult Abuse Work* (Pritchard 2001a) and for workers working with older people there are numerous case studies in *Working with Elder Abuse* (Pritchard 1996). The questions which need to be used in group work when focusing on recognising abuse are:

1. What types of abuse could be happening?
2. What are the indicators for each category you have listed?
3. What do you think should happen next?

 Handout 4.15, p.138

Key learning points from this chapter

- Abuse can happen anywhere – in the community or in institutional/communal settings.

- It is wrong to stereotype the victim and abuser.

- Anyone can be a victim; anyone can be an abuser.

- Men can be victims.

- Women can abuse.

- There can be many causal factors of abuse: historical, social, economic, environmental, political.

- The root cause of abuse can relate to the past as well as the current situation.

- The abuser rather than the victim may have problems.

- Domestic violence is a form of adult abuse.

- There can be a link between child abuse, domestic violence and adult abuse.

- It is crucial to monitor changes in behaviour and appearance over time.

- What may be indicators of abuse can also be signs and symptoms of other things, for example medical conditions.

- Do not label people; ask why they behave as they do.

- Never make assumptions.

- Keep an open mind.

- Don't jump to conclusions.

Suggested reading

Read the section in your local policy and procedures on vulnerable adults/adult abuse about signs and symptoms/indicators of abuse.

Decalmer, P. and Glendenning, F.J. (eds) (1997) *The Mistreatment of Elderly People.* London: Sage. (Even though this book is concerned with older people a lot can be learnt about identifying abuse in general. It is a valuable resource.)

Pritchard, J. (ed.) (2001b) *Good Practice with Vulnerable Adults.* London: Jessica Kingsley Publishers.

Video

WAA2: Recognising Adult Abuse

This video takes workers a stage further on from definitions. Case studies across the specialisms illustrate how the various categories of abuse can be recognised.

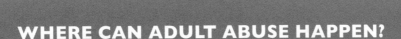

WHERE CAN ADULT ABUSE HAPPEN?

Objective

To make participants think about exactly where abuse can happen.

Participants

In small groups.

Equipment

Flipchart paper and pens.

The trainer will have prepared flipchart sheets with the headings 'Community' and 'Institutions'.

Copies of Handout 4.1.

Time

10 minutes.

Task

1.   The large group is divided into either two or four groups.

2.   The groups are given a flipchart sheet which is marked *either* 'Community' *or* 'Institution'.

3.   Participants have to list exact locations where they think abuse could happen.

Feedback

1.   Each group feeds back their lists.

2.   Participants are given Handout 4.1.

3.   There is general discussion.

© Jacki Pritchard 2007

STEREOTYPING VICTIMS AND ABUSERS

Objective

To get participants to realise that they have stereotyped people on occasions, but also to think about how society can stereotype as well.

Participants

Two or four groups.

Equipment

Flipchart paper and pens.

The trainer will have prepared the flipchart sheets with the headings 'Victim' and 'Abuser'.

Time

15 minutes.

Task

1. The groups are given a flipchart sheet which is marked *either* 'Victim' *or* 'Abuser'.

2. Participants write down the characteristics of a victim or abuser but also how they envisage they will look, for example colour of hair/eyes; what they wear.

3. The groups draw the face of either the victim or abuser.

Feedback

1. Each group talks through their list and explains why they drew their victim/abuser as they did.

2. Discussion about how society views certain groups of people.

Note for trainer

Some participants find this exercise very hard to undertake as they do not believe they stereotype in any way. In explaining the task, the trainer should encourage groups to also think about how other people/society in general stereotype. Participants should think about their family, friends, colleagues and what may have been said to them earlier in life.

 © Jacki Pritchard 2007

HAVE I SEEN ABUSE?

Objective

To make participants who have worked in health and social care reflect back on what they have seen in the past.

Participants

In small groups.

Equipment

Flipchart paper and pens.

Time

15 minutes.

Task

1. Participants will think back to service users they have worked with in the past or those they are working with now.

2. Participants are asked to think about whether they now think they may have missed any indicators of abuse.

3. List the indicators and discuss whether they could be signs of anything else.

Feedback

1. Each group feeds back their lists.

2. Discussion about how the participants now feel and what they have learnt from reflecting back.

Note for trainer

The trainer should emphasise at the outset that this exercise is not being undertaken to criticise workers. The aim is to encourage reflection but also to make participants think about whether they take things at face value.

WHERE ABUSE HAPPENS

You must remember that abuse can happen anywhere, i.e. in the community or in institutional/communal settings. Some examples might be:

- a person's home – bedsit, flat, house, supported or sheltered accommodation

- a public place – street, alleyway, corridor, hallway, shop, post office, cinema, club

- a workplace

- a day centre

- a day hospital

- a hospital ward

- an education/training establishment

- a care home

- prison.

© Jacki Pritchard 2007

THINGS TO THINK ABOUT

Relevance of the past

The past may be relevant to the current abusive situation. The following should be considered:

- past relationships

- past experience of violence/abuse/neglect

- past problems

- history of offending.

Problems: past and current

- addictions

- financial problems

- losses

- physical and mental health problems

- stresses

- dependency (emotional and physical)

WHY A CARER MIGHT BE STRESSED AND THEN ABUSE

- The high dependency levels of the vulnerable adult

- The behaviour traits of the dependent person

- The nature of the tasks which have to be performed on a daily basis

- Monotony

- Boredom

- Frustration

- Isolation – little social contact with other people; being stuck in the house all day and night; little meaningful conversation

- Little/no support

- Lack of services

 © Jacki Pritchard 2007

ROOT CAUSES OF ABUSE IN INSTITUTIONAL SETTINGS

- The manager

- Existing regimes

- Lack of education/training

- Staff groups/factions

- The environment

- Low staffing levels

- Low staff morale

- The characteristics of staff

- The characteristics of service users

PRINCIPLES OF CARE

- Privacy

- Dignity

- Independence

- Choice

- Rights

- Fulfilment

- Respect

- Partnership

- Individuality and identity

© Jacki Pritchard 2007

CHANGES IN BEHAVIOUR

- Withdrawal

- Confusion

- Aggression

- Fearfulness

- Resignation, lethargy, depression

- Making inappropriate attachments

- Denial

- Seeking help from numerous sources

© Jacki Pritchard 2007

INDICATORS OF EMOTIONAL ABUSE
(THIS INCLUDES EMOTIONAL NEGLECT)

- Insomnia/deprivation of sleep or need for excessive sleep

- Change in appetite

- Unusual weight gain/loss

- Weepiness/unusual bouts of sobbing/crying

- Unexplained paranoia

- Low self-esteem

- Excessive fear/anxiety

- Flinching in the presence of someone

© Jacki Pritchard 2007

PHYSICAL INDICATIONS OF ABUSE
(THIS INCLUDES PHYSICAL NEGLECT)

- Multiple bruising not consistent with a fall

- Black eyes

- Unexplained marks

- Cuts/lacerations

- Burns not consistent with scorching by direct heat

- Fractures not consistent with falls

- Stench of urine/faeces; incontinence

- Drowsiness; excessive sleep

- Loss of weight

- Hunger/thirst

- Lack of personal care

INDICATORS OF SEXUAL ABUSE

- Genital or urinary irritation

- Frequent infections

- Pain/itching in genital/anal area

- Bleeding from vagina or anus

- Sexually transmitted infections

- Stains on underwear, nightwear

- Wetting/soiling

- Bruising on inner thighs/upper arms

- Difficulty in walking/sitting

- Sudden onset of confusion

- Wearing extra layers of clothes

- Depression

- Nightmares/flashbacks

- Severe upset or agitation when there is personal contact

- Conversation regularly becomes of a sexual nature

© Jacki Pritchard 2007

INDICATORS OF FINANCIAL ABUSE

- The vulnerable adult lacks money

- The person does not manage his or her own finances although he or she is capable

- A power of attorney has been obtained when the adult cannot comprehend

- The person is reluctant/refuses to buy things which are necessary when finances should not be a problem

- The person is unable to pay bills or buy food or other essential things

- There are unexplained or sudden withdrawals of money from the vulnerable adult's post office/bank/building society accounts

- There is a disparity between the person's income/assets and satisfactory living conditions

- There is extraordinary interest by family members or other people in the vulnerable adult's assets/will

INDICATORS OF NEGLECT

- Inadequate heating, lighting

- Accommodation, environment in general is poor

- Ulcers, pressure sores

- Smell of urine/faeces

- Weight loss

- Malnutrition

- Dehydration

- Unkempt, for example clothing in poor condition; wears same clothes; soiled clothing

- Absence of mobility aids, hearing aid, glasses

- Objects used to restrict movement

- Difficulty in gaining entry/access to adult

- Reluctance/failure/prohibition to access services

 © Jacki Pritchard 2007

INDICATORS OF DISCRIMINATORY ABUSE

- Reluctance to go out

- Refusal to attend places previously visited frequently

- General withdrawal

- Crying

- Fear

- Anxiety

- Depression

- Anger

- Questioning of self

GENERAL INDICATORS OF ABUSE

- Changes in behaviour

- Changes in appearance

- Change in usual routine/lifestyle

- Victim becomes over-protective/defensive

- Someone shows extraordinary interest in the vulnerable adult

- Repeated requests for GP (or other professional/worker) to visit

- Frequent visits to casualty

- Regular admissions to hospital

- Repeated falls, injuries

- Carer has negative perception of vulnerable adult

- Carer goes to see GP regularly

 © Jacki Pritchard 2007

SOME INDICATORS OF INSTITUTIONAL ABUSE

- Service users have no choice about when and how to do things

- Set times for getting up, going to bed, toileting, meals, and so on

- No menu or choice of alternative meals

- No opportunity for getting drinks and snacks when required

- Lack of organised activities

- Minimal interaction between workers and service users

- Lack of personal possessions

- Service users appear unkempt

- Smell of urine/faeces

- Poor standard of cleanliness in the surrounding environment

- Complaints not followed through

© Jacki Pritchard 2007

RECOGNISING ADULT ABUSE

Read the case study, then answer the following questions:

1. What types of abuse could be happening?

2. What are the indicators for each category you have listed?

3. What do you think should happen next?

 © Jacki Pritchard 2007

Chapter 5

Handling Disclosure

Disclosure usually comes when a worker least expects it. Consequently, he or she can be taken aback and may not act in the best possible way. Learning how to handle a disclosure about abuse is vital because workers can contaminate evidence without realising they are doing so. The main danger is that workers will ask too many questions and delve too deeply at this early stage. The purpose of this chapter is to take the reader back to basics; that is, to revisit good listening skills and responding skills. As these are fundamental skills to most jobs in health and social care it is important that all workers (no matter how long they have been practising) return at regular intervals to evaluate current practices. We all develop bad habits over time; driving a car is a good example. Most of us who passed our test years ago would probably fail if we retook a test today. It is the same with listening and responding skills; we can unconsciously become stale and develop bad practices.

When talking about disclosure many readers may automatically assume that we are going to be thinking about disclosures from victims of abuse. What people often do not give enough thought to is the fact that an abuser can give a disclosure. There will be the remorseful abuser; a good example being a carer under stress who has lashed out in a fit of temper. However, there is also the unrepentant abuser who may disclose for all sorts of different reasons. It may be hard for some workers to get their head around the fact that some people enjoy abusing other human beings and they get a kick out of talking about what they have done. Because a disclosure can come from a victim or abuser I shall use the term 'service user' in this chapter to relate to anyone who might disclose.

Going back to basics

As a trainer I feel very strongly that all workers should be given the opportunity to attend courses which revisit basic skills; this enables workers to evaluate their day-to-day practice and so keeps them fresh and prevents them from becoming stale and maybe responding like a robot. I have written elsewhere about good communication skills (Pritchard 2003b) but in this chapter I think it is important to return to consider what good listening and responding skills are in order to receive a disclosure in an appropriate way.

The storyteller and listener

A good starting point when delivering training on handling disclosure is to introduce the concept of the storyteller and the listener. Because of the way many workers have to assess nowadays, it can be common practice for them to have an agenda which involves asking a lot of questions rather than sitting back and listening to the service user.

KEY QUESTIONS

Do you talk too much?

Do you let other people speak while you sit back and listen?

Do you ask a lot of questions?

Do you use 'Why?' questions a lot?

All too many of us rely on questions when we talk rather than developing the art of good conversation. A mini exercise which I usually set for course participants (if I have them on a course for longer than a day) as a bit of 'homework' overnight is as follows.

HOMEWORK

Workers are asked to choose a half-hour period of time when they are either at home with friends/family or out socially. In that half hour they have to count how many questions they ask during the course of a normal conversation and how many of them are 'Why?' questions.

I shall never forget the worker who told me she lived alone and would not see anyone that evening so could not do the exercise. The next morning she told me she would be contributing to the feedback because she had asked her cat 62 questions in her first hour at home.

Exercise 5.1 introduces the concept of the storyteller and the listener. It will help workers to start thinking about how they communicate with people, whether they do listen enough and how they use their body language. The trainer needs to keep reinforcing throughout a course on handling disclosure the point that it is important to get the service user to give a disclosure in their own words with few interruptions.

✍ Exercise 5.1, p.152

Body language

We have all heard the phrase or been trained to 'adopt a relaxed open position' when communicating with people, and we know that it is wrong to cross arms and legs as this may be interpreted as a barrier. The reality is that many of us feel more relaxed when our arms and legs are crossed. I find when I train workers many of them are resistant to trying to change their posture. It is important for workers to understand that a service user must be given the right messages; that is, the disclosure is welcomed. The real situation might be that the worker is wishing he or she was not receiving a disclosure; perhaps thinking 'Why me?'; 'Oh no, not another abuse case!' The body language must not show this.

Very often disclosure comes when you least expect it, frequently when a worker may be bathing or toileting a service user. Another classic scenario for disclosure is when a social worker has been with the service user for about an hour and just as he or she is going out of the door, the disclosure comes.

THINK ABOUT

What would you do if a service user started giving you a disclosure and you had to be somewhere else in the next 30 minutes (e.g. picking a child up from school; attending a case conference)?

It is important to stress that a worker should not show shock or horror when they are given the disclosure. Many victims are fearful that they are not going to be believed; some will be worried that they are going to upset the worker. It is so important for the worker to indicate verbally and visually that he or she is willing to receive the disclosure. This is equally important when an abuser discloses. Some abusers may enjoy seeing the worker feeling uncomfortable. Therefore, workers need to think about how parts of their body are responding when they are listening to a disclosure and the effects these might have on the discloser:

- head movements
- facial expressions
- eye contact/eyebrows
- arms
- hands
- legs
- feet.

 Handout 5.1, p.156

A worker should never use quick, jerky movements – which many of us do when we are taken aback. As has been said already, it is important to try to get the service user to tell their story in their own words and at their own pace. Workers should not introduce their own agenda, which is easily done when panic is setting in and thoughts are going to the alerter role and what may follow. While listening it can be encouraging for the service user if the worker uses certain gestures:

- nodding
- tilting the head to one side
- showing the palm of hand upwards
- beckoning with one hand.

We all have bad habits regarding body language. We may do things without realising it. It is important to try to identify these habits and they often come to light during role play on a training course. Typical distracting things can be:

- fiddling with rings, earrings, hair or a pen
- fidgeting
- moving one's glasses up and down the nose or onto the head
- jogging one's foot
- making too much hand movement.

KEY QUESTION

In regard to body language, what are your bad habits?

Other things to think about

There are so many things to think about when a disclosure suddenly starts happening. It is very natural for any worker to feel a little bit of panic and get distracted because all sorts of things are going through the mind. Workers should try to think about their:

- voice
- eye contact
- facial expressions
- position and use of body
- breathing.

 Handout 5.2, p.157

The voice

The voice is a very important tool which a worker must use effectively. There are many things to think about in using the voice:

- tone
- pitch
- inflection
- spacing of words
- use of emphases
- pauses
- silences.

 Handout 5.3, p.158

The service user must understand what the worker is saying and in times of stress a person may not remember what has been said to him or her – no matter how succinctly it has been put. A worker must aim to speak at an appropriate pace; it is very easy to speak too quickly if you are nervous or feeling panicky. If taken aback, a worker may speak too quietly. So workers need to think about how they project their voice and about using emphasis to convey what they want from the service user. The voice is important but it is just as important for a worker to make effective use of pauses and silences. Many people feel uncomfortable with silences and develop a tendency to jump in with a question. If you are a person who knows you do this you should start practising the *counting technique* in your day-to-day practice. When there is a pause or silence you need to count seconds before you start talking. In regard to adults (it is totally different when communicating with children) a pause is up to 20 seconds and a silence is between 20 and 45 seconds.

Eye contact

It is important to maintain eye contact with the service user who is disclosing but not to glare! It is all right to make slight eye movements. However, the service user who is disclosing may *not* look at the worker. If he or she is looking out of the window or at the floor, it is imperative that the worker keeps looking at the service user, because he or she will feel that.

Facial expressions

I think it is incredibly difficult to know what your own face looks like and our faces can react very quickly when we hear something. It is important not to show shock or horror when receiving a disclosure but this can be very hard if you really are shocked. Workers need to remember to make a mental note to ask themselves the following question:

> ### KEY QUESTION
>
> What is my face showing now?

Position and use of body

Body language has been discussed at length above, but here I just want to introduce the concept of the *five-minute body rule*. It is something workers can start practising in their day-to-day work so it becomes natural to do this. The idea is that, when interacting with a service user, the worker looks at the position of the body every five minutes to see if it has moved and whether it is in a good position. If it is not positioned correctly then the body should be repositioned.

TASK

Next time you are in a team meeting, decide which colleague you are going to watch. Do the five-minute body rule watching yourself and your colleague. See how much both of you move during the course of the meeting.

Breathing

One hopes that breathing comes naturally but funny things happen when we are nervous; for example, someone can take a breath and forget to let go. It is important to remain calm when handling a disclosure, so the worker needs to breathe deeply not shallowly. Pauses and silences can be used to restore a worker's equilibrium – this is the chance to breathe deeply and think about what is being said by the service user and how to respond to this correctly. The worker must also be observing the breathing patterns of the victim because this may give some indication of how he or she is feeling.

Verbal communication

We are going on to consider how to respond appropriately in a disclosure, but in the first instance it is good for a worker to think about what makes good verbal communication. Below is a list of good practice points:

- Think before you speak.

- Be clear about what you are saying.

- Speak loud enough/not too loudly.

- Do not speak too fast.

- Think about the language you use: avoid jargon, complex words and long sentences.

 Handout 5.4, p.159

Responding without contaminating evidence

Because many workers talk a lot there is always the danger that when a service user gives a disclosure a worker will start asking questions and may unintentionally go into investigation mode. There has to be a balance, and many workers feel they are in a Catch 22 situation because they need to get enough good quality information to take back to their manager but, on the other hand, they must not go in too deep and mess things up for the police if they are brought in to investigate in the future.

A lot of things will be going through a worker's head when they realise that they are receiving a disclosure. Workers should remember the following good practice points:

- Do not go into investigation mode.

- Be honest.

- Explain about the limits of confidentiality and sharing information.

- Encourage the disclosure.

- Reassure the service user he or she is doing the right thing in talking about the abuse.

- Do not make false promises (i.e. do not say things that you cannot guarantee, e.g. 'You'll be safe now', 'No one is going to hurt you any more' etc.).

 Handout 5.5, p.160

Types of disclosure

My own practice has led me to believe there are two types of disclosure:

1. flowing
2. fits and starts.

The flowing disclosure will be given *either* when a service user has psyched themselves up and decided today is the day to tell someone they trust about the abuse *or* when a service user is in crisis and they blurt it out – a sort of a knee-jerk reaction. It is important that a worker structures the handling of either type of disclosure.

Structuring a disclosure

Giving structure to a disclosure does not mean that the worker leads the service user. Having a structure in mind just gives the worker a framework – it acts as a reminder of what needs to be covered. It is helpful to think in very simple terms – beginning, middle and end (this can also be helpful when it comes to recording, which we shall discuss in detail in Chapter 9).

 Handout 5.6, p.161

Flowing disclosure
THE BEGINNING

As soon as the worker realises or senses that the service user is telling something very sensitive and important, he or she must give a reminder and explanation about confidentiality. The worker may need to stop the service user mid flow and this may feel uncomfortable. However, it is being honest. It is very unfair to let someone give a full disclosure and only after he or she has finished to give an explanation about confidentiality and the need to share information. Explaining these things is something workers should be doing *regularly* when they are involved with someone on a long-term basis. When a service user first meets a worker he or she may not always take in everything that is said so it is good practice to remind the service user about the limits of confidentiality. A worker needs to make it clear to all service users that:

- any information which is given to a worker belongs to the agency not to the individual worker; a worker cannot keep secrets

- if a worker thinks a service user could be at risk of harm then he or she has to share these concerns with his or her line manager.

If the service user continues to give the disclosure, the worker should try to listen without interruption.

THE MIDDLE

When the service user has finished, it is always good to give him or her some reassurance; that is, that it was the right thing to tell you about the abuse. The worker then needs to give another reminder about confidentiality and after that explain that he or she is going to ask a few questions just to make sure he or she has got the facts correct. This is where workers have the tendency to ask too many questions. Ideally the worker needs to have basic information about the:

- alleged victim

- alleged abuser

- types of abuse being alleged – what has happened

- time of the abuse – duration, frequency

- location – where the abuse happened (crime scene).

 Handout 5.7, p.162

It is during this middle stage that the worker can respond in order to clarify what he or she has been told and how he or she perceives the feelings of the service user, but is also the opportunity to gain information if there are gaps in the story. The worker can use:

- questions

- the reflection technique

- prompts.

These techniques will be discussed further below. Usually during this stage of the disclosure the worker will ascertain the feelings and wishes of the service user. If this does not come out naturally then the worker must ask direct (not leading) questions. There must be some discussion around contacting the police and this brings us back again to the sticky issues surrounding confidentiality. Many service users will not want the police involved, but if a crime has been committed this should be pointed out to them. Workers must also be honest about the fact that their line manager may decide to share this information with the police. However, it is unlikely that the police will dash out and land on the doorstep if they know a person is not willing to take proceedings against their abuser. These sorts of issues have to be discussed at a strategy meeting, but explanation and discussion is needed with the service user at this point in the disclosure.

This is also the time in the disclosure to find out if the victim wants to leave an abusive situation and requires a place of safety. Some victims might not know what is available to them, so the worker might have to give them some options. However, it is important not to go into problem-solving; at this stage it is about focusing on and assessing the person's immediate safety.

THE END

To draw the disclosure to an end the worker must summarise the key points from the disclosure. In order to do this without contaminating evidence, the worker should use the reflection technique (see below). The worker should explain what he or she is going to do next and, most important, when the next point of contact will be and how this will be done – by a visit or telephone. A service user should never be left up in the air not knowing when he or she will see or hear from the worker again. It is also vital that the worker never leaves the service user in a distressed state.

Fits and starts disclosure

There is a lot of pressure on a worker when they are getting a fits and starts disclosure because there will be a limited amount of time to get the information needed. A disclosure should never be prolonged; every effort must be made to avoid the service user becoming extremely upset or distraught. If the service user is struggling the worker needs to get enough information very quickly.

Sometimes a service user will present as though they are giving a fits and starts disclosure but then suddenly it becomes a flowing disclosure. Others will struggle and not gain confidence. A worker should give the service user between three and four minutes – using the odd prompt – and if the disclosure is not then flowing the worker should start using questions, the reflection technique and prompts. The worker will probably only get one go at this, hence the reason for saying that there is a great deal of pressure put on the worker. Before using questions, it is once again important for the worker to explain about the limits of confidentiality.

The difference with this type of disclosure is that it is not going to have a middle; that is, the worker is not going to go deeper. After getting as much as is reasonably possible without putting the service user under too much duress, and finding out what he or she wants to do, the worker needs to go straight to the end stage; that is, summarising what has been said and explaining what will happen next.

Questions, reflection and prompts

Most workers are frightened to death that they are going to use leading questions, and I find when I deliver training a lot of workers do not realise when they *are* using leading questions. Simply, a leading question is suggestive. It gives the idea or option for an answer; in other words, it puts words into the service user's mouth. Some examples:

- Did she hit you with her hand or did she use something else?

- Did you feel angry?

- Did this happen after you had gone to bed?

- Was it painful?

It is always better to use *open* rather than *closed* questions. An open question will encourage the service user to tell the story in his or her own words; a closed question may only elicit a 'yes' or 'no' answer. Some useful words (which will also help to remind a worker of what information they need to get) are:

- How?

- Who?

- What?

- When?

- Where?

 Handout 5.8, p.163

Workers should always avoid the use of 'Why?' questions. It is an extremely irritating word (those of you who are parents will testify to this I am sure) but also it will give the service user the impression that the worker is seeking a reason for the abuse. This is not the case; at this stage the worker is gathering facts and information – not looking for causal factors.

A useful way to avoid leading a service user but encourage him or her to keep disclosing is to use the *reflection technique*. This involves repeating the exact words which have been said but putting them with inflection in the voice so it sounds like a question:

'I feel so frightened.'

'You feel so frightened?'

The trouble with the reflection technique is that if you use it a lot you can start sounding like a parrot, so it needs to be intermingled with *prompts*. A 'prompt' is between one and four (maximum) words in length. It is useful for workers to develop and use what I call 'bog standard' prompts; again to mix them up:

'In what way?'

'Tell me more.'

Another useful technique to remember is *TEDPIE*. This is most useful when conducting investigation interviews but the first half, TED, can be helpful for prompting in disclosure. It stands for:

Tell me

Explain

Describe

Precisely

In detail

Exactly.

 Handout 5.9, p.164

Receiving a disclosure from an abuser

It is important to say something about receiving a disclosure from an abuser. Again these can be flowing or come in fits and starts. Workers receiving such a disclosure must be mindful of their own health and safety. Much of what has been said regarding structuring a disclosure from a victim applies to handling a disclosure from an abuser. However, if the worker thinks an abuser could become violent then he or she must be careful which words he or she chooses when explaining what must be done (i.e. as regards reporting). If a worker feels in danger then he or she must leave the situation as soon as possible. It is also important to stress – yet again – that the worker must not go too deep. This is even more important when an abuser discloses because the police may very well have to interview him or her later and the worker must not have taken on the police role and asked questions that are in the remit of the police. Consequently, the worker may feel it is better to keep the disclosure to a minimum.

Taking notes

I am often asked on courses whether it is all right to take notes during a disclosure. The answer is 'yes', as long as they are only notes. It is important to do this if you think you might forget something – especially if the service user is giving a lot of detail (e.g. amounts of money which have gone missing on different dates). If a worker is going to jot down some notes then he or she should explain to the service user why; that is, that this is to ensure that all the details have been taken correctly and that nothing will be forgotten. It is important to say that a worker must *not* write down the disclosure verbatim because this could be deemed to be the first statement by the Crown Prosecution Service. Also, if notes are taken they should *never* be thrown away – even when they have been written up on the service user's file. These notes are known as contemporaneous notes and in the future may have to be sent to the Crown Prosecution Service.

Role play

I think the best way for workers to learn is to rehearse in a safe environment, where they can botch up and learn from their mistakes. As a trainer I am very well aware that many people hate role play. It is important for a trainer to make a participant feel safe and people will not learn if they are scared to death. I have found the best way to conduct role play is for participants to work in pairs and not be watched. Certain ground rules have to be set which are summarised in Handout 5.10.

Handout 5.10, p.165

I have designed various role plays which are included at the end of this chapter. The trainer should prepare the roles for participants by cutting the handouts into two parts, so participants do not see or read each other's briefs.

Handouts 5.11, 5.12, 5.13, 5.14, 5.15 and 5.16, pp.166–171

These role plays can be used in a variety of ways. A manager can use them to undertake role play in a supervision session. A trainer can use them at different stages of a course on handling disclosure, but the objective of undertaking the role play must be clearly stated at the outset. For example, it needs to be explained that the worker's objective should be to practise any of the following:

- listening skills

- body language

- responding skills using non-leading questions and prompts

- reflection technique

- summarising the disclosure which has just taken place (this can be done as a separate role play directly following on from a role play which has taken place).

Emotions

There has been a lot of discussion about communication in order to handle a disclosure correctly. It is also important to give some consideration to emotions; there will be whole gamut of them flying about during a disclosure. Exercise 5.2 can be introduced into a training course fairly early on so that workers are thinking about this topic, but also the flipchart sheets which are produced can be used after a role play has taken place. The main objective is for workers to think what emotions victims or abusers may feel when they are giving a disclosure but also to consider how workers may feel when they are receiving a disclosure from either a victim or abuser.

 Exercise 5.2, p.154

Recording

A worker should record a disclosure as soon as possible after the event, while it is fresh in his or her memory, and keep any notes taken. It is important to record the content of the disclosure, but also what the worker has observed regarding feelings and emotions of the service user during the disclosure.

Key learning points from this chapter

- There can be two types of disclosure: flowing and fits and starts.

- Remember the concept of the storyteller and the listener; in other words, try to let the service user give the disclosure with few interruptions.

- Do not show shock or horror when receiving a disclosure.

- Body language is important in conveying to the service user the message that a worker is willing to listen.

- Remember the five-minute body rule – a worker should check his or her body position regularly.

- Structure a disclosure – think beginning, middle and end.

- Remind a service user about the limits of confidentiality at the beginning of a disclosure.

- Do not contaminate evidence by asking too many questions and going too deep.

- Do not go into investigation mode.

- Use open questions rather than closed; avoid using *Why?* questions.

- Vary your responses by using the reflection technique and short prompts.

- Always explain what is going to happen next and when the next point of contact will be (either by telephone or visit).

- Record a disclosure as soon as possible after the event.

- Do not throw away any notes taken during a disclosure.

Suggested reading

Kirkpatrick, S. (2001) 'What is good interviewing in adult abuse work? A police view.' In J. Pritchard (ed.) *Good Practice with Vulnerable Adults*. London: Jessica Kingsley Publishers. (Although this chapter is about interviewing much of this knowledge is relevant to disclosure.)

 Videos

WAA1, WAA2, WAA3, WAA4, WAA5, WAA6

All the videos in the series portray disclosures from victims and how they are handled (examples of both good and bad practices are shown).

THE STORYTELLER AND THE LISTENER

Objective

To practise listening skills.

Participants

To work in pairs.

Equipment

None.

Time

15 minutes.

Task

1. The pairs decide who will be Number 1 and who will be Number 2.

2. The trainer introduces the concept of the storyteller and the listener.

3. Participants are asked to reflect for 30 seconds exactly on a time in their life when they experienced real fear. They should think about what they were doing before the incident, what happened during it and how they felt afterwards.

4. Number 1 is the designated storyteller. He or she talks about his or her experience for three minutes. Number 2, who will be the listener, can only say 'mm', 'yes' and 'right', and the aim is that he or she uses body language to communicate.

5. If the storyteller finishes the tale before the trainer indicates three minutes is up, he or she should go back to the beginning and repeat the story again (and yet again if necessary).

 © Jacki Pritchard 2007

THE STORYTELLER AND THE LISTENER

6.   The exercise is repeated with Number 2 being the storyteller and Number 1 being the listener. This time round, the listener is allowed to be disruptive (within reasonable limits); in other words, he or she can ask questions, make statements etc. The same rules apply to the storyteller as before: if the tale is finished before the three minutes are up he or she should start again.

Feedback

Discuss in large group:

1.   What it felt like to be the storyteller.

2.   What it felt like to be the listener.

3.   The advantages and disadvantages of the listener:

> (a)   not being able to speak
>
> (b)   being able to interact freely.

4.   Body language – what was good/bad; identify bad habits.

Note for trainer

1.   A time of thirty seconds is specifically set for participants to think of an incident because the trainer can use this set time period for discussion later in the course; that is, when thought is given to what constitutes the time difference between a pause and silence. After they have thought of an incident (and before they start the role play) the trainer should ask whether they thought it was a long or short period of time. There is usually a mixed response.

2.   The trainer should emphasise that participants should think of a fairly simple incident when they experienced fear; not something horrendous. Before taking feedback the trainer should ask if everyone is feeling OK as sometimes participants' memories do go back to something which was traumatic for them.

EMOTIONS

Objective

To think about how a victim, abuser and worker feel when a disclosure is given.

Participants

Three groups.

Equipment

Flipchart sheets and pens.

Time

10 minutes for the exercise.

Task

To make a list of emotions experienced when giving or receiving a disclosure on the flipchart sheet.

> Group 1 will focus on the victim – how they feel when *giving* a disclosure.

> Group 2 will focus on the abuser – how they feel when *giving* a disclosure.

> Group 3 will focus on the worker – how they feel when *receiving* a disclosure.

Feedback

Each group will feed back their list of emotions in turn. After a group has read out and explained the emotions the other two groups are asked if they have any other suggestions to add to the list.

 © Jacki Pritchard 2007

EMOTIONS

Note for trainer

1. The trainer needs to emphasise the following points before the exercise begins:

    (a) Group 1 should not forget to list the positive emotions; participants tend to focus on the negative side of disclosure.

    (b) Group 2 should consider both the remorseful and unrepentant abuser.

    (c) Group 3 should be asked to consider whether workers might experience different emotions when they receive a disclosure from a victim compared to when an abuser discloses.

2. Groups 2 and 3 sometimes divide the flipchart into two sections if emotions are different regarding the remorseful and the unrepentant abuser, and receiving disclosure from a victim and an abuser. It is up to them if they wish to do this.

3. If role play is to be undertaken on a course, it is useful to pin the flipchart sheets on the wall after this exercise has taken place. After each role play and before debriefing, participants are asked to tick the emotions they felt during the role play. It should be stressed that participants can add emotions to the lists; very often they experience emotions that the groups had not considered during this exercise.

BODY LANGUAGE

When receiving a disclosure a worker needs to think about:

- head movements

- facial expressions

- eye contact/eyebrows

- arms

- hands

- legs

- feet.

© Jacki Pritchard 2007

THINGS TO THINK ABOUT

When receiving a disclosure think about:

- voice

- eye contact

- facial expressions

- position and use of body

- breathing.

THE VOICE

Think about:

- tone

- pitch

- inflection

- spacing of words

- use of emphases

- pauses

- silences.

 © Jacki Pritchard 2007

VERBAL COMMUNICATION

To improve handling disclosure remember:

- think before you speak

- be clear about what you are saying

- speak loud enough/not too loudly

- do not speak too fast

- think about the language you use: avoid jargon, complex words and long sentences.

GOOD PRACTICE POINTS FOR THE INITIAL STAGES OF A DISCLOSURE

- Do not go into investigation mode

- Be honest

- Explain about the limits of confidentiality and sharing information

- Encourage the disclosure

- Reassure the service user he or she is doing the right thing in talking about the abuse

- Do not make false promises

 © Jacki Pritchard 2007

STRUCTURING DISCLOSURE

Flowing disclosure

Beginning:

- Service user starts disclosure
- Reminder about confidentiality
- Listen
- Do not interrupt
- Think about your body language

Middle:

- Reassure the service user that it is good to receive the disclosure
- Remind again about confidentiality
- Explain that you are going to ask a few questions for clarification
- Use questions, reflection technique and prompts
- Ascertain the service user's wishes, explain options (e.g. place of safety) if necessary

End:

- Summarise the disclosure
- Explain what will happen next
- Arrange the time of next contact (visit or by telephone)

Fits and starts disclosure

Beginning:

- Service user tries to disclose
- Listen but if service user is struggling use a few prompts
- If after three or four minutes service user is still struggling use questions, use reflection technique and prompts
- Ascertain the service user's wishes, explain options (e.g. place of safety) if necessary

Middle:

MISS OUT – DO NOT GO DEEPER

End:

- Summarise the disclosure
- Explain what will happen next
- Arrange the time of next contact (visit or by telephone)

© Jacki Pritchard 2007

GETTING ENOUGH INFORMATION

When receiving a disclosure a worker must remember not to go into investigation mode. Basic information is needed about the:

- alleged victim

- alleged abuser

- types of abuse being alleged – what has happened

- time of the abuse – duration, frequency

- location – where the abuse happened (crime scene).

© Jacki Pritchard 2007

SOME USEFUL WORDS

Try to avoid using the word 'Why?' to start a question. It is better to use:

- · HOW?

- · WHO?

- · WHAT?

- · WHEN?

- · WHERE?

© Jacki Pritchard 2007

TEDPIE

Tell me

Explain

Describe

Precisely

In detail

Exactly

© Jacki Pritchard 2007

GUIDE TO DOING THE ROLE PLAYS

1. Don't be frightened – the role plays will be done in a safe environment – no one will watch you.

2. You will be given a role – you have five minutes to think about the information you have been given on the sheet. Ask the trainer if you are unsure about anything.

3. The role play will run for ten minutes.

4. If you botch up (say something wrong, get the giggles, find that the body language is wrong), stop the role play, discuss what happened with your partner(s) and restart from where you left off.

5. At the end, you will have five minutes to debrief with your partner.

6. General feedback will be taken in a large group. Think about what you learnt from doing the role play.

© Jacki Pritchard 2007

ROLE PLAY

Role: Janet (aged 25)

You have lived in supported accommodation for the past three years and have been very happy and settled. You have a learning disability, but can communicate reasonably well in very simple short sentences. You get very frustrated when you cannot express what you want to say.

Today, you are going to disclose to one of the workers in the house that another service user, Tom, has been hitting you regularly with a belt. This has been happening for about a month. You can show bruises on your arm.

Last night, Tom came into your room and got into your bed. He did *not* have sexual intercourse with you, but he did touch your breasts and put his finger in your vagina. You are very frightened of Tom. You are going to tell the worker everything after he or she comes into your room to see you. You will be crying when the worker comes into the room.

- -

Role: Worker

You work in a supported accommodation project. Today you go into one of the bedrooms to see a service user, Janet (aged 25). Janet has lived in the house for three years and has always been very happy and settled. Janet can communicate reasonably well, but only in short simple sentences. When you walk in the bedroom you see that Janet is crying. Janet will talk to you about Tom, who is another service user.

© Jacki Pritchard 2007

ROLE PLAY

Role: Eamon (aged 40)

You find it very difficult to communicate verbally. You have only been living in supported accommodation for a short while (four weeks) and you don't like it. You want to leave. You have been having temper tantrums and lashing out at both staff and other service users. The reason for this is that one of the members of staff, Joe, is very cruel to you emotionally. He laughs at you a lot (but *never* in front of other people) and makes fun of you because you find it difficult to talk. He knows you are scared of the dark and often switches the lights off in your room, or he comes into your room at night and frightens you by making silly noises. On one occasion he has thrown cold water over you when you were having a bath. Today you have really lost your temper with another service user, Frank, and hit him. You are now sitting down talking to your key worker after the incident. You are going to try to tell this worker what Joe has been doing to you.

Role: Key worker for Eamon (aged 40)

Eamon has only been living in supported accommodation for four weeks. He has not settled in at all and it is clear he does not like living here. He has severe temper tantrums and lashes out at other service users and staff members. Today he has lost his temper with another service user, Frank, and hit him. You are now sitting with Eamon after the incident. Eamon may mention another worker in the project, Joe.

© Jacki Pritchard 2007

ROLE PLAY

Role: Home carer

Carmel is 55 years old and is severely disabled, having had a stroke a few years ago. She lives with Hannah, who was her daughter's best friend (her daughter died eight years ago). Hannah is single and works during the day. She moved in after Carmel had the stroke. You have noticed a decline in Carmel during the past year. She has become very thin and on occasions it seems she has not been washed. When you arrive this morning Carmel is crying.

Role: Carmel (aged 55)

You are severely disabled after having a stroke a few years ago. You live with Hannah, who was your daughter's best friend (your daughter died eight years ago). Hannah is single and works during the day. She moved in after you had your stroke. Hannah has been neglecting you. She does not feed you properly, as she says she is too tired to cook when she comes in and she does not like helping you to get ready for bed or to use the commode. She insists that you go to bed at 8.00 p.m. You have found it difficult to say anything because she has offered to look after you and you have no one else. You are also worried because Hannah manages your finances and recently she has refused to show you the bank statements. Your bank account is in joint names and you fear Hannah is spending your money. All the worry and stress has suddenly got too much for you and you are crying when the home carer arrives this morning. You are going to tell her everything.

© Jacki Pritchard 2007

ROLE PLAY

Role: Stuart Roberts (aged 45)

You have schizophrenia and have been sectioned numerous times. You live with your mother, Angela Roberts, whom you hate. She has been extremely cruel to you ever since being a child. You have had many different social workers and seen many doctors, all of whom think your mother is kind, considerate and understanding of your mental health problem. You have said on many occasions that you would like to live elsewhere but you always have been persuaded to stay with your mother. You are going to meet a new support worker today and you have decided to disclose about the abuse you have experienced from your mother in the past and about the abuse you are still experiencing. She regularly beats you, locks you in the bedroom and refuses to feed you for days at a time.

Role: Support worker

Today you are going to meet a new service user, Stuart Roberts. You have been allocated this case suddenly and have not had time to read the file properly. All you know is that Stuart is 45 years old and has schizophrenia. He has been sectioned numerous times and lives with his mother, Angela Roberts.

ROLE PLAY

Role: Olivia (aged 70)

You are slightly confused but you do have very good days when you can remember everything. You have one son, Bobby, whom you dote on but he is physically abusing you. Bobby lives with his family on the other side of the city; he visits once a week.

A social worker is coming to assess you today because your GP is concerned about you. He knows you have been getting a lot of injuries which you have told him are due to being unsteady on your feet and falling. In fact it is Bobby who hits you when he gets annoyed with you. You will tell the social worker that he has a bit of a temper but you put this down to you being a bit of a burden to him when he is so busy. The social worker will notice that you have a black eye. You will admit that Bobby hit you last week.

The other thing you are worried about is that money keeps going missing. You do tend to leave the back door open. You think some of the local teenagers may be sneaking in from the entry at the back of the house.

- -

Role: Social worker

You have been allocated the case of Olivia, who is 70 years old. The referral came from her GP who is concerned that she has had so many falls recently and sustained a lot of injuries. The GP said that she is becoming slightly confused. Olivia lives alone, but has one son who lives the other side of the city with his family. When you meet Olivia you will notice that she has a black eye. You need to ask her about this.

© Jacki Pritchard 2007

ROLE PLAY

Role: Care worker in care home

Hugh McDonald (aged 78) has been very ill for months now but says he wants to die in the care home not in hospital. The care workers and manager feel they can cope with support from the nurses who come in daily. This morning you have just come on duty and are going in to see how Hugh is today. It was thought yesterday he would not see the night out. You walk into Hugh's bedroom.

Role: Hugh McDonald (aged 78)

You have been very ill for months now but have said all along you want to die in the care home not in hospital. You know the end is very near and you want to confess what you have done to another resident, Clara, and to other people in your lifetime. A care worker comes in to see you this morning. You are going to tell her that you have been sexually abusing Clara (who has dementia) ever since you came into the care home nine months ago. You will also admit that years ago you sexually abused female children, including your own daughters.

Chapter 6

Investigating Adult Abuse

This chapter considers how allegations or suspicions of abuse should be investigated.

Knowing the local policy and procedures

For most people, reading policies and procedures is not their favourite pastime. However, in order to practise well in the field of health and social care, all workers must become familiar with relevant policies. When the Department of Health's guidance *No Secrets* was launched in March 2000, a Circular stated: 'Directors of Social Services will be expected to ensure that the local multi-agency codes of practice are developed and implemented by 31st October 2001'(Department of Health 2000b, p.2).

Most areas complied and local policies should have been widely circulated once implemented. Titles of policies can differ – vulnerable adult, adult abuse, adult protection and safeguarding adults. Nowadays a lot of people are using the term 'POVA' – protection of vulnerable adults.

KEY QUESTION

Do you have a copy of your local vulnerable
adult/adult abuse policy in your workplace?

Around the UK there is a general consensus about what constitutes good practice regarding investigations into allegations of abuse. However, there will be differences within local policies; for example, regarding time limits, who can investigate etc. Therefore, it is very important that all workers (no matter what job they are doing) become familiar with their local policy and procedures.

In this chapter we are going to consider what to do if it is thought there might be a need to start an adult abuse investigation. Handout 6.1 is a flowchart which indicates what might be considered to be good practice.

 Handout 6.1, p.193

What is alerting?

Jargon comes in and out of fashion and two terms are now used a great deal in adult protection work – *alerter* and *alerting*. Some explanation is needed. An 'alerter' is someone who may report that they suspect abuse has happened or is still occurring. 'Alerting' really means reporting.

Anyone who works with a vulnerable adult could become an alerter. Grassroots workers often undervalue themselves and may not think that they will have to deal with abuse: 'We'd never deal with anything like this. It's something social workers do. They're the professionals' (Home care worker). On basic awareness training it must be stressed how valuable *all* workers are – at any level. It is not just professionals who will deal with abuse. For example, key people who may identify physical abuse will be those who are involved in helping with personal care tasks – home carers, residential/day care workers, and so on. Vulnerable adults often build trusting relationships with workers they see on a regular basis. Volunteers and advocates could also be alerters. So in this chapter the term 'worker' will be used generically to include anyone who might work with a vulnerable adult.

A worker needs to alert when he or she:

- suspects abuse (even if it is just a gut-feeling – the worker should talk about it)

- witnesses an incident

- receives a disclosure.

Ideally, the worker should tell the service user that he or she has concerns and will speak to his or her manager. A worker should not report something behind the service user's back; we are dealing with adults who have human rights (this is very different to working with children under the Children Act 1989). Many workers feel very uncomfortable doing this. It can be because they lack confidence in broaching the subject and in asking direct questions. Workers can also be scared of asking leading questions. Something for all workers to think about on a daily basis is how they introduce themselves and explain the boundaries of confidentiality when they first get involved with a service user. It should be made clear to the service user that if a worker has concerns (about anything) then he or she must report this to his or her manager. A service user needs to know that any information he or she gives belongs to the agency not to the individual worker.

If a worker needs to alert the manager, they should do this as soon as possible. Some policies state actual time limits for doing this (e.g. within two to four hours). Workers must never keep concerns to themselves. Even when there is no obvious evidence of abuse, sometimes just talking things over with a manager will clarify them.

KEY QUESTIONS

When you first get involved with a service user do you spend enough time explaining the limits of confidentiality, when you would talk to your line manager and the records you keep?

Do you revisit the subject of confidentiality often enough with your service users?

Exercise 6.1 will get workers thinking about when they would alert.

✍ Exercise 6.1, p.190 and 📋 Handout 6.2, p.194

Additional scenarios for alerting exercises can be found in Chapters 10, 11 and 12.

✍ Exercises 10.4, p.318; 11.4, p.339; 12.10, p.370

What the line manager should do

If the line manager receives an alert they have to decide what to do about it. Some managers may feel they have not got enough information at this stage to decide whether the abuse policy should be followed. In this situation they may suggest the situation needs to be monitored for a while. However, if there are real concerns action must be taken immediately. If the manager is working outside social services (e.g. in the voluntary or independent sector) they will need to make a referral to social services because since the advent of *No Secrets* in 2000 it has been clear that social services should *manage* investigations (this is very different to taking the *lead*, which will be discussed below).

If the alleged victim is known to social services, the manager will usually make the referral to the worker involved (e.g. social worker, community psychiatric nurse). On the other hand, if the alleged victim is not known or the case is closed the referral will go through to a duty worker or the central point for referrals.

Taking a referral

It is important to state early on that adult protection work is very different to child protection work. Because there is no equivalent to the Children Act 1989 in adult protection, workers cannot share information in the same way. Workers in child protection can share information between agencies if it is in the child's best interests. Adults have the right to know what is being said about them and have the right to deny access to information. Workers need to have training on the Data Protection Act 1998, Freedom of Information Act 2000 and the Human Rights Act 1998. If it is thought the service user may lack capacity this needs to be stated clearly and written on the service user file that a worker/manager is sharing information because they are acting in their 'best interests' as defined in the guidance *Making Decisions* (Lord Chancellor's Department 1999).

The person taking a referral should take very basic information from the alerter (or their line manager):

- the alleged victim (e.g. name, address, date of birth)

- the alleged abuser (e.g. name, address, date of birth)

- the incident/allegation (dates/times)

- the alleged type(s) of abuse

- other workers/agencies involved

- confirmation that the service user knows the referral is being made.

 Handout 6.3, p.196

The worker taking the referral should not start ringing round agencies or organisations for more information without permission from the alleged victim. If it is thought that the alleged victim lacks capacity, then it is rather different as the worker can act in a person's 'best interests'; that is, the worker can justify his or her actions. Once the basic information has been gathered, the worker should go directly to his or her own line manager. Exercise 6.2 has been designed for managers so that they think about what they would say to a worker who has taken the referral and what they would do next.

 Exercise 6.2, p.191, and Handout 6.4, p.197

The manager of the worker who takes the initial referral primarily must think about implementing the policy.

KEY QUESTION

Has a crime been committed?

If it is thought a crime has been committed, then the police must be informed. This is made clear in most policies. However, in reality workers often struggle with this when victims have said they do not want to do anything about the abuse. This is where the concept of the professional dilemma comes in. When working with adults we always stress the importance of self-determination. Consequently workers feel very uncomfortable when they have to override that principle and break confidentiality. This reminds us again of how all workers must spend time with service users explaining the limits within which they have to work regarding confidentiality and the sharing of information.

Sharing information

We need to consider further the difficulties regarding the sharing of information. Problems arise because, as has been stated previously, in adult protection work there is no equivalent to the

Children Act 1989. Therefore, workers have to be aware of the fact that information cannot be exchanged in the same way. An adult has the right to know what information is being shared. Most local areas will have some form of sharing information protocol. There is inconsistency around the UK regarding such protocols. Some areas have developed protocols in relation to sex offenders; others will have more comprehensive protocols which relate to other service users. Also there are differences regarding who signs up to and uses the protocols. All workers should find out about their local protocols.

KEY QUESTION

Do you know if you have a local sharing information protocol?

Workers should also be aware of the useful legislation Section 115 of the Crime and Disorder Act 1998. In order to prevent a crime occurring in the future, a worker has the *power* to share information with personnel within the following agencies:

- local authority

- health authority

- police

- probation.

A worker can use this section when he or she thinks a crime has been committed or could be committed in the future. This is really helpful; however, it is *not* a *duty*, so someone can still refuse to give information. If a worker does decide to act under Section 115 it is important that he or she records this clearly on the service user's file and explains the reasons why they have decided to do this. Any decision to use this Section should have been discussed with the line manager in the first instance.

It has been obvious to me on training courses I deliver that many workers are unsure about when an investigation actually starts. This is important because the beginning of an investigation must be recorded on a service user's (i.e. the alleged victim) file. Most policies refer to a strategy meeting. In the past many managers liaised with other key professionals (e.g. the police) and then made a decision about what to do. Nowadays most people refer to a strategy meeting and immediately people think about having a sit down, formal meeting; it does not have to be so.

What is a strategy meeting?

KEY QUESTION

Do you know the purpose of a strategy meeting?

Again, from my own experience of training all kinds of workers, I know that people can get very confused about what a strategy meeting is meant to achieve. There can also be uncertainty about the difference between a strategy meeting and a case conference. It can be explained simply. A strategy meeting comes at the beginning of the investigation; a case conference happens at a later stage in the investigation when evidence has been gathered.

The fundamental considerations for the strategy meeting are:

- Does the adult abuse policy need to be implemented?

- Is the alleged victim in immediate danger of harm (i.e. carry out a risk assessment)?

- Is a place of safety needed?

- Should there be a joint investigation – if so, which agencies will work together?

- Who will interview the alleged victim; in other words, who will be the investigating officers?

- When and where should the interview take place?

- Does the alleged victim have special needs?

- Are Special Measures required?

 Handout 6.5, p.198

The main objective is to decide whether the vulnerable adult/adult abuse policy should be implemented. It needs to be stressed that a strategy meeting can take place on the telephone. Time can be wasted when trying to get people together for a formal sit down meeting. Managers should also be aware of the Human Rights Act 1998. Many human beings would be very annoyed if they found out a group of professionals had convened a meeting about them and they had never been informed. Obviously some vulnerable adults will lack capacity (so, as stated above, the argument would be that professionals were acting in their best interests and this should be recorded on the service user's file and in the minutes of a strategy meeting), but many vulnerable adults will be perfectly mentally sound and some will feel they could make their own decisions about their life.

A manager has to consider first of all whether the alleged victim is in immediate danger and whether a quick response is needed. This is what I call a 'mini risk assessment'. Many policies state that there has to be a response to a referral within 24 hours. Other policies go to the other extreme and say that a strategy meeting should be convened within five working days. Another key consideration for a manager is whether a crime has been committed. Good practice involves liaising with the police to seek their advice and opinion. Police officers find it very frustrating if they are brought in too late in the investigation, when perhaps evidence has been contaminated.

As has already been stated – a strategy meeting can take place on the telephone. The manager should ensure that a written record is kept of all the conversations and decisions made. If a formal meeting is convened it should be chaired by the manager and a minute-taker should be appointed.

If the meeting decides that an investigation will take place, then the next consideration is about who should undertake it. *No Secrets* stresses the importance of inter-agency working. As stated previously, social services will manage the investigation but other agencies could carry out the investigation; that is, take the lead.

Implementing the policy and the importance of recording

Recording has already been referred to several times in this chapter. It cannot be emphasised enough how important this is. Good recording includes stating:

- the date and time of the 'event' (i.e. conversation, meeting, debriefing)
- the content
- decisions reached (including the reasoning behind the decision-making).

Once it has been decided to implement the abuse policy this must be written on the service user's file. It is then clear under which policy workers are functioning. This is vital and very important should the case proceed as far as the Crown Prosecution Service.

Risk assessment

Risk assessment is an important activity during an abuse investigation and is discussed in full in Chapter 8. In the early stages it is imperative to consider whether the alleged victim is in immediate danger and whether a quick response may be needed. Throughout an investigation workers should always be thinking about assessing the risk of significant harm. When assessing risk a worker must think about risk of harm to:

- the service user
- the general public
- property.

Adult protection workers have no right of entry into a house unless it is suspected an adult has a mental health problem or someone may be lying injured or dead (in which case assistance from the police would be required to gain entry). It is also impossible to remove someone who is of sound mind from a situation if they refuse intervention. Nevertheless, it is crucial that risk assessment is at the forefront of a worker's mind, even before the investigation has begun; that is, at the point of referral.

Place of safety

Some victims of abuse do decide they want to leave the abusive situation and need somewhere to go. In other situations once the investigating officers are involved and they offer options, a victim may say they want to go to a place of safety. If a victim does make the decision to leave, it is important that resources are readily available. It takes a great deal of courage to leave an abusive situation, so it is not helpful if the victim then has to wait while a place of safety is found.

KEY QUESTIONS

Do you have places of safety available at short notice in your local area?

Where are these places?

Who can investigate?

The Department of Health's guidance *No Secrets* clearly recommends joint investigations; that is, various agencies could become involved. Social services will still manage an investigation even if different agencies are involved.

KEY QUESTION

Which agencies do you think could become
involved in an adult abuse investigation?

It is so important to emphasise that a worker should *never* be sent out alone to investigate. There should always be two investigating officers. In the past policies have usually suggested that a *qualified social worker* should investigate with someone else. However, nowadays, with the development of multidisciplinary teams in many specialisms (especially mental health and learning disabilities), some policies suggest that other professionals can take the lead – for example a nurse on a learning disabilities team or a community psychiatric nurse from a community mental health team – as long they have undergone investigation training.

It is important to acknowledge at this point that practices do differ around the UK. *No Secrets* emphasises the importance of inter-agency working and in many areas police work closely with other professionals. Police and social workers can and do interview together. In other cases, a social worker will go out with a community psychiatric nurse or other professionals will interview together. Nothing is written in tablets of stone; we can be creative in how we work. However, in some areas the police will do their own criminal investigation and will not interview with social workers, who sometimes feel they have been left in the dark. Good communication is essential; workers should not be left wondering what is happening to the abuse investigation. Everyone has to be very clear about their roles and responsibilities.

Before going on to consider the importance of preparing for an investigation it is necessary to give some consideration to *Achieving Best Evidence* (Home Office 2002).

Achieving Best Evidence – the history

In 2002 the important guidance *Achieving Best Evidence* was produced by the Home Office. It is essential that workers have some knowledge about this guidance – no matter what job they are doing – in addition to *No Secrets* and the local policy and procedure on vulnerable adults/adult abuse. First, *Achieving Best Evidence* should be put in a context since it can be helpful for workers to understand how it was developed. To do this we need to give a bit of history. In the 1990s the Home Office had a working party which was looking at how a vulnerable witness could be helped through the criminal justice system. I shall continue to use the term 'vulnerable witness' rather than 'vulnerable adult' in this chapter only. The working party made 78 recommendations which were put forward in a report – *Speaking Up for Justice* (Home Office 1998). The recommendations were accepted and an implementation programme developed which was called *Action for Justice* (Home Office 1999). The programme did not go as planned; originally the objective was to have the recommendations in place by 2003. When it was realised this was not going to be reached *Action for Justice* was rewritten and published in 2002. At the same time *Achieving Best Evidence* was launched (Home Office 2002).

Speaking Up for Justice acknowledged that vulnerable witnesses may need help in order to give their 'best evidence'. It was recognised that some vulnerable adults may have communication difficulties or they may feel intimidated if they had to face their abuser in the courtroom.

Who is a vulnerable witness?

We know that the definition of a vulnerable adult in *No Secrets* is someone:

> who is or may be in need of community care services by reason of mental or other disability, age or illness; and who is or may be unable to take care of him or herself, or unable to protect him or herself against significant harm or exploitation. (Department of Health 2000a, pp.8–9)

Those who may be considered to be vulnerable are defined in the Youth Justice and Criminal Evidence Act 1999 as:

- children under 17 at the time of the hearing

- individuals with a mental disorder

- individuals with an impairment of intelligence and social functioning (disorders of communication)

- individuals who have a physical impairment (including sensory impairments) or who are experiencing a physical disorder

- individuals who have become vulnerable due to circumstances (e.g. domestic violence; harassment; bullying; self-neglect; self-harm; the nature of the offence; racially aggravated offences; racial or ethnic origin or religious beliefs of the witness; domestic, social and employment circumstances of the witness; any religious beliefs or political opinions of the witness; those who are eligible due to their age)

- individuals who are likely to be or who have been subject to intimidation.

The Youth Justice and Criminal Evidence Act 1999 recognises four categories of vulnerability amongst adults who:

- are learning disabled

- are physically disabled

- have a mental disorder or illness

- are suffering from fear and distress.

 Handout 6.6, p.199

Special Measures

Special Measures are provided in order to help the witness give their best evidence either in initial interview or in a court of law: 'the measures specified in the Youth Justice and Criminal Evidence Act 1999 which may be ordered in respect of some or all categories *eligible* witnesses by means of a *special measures direction*' (Home Office 2002, p.134). There can be all sorts of Special Measures; their objective is to help the vulnerable adult give their best evidence. Some examples are:

- video-recorded interview

- live link

- use of screens

- lawyers removing wigs and gowns

- examination of a witness through an intermediary

- aids to communication

- evidence given in private.

Many vulnerable adults are now interviewed in a video suite. The idea is that the witness will be in a relaxed environment – not in a traditional police interview room. Video suites are usually located in a traditional house within the community. They do vary within areas but will usually comprise of a comfortable room for interview, a waiting room, a monitoring room (where another police officer can watch/hear the interview), a medical room, a bathroom and an office.

Victims may be helped in other ways. They can have a *supporter* with them who is there to give emotional support; supporters cannot prompt or communicate on behalf of victims. The supporter cannot be anyone who might have to give evidence in the proceedings or who has any connection with the alleged abuser.

If the vulnerable witness has communication difficulties, a person can be appointed who is allowed to communicate for the witness; that is, interpret. This person is known as an *intermediary*. The intermediary's role is 'to assist the witness to understand the interviewer, and the interviewer to understand the witness' (Home Office 2002, p.62). There is scope to be creative here. Workers who know the witness may understand their way of communicating (e.g. a support worker who helps an adult with learning disability use a Makaton board), but art and music therapists could also have a role.

Workers can get confused with these two terms but also with the term *appropriate adult*, a person appointed for the alleged offender (not the victim) if he or she is vulnerable.

There is a lot to be learnt from *Achieving Best Evidence*. Not all workers need to know everything in the guidance but some basic knowledge is essential and Handout 6.7 summarises just a few key terms which a worker should understand:

- vulnerable or intimidated witness
- supporter
- intermediary
- appropriate adult

- Special Measures
- video interview/recording
- Youth Justice and Criminal Evidence Act 1999.

 Handout 6.7, p.200

Preparation

Workers across the sectors can come under all sorts of pressures in their day-to-day work and they may feel that there never seems to be enough hours in the working day. However, if workers are not given enough time to prepare to go out on an abuse investigation then bad practice can occur. I know from the training I deliver that many workers feel very unconfident about undertaking investigations. If they are not doing this type of work on a regular basis then they can forget what they have learnt in between the investigations they have undertaken. When training on investigations is given, a lot of emphasis should be put on the fact that workers must not ask leading questions. If the police are involved in an interview they will usually take the lead in questioning. However, the police are not always there so workers must be prepared to take the lead.

Time

There will always be referrals that come through at a quarter to four on a Friday afternoon and if someone is deemed to be at risk workers will probably dash out before the weekend starts. In day-to-day practice it is imperative that workers are given adequate time to prepare. When I announce on a training course that I think investigating officers need at least two hours to prepare, I am usually met with laughter or the comment 'You've got to be joking. We'd never be allowed that amount of time.' After undertaking Exercise 6.3 workers realise just how much time it can take to prepare properly.

Changing hats

When undertaking an investigation workers have to wear a different hat; they find it difficult to think in terms of investigating rather than assessing. Assessment skills are still needed but it is necessary to think in a different way. The objective of an investigation is to find out if abuse has happened and to gather evidence. There can be a danger that workers go 'around the houses' rather than asking direct questions; possibly because they are feeling uncomfortable in the role of investigating officer. It should be remembered there is a difference between a *leading* question and a *direct* question, and it is all right to ask direct questions. It is always better to ask 'open' rather than 'closed' questions, but sometimes it will be necessary to ask the latter. Investigating officers need to be realistic; some vulnerable adults just will not understand what they are being asked or they will lack the ability to respond. In some cases the investigating officers will eventually have no option but to ask what may be considered leading questions; this will be a last resort.

Things to think about

Investigating officers should refer regularly to the manager of the investigation, who is there to advise and support them. A simple checklist like that shown in Handout 6.8 may help with the preparation as well as for conducting the interview and afterwards:

- video interview
- appropriate venue
- special facilities
- roles in interviewing – lead and back-up
- supporter
- intermediary
- appropriate adult

- note taking – contemporaneous notes
- going at victim's pace
- taking breaks
- number of interviews
- debriefing
- writing up interviews.

 Handout 6.8, p.201

Video interview

If the police are involved then a video interview may take place and this will be undertaken in a special video suite, as discussed above.

Venue

If the police are not involved it will be important for the investigating officers to think about where the interview should take place. Health and safety issues are of paramount importance. Both the victim and the investigating officers need to be safe.

> ### KEY QUESTION
> Is the alleged abuser likely to walk in when the interview is taking place?

Sometimes it will be appropriate to interview the victim in his or her own home; in other cases the victim will have to be taken elsewhere (e.g. to a day centre, care home). The investigating officers must ensure that privacy will be maintained. The interview should not be interrupted. Facilities such as easily accessible toilets and refreshments are another important consideration.

Special facilities

Some vulnerable adults will need special facilities in addition to those mentioned above. For example:

- Someone from a different minority ethnic group may need an interpreter.

- An adult with learning disabilities may need to use a Makaton board.

- An adult with a hearing impairment may need a loop system or someone to sign.

- Someone who has diabetes may need to take a break at a certain time in order to eat.

Taking the lead

During an interview a victim should never be bombarded with questions by the two investigating officers. Good practice involves deciding who will take the lead in questioning the victim. The second person will take notes and observe; they will only question the victim if the lead person botches up or fails to pick up on something which is important.

Other people

Other people may be involved in the interview. The roles of supporter, intermediary and appropriate adult in a video interview were discussed above. Even if a video interview is not taking place the victim may want someone to support them. It is important to emphasise that this supporter should not be anyone who might have any connection with the alleged abuser.

Contemporaneous notes

As I mentioned in Chapter 5, I come across a lot of workers who have never been told about the importance of contemporaneous notes. Any notes which are taken during an interview must never be destroyed or thrown away. Many workers think that it is all right to throw away the original notes once they have been written up on the service user's file. The original notes *must* be kept. This also applies to when a worker receives a disclosure. Even if something was scribbled on the back of an envelope, cigarette packet or napkin, it must be kept as it is evidence. Such evidence has to be sent to the Crown Prosecution Service as part of the Evidential Test.

During the interview

It can be extremely stressful for victims to recount what has happened to them. The interview should always go at the victim's pace; he or she should never be rushed. Investigating officers must explain at the outset that the victim can ask for a break at any time.

Number of interviews

In an ideal world it is good if all the information can be gleaned from the victim in just one interview. In reality, many vulnerable adults will have communication problems or they will become extremely upset and distressed during an interview. Great sensitivity needs to be exercised here and if it seems that the interview should be stopped then so be it. It can be continued at another time.

Debriefing

A primary concern is to help and support the victim to give their best evidence, but we must not forget about the well-being of the workers involved. I believe very strongly that adult protection work can be just as stressful as working with child abuse cases. Therefore, workers need to be well supported and given the opportunity to talk about how they feel. Investigating officers can debrief each other but the manager of the investigation *must* also debrief them as soon as possible after the interview has taken place (preferably the same day). The purpose of debriefing is to:

- feed back what happened during the interview

- discuss what needs to happen next

- give workers the opportunity to talk about how they feel.

If workers are sent out to investigate and it is likely that they will finish after normal office hours, the manager of the investigation must give them his or her home number. If the manager is not available in the evening another manager must be made aware that the workers are out and take responsibility for them. This is a health and safety issue. Management needs to know that workers have got home safely and to offer a short debriefing session, which will be followed up by an in-depth debriefing session the following day.

A culture needs to be developed within every organisation which encourages workers to talk freely about their feelings. They should not be afraid to speak out – whether it is about being scared, angry, feeling inadequate etc.

KEY QUESTIONS

How did you feel during the interview?

What emotions did you experience?

How do you feel now?

Recording

It is vital that investigating officers write up the interview as soon as possible. If there is a time lapse the memory can become distorted, especially when there is so much going on during an abuse investigation on top of the normal workload. A good rule of thumb should be that records should be written up within 48 hours maximum.

An exercise for preparation

Exercise 6.3 is an excellent way of getting workers to structure their preparation for an investigation. Trainers can decide how long they want to give workers to undertake the exercise, remembering that in the real world ideally it should take at least two hours. Therefore, at least half a day is needed for this.

 Exercise 6.3, p.192, and Handout 6.9, p.202

 Four case studies have been included at the end of this chapter for use in Exercise 6.3:

Handouts 6.12, 6.13, 6.14, 6.15, pp.205–208

In addition, extra case studies can be found in Chapters 10, 11 and 12.

Initial thoughts and writing the script

We all have naughty thoughts (although many people will deny this – especially on a training course!). By this I mean that we all can read things into situations or information we are given and perhaps jump to a conclusion – we write the script. A simple example is when you watch a murder or mystery movie, you tend to try to work out 'who did it'. One hopes that workers will always practise in a totally professional and non-judgemental way, but this does not mean that initially they will have thought of something. Investigating officers need to be honest with each other and admit if they had any initial thoughts or jumped to a conclusion.

The facts: what is known already

A good way to get focused is to make a list of things which are known to be true, the facts. This precedes what needs to be found out during the interview. For example, a referral may say an older person has dementia. Is this a fact? It may not be if a diagnosis has not been made; the person may have been labelled because he or she is confused. On the other hand, a fact may be that the victim lives with the alleged abuser.

What needs to be found out: subject areas to be covered

This is the hard bit and it is here that workers need to adopt a different way of thinking and working. First of all, the investigating officers may need to clarify certain things; for example, what are the victim's capabilities in regard to communicating? Sometimes the victim will be known already but in other cases little may be known about the person's level of functioning. It is important at this point for the investigating officers to be cautious; they should not contact people unless it is absolutely necessary. It is necessary to reiterate that we cannot communicate in the same way as under the Children Act 1989. A vulnerable adult should know if a worker is seeking information from other sources. If it is thought someone lacks capacity then the investigating officers will contact people in order to act in the person's 'best interests' as stated in *Making Decisions* (Lord Chancellor's Department 1999).

The investigating officers really need to spend a lot of time thinking about what they need to find out from the victim. They should never lead the victim; it is imperative to get the victim to tell 'their story' in their own words. A useful concept is to think about the storyteller and the listener, which was discussed in full in the previous chapter. Nevertheless, the investigating officers need to prepare themselves in regard to what questions they might need to ask.

You can never predict totally what is going to happen in an interview. Very often the interview will take you off in a direction that you never expected. When undertaking Exercise 6.3 workers often moan that it is really hard because you do not know what the victim is going to say back to you. This is true, but also the whole point of preparing – that is, to anticipate what may occur during the interview.

The investigating officers need to list possible subject areas to be covered in the interview. The struggle they will encounter is that they will immediately want to ask questions. This is where they have to change hats (as discussed earlier). A subject area should not be more than two or three words. These should be listed in a column as headings and then sub-headings can be drawn from the main subject areas. Some examples are given in Handout 6.10.

 Handout 6.10, p.203

There will some common subject areas which will be pertinent to most cases:

- types of abuse
- abuser
- location
- time of incident
- duration of incident
- frequency
- before incident
- during incident
- after incident
- witnesses.

 Handout 6.11, p.204

Questions

Once a long list of subject areas has been developed the investigating officers then develop questions from each subject area. They do not have to be in any particular order. Once all the questions have been written down, they are then put into some sort of logical order. The investigating officers have this list of questions with them during the interview, and it acts as a checklist or aide-mémoire. As stated previously, the interview may go in other directions but it is essential that the important subject areas are covered.

The next stage

An investigation will involve interviewing the victim and the alleged abuser and gathering information from other people where appropriate. If the police are involved they will interview the abuser. Confusion about processes often arises when allegations are made against paid workers. A common question is 'What should come first?' – the criminal investigation, abuse investigation or the disciplinary procedures? All this should be discussed at the initial strategy meeting to plan the investigation – who is going to do what. After evidence has been collected by the investigating officers, the next stage of the abuse investigation is the case conference, which is the subject of the next chapter.

Key learning points from this chapter

- It is vital that workers familiarise themselves with the local vulnerable adult/adult abuse policy and procedure, and also with the Home Office guidance *Achieving Best Evidence* (Home Office 2002).

- Anyone working with a vulnerable adult could be an alerter.

- Suspicions need to be reported to a line manager immediately.

- A worker needs to be upfront and honest with the service user and explain what he or she is going to do.

- All allegations of abuse should be taken seriously.

- A manager has to decide whether to convene a strategy meeting (either on the telephone or by having a sit-down meeting).

- A strategy meeting comes at the beginning of an investigation (it is the planning stage).

- A fundamental question is 'Has a crime been committed?'

- The safety of the victim is of paramount importance. Risk assessments should be carried out at the referral stage and during the investigation process.

- It is important to maintain the safety of the victim throughout an investigation.

- Agencies and organisations need to work together.

- The victim should be kept informed at all stages of the investigation (as should other people involved in the investigation).

- Workers should check if there is a local sharing information protocol in place.

- They should also be aware of the powers to share information under Section 115 of the Crime and Disorder Act 1998.

- No worker should ever be sent out alone to investigate an allegation of abuse.

- Joint investigations can promote good practice in adult abuse work.

- Preparation and planning are essential in an abuse investigation.

- Think about Special Measures.

- Do not lead the victim in the interview.

- Keep contemporaneous notes.

- Record in detail, fully and regularly.

- A case conference should be convened to present the findings of the investigation, assess the risk of significant harm and develop a protection plan.

- Investigating officers must be debriefed regularly and properly during an investigation.

- Workers should never be afraid of venting their true feelings about a case of abuse.

Suggested reading

Workers must read the procedures within their local vulnerable adult/adult abuse policy.

Brown, H., Skinner, R., Stein, J. and Wilson, B. (1999a) *Aims for Adult Protection: The Alerter's Guide and Training Manual.* Brighton: Pavilion Publishing.

Brown, H., Skinner, R., Stein, J. and Wilson, B. (1999b) *Aims for Adult Protection: The Investigator's Guide and Training Manual.* Brighton: Pavilion Publishing.

Home Office (2002) *Achieving Best Evidence.* London: Home Office Communication Directorate.

Kirkpatrick, S. (2001) 'What is good interviewing in adult abuse work? A police view.' In J. Pritchard (ed.) *Good Practice with Vulnerable Adults.* London: Jessica Kingsley Publishers.

 Video

WAA3 Investigating Adult Abuse – Two-video set

Video 1 supports all the information given in this chapter; Video 2 presents five case studies each representing a different service user group.

WOULD YOU MAKE AN ALERT?

Objective

To get participants to think about when they would alert their line manager that abuse might be occurring.

Participants

Individual work, discussion with line manager or in training group.

Equipment

Paper and pens.

Copy of Handout 6.2.

Time

10 minutes' individual work.

Task

1. The participants are asked to consider the scenarios on the questionnaire. They are asked to put themselves in the position of the worker.

2. The participants choose a response to each scenario on the questionnaire.

Feedback

1. If this exercise is carried out by a worker and set by a line manager, they both discuss the worker's responses on the questionnaire.

2. If this exercise is carried out during a training course, participants can share their responses in pairs and then there is a large group discussion.

© Jacki Pritchard 2007

MANAGER'S ALERT EXERCISE
WHAT WOULD YOU SAY AND DO?

Objective

To get managers to think how they would respond when a worker brings a referral of abuse.

Participants

Small groups.

Equipment

Flipchart paper and pens.

Copy of Handout 6.4.

Time

30 minutes.

Task

1. The participants are asked to consider the referrals on Handout 6.4.

2. Participants are asked to discuss how they would respond to the worker: what questions would they ask, what other information would they want to know, and so on.

3. Participants discuss what they would do next. Would they implement the vulnerable adult/adult abuse procedures?

Feedback

1. Each group feeds back its responses and actions.

2. Other groups make comments and make suggestions.

Note for trainer

It must be emphasised that participants must discuss whether they would be thinking about following the vulnerable adult/adult abuse policy. If they are not, what are their reasons for this?

PREPARING FOR AN INVESTIGATION

Objective

To train participants on how to prepare for an interview by using a definite structure.

Participants

In small groups.

Equipment

Flipchart paper and pens.

Copies of Handout 6.9.

Case studies (Handouts 6.12–6.15) – see 'Note for trainer' below.

Time

Half-day training session (about three hours).

Task

1. Each group is given a different case study plus a copy of Handout 6.9.

2. Participants work through the tasks listed on Handout 6.9.

Feedback

1. One case study is taken at a time. Each group will feed back their work.

2. The other participants will then comment on the questions which have been developed. Discussion should be encouraged around whether the questions are appropriate or leading. Participants are also encouraged to put forward other questions.

Note for trainer

1. Trainers will need to prepare case studies for this exercise.

2. Additional case studies are included in Handouts 6.12 to 6.15 and in Chapters 10, 11 and 12. Alternatively trainers may have their own case studies or may ask participants to use cases they have worked on previously for materials. However, if more case studies are needed, a trainer may want to use case studies presented in *Becoming a Trainer in Adult Abuse Work* (Pritchard 2001a); there are 20 in total. Case studies can also be found in *Working with Elder Abuse* (Pritchard 1996).

  © Jacki Pritchard 2007

FLOW CHART – INVESTIGATION

TIME SCALE	ALERTER
	Report to own line manager
Immediate or **within 24 hours**	
	Social Services (Allocated Worker or Duty Worker)
Policies vary – **24 hours** to **5 working days**	**Referral taken –** **information gathered**
	Discuss with manager
	Strategy meeting (Telephone or formal meeting)
	Interview(s) Including risk assessment
10–15 working days **(either from referral or strategy meeting)**	**Case Conference**
	Protection plan
	Monitor
Date depends on level of risk assessed	**Review Case Conference**

© Jacki Pritchard 2007

WOULD YOU MAKE AN ALERT?

Imagine you are the worker in each scenario.

1. You hear a daughter shout and swear at her mother who has Alzheimer's disease.

   Yes ☐ **No** ☐ **Don't know** ☐

2. A support worker knows that a colleague is borrowing money from service users who have mental health problems.

   Yes ☐ **No** ☐ **Don't know** ☐

3. A home carer finds extensive bruising on Catrina's body when she helps her get out of bed. Catrina is physically disabled and says she falls a lot. Catrina lives with her younger sister who goes out to work.

   Yes ☐ **No** ☐ **Don't know** ☐

4. Agatha is 80 years old. She tells you that her husband has always beaten her and continues to do so, but she does not want you to do anything about it.

   Yes ☐ **No** ☐ **Don't know** ☐

5. Julie has learning disabilities and lives in supported accommodation. She tells her key worker that another service user touches her breasts on a regular basis. She has made similar allegations about other service users before, none of which have been proven.

   Yes ☐ **No** ☐ **Don't know** ☐

© Jacki Pritchard 2007

WOULD YOU MAKE AN ALERT?

6. Michael has been diagnosed as having schizophrenia. When he stops taking his medication he hears voices. Today he tells you that people are coming into his house and taking his money, but he says he does not know who they are.

   Yes ☐ **No** ☐ **Don't know** ☐

7. Mr Singh is a Sikh man who is very frail. He has recently had a major operation and has come into the care home for a short while. The night staff insist that he remove two of his sacred symbols, the bangle and small dagger, when he goes to bed. Mr Singh tells you, a care worker who works the day shift, that this happens.

   Yes ☐ **No** ☐ **Don't know** ☐

8. You see that an older woman flinches every time her daughter comes near her and becomes very quiet when normally she is very chatty.

   Yes ☐ **No** ☐ **Don't know** ☐

9. A district nurse suspects that a husband is leaving his wife alone for long periods of time. When questioned he denied this. His wife has Huntington's disease and cannot communicate.

   Yes ☐ **No** ☐ **Don't know** ☐

10. A neighbour tells the community psychiatric nurse that she regularly hears shouting and screaming from next door where a father and son live. The father has Wernicke Korsakoff's syndrome, which is the reason why the community psychiatric nurse is involved.

    Yes ☐ **No** ☐ **Don't know** ☐

© Jacki Pritchard 2007

TAKING A REFERRAL

The person taking the referral needs the following information from the alerter:

- the alleged victim (e.g. name, address, date of birth)

- the alleged abuser (e.g. name, address, date of birth)

- the incident/allegation (dates/times)

- the alleged type(s) of abuse

- other workers/agencies involved

- confirmation that the service user knows the referral is being made.

© Jacki Pritchard 2007

MANAGER'S ALERT EXERCISE: WHAT WOULD YOU SAY AND DO?

1. Mr Richardson rang a worker to say he is not happy with the care his wife is receiving in a care home. She was admitted there four weeks ago; the first review is due to take place in a couple of weeks. He is concerned about her hygiene and believes that she is not being washed and bathed regularly. Also, he does not like the attitude of the staff, claiming that they are 'short and sharp' with both him and his wife.

2. A worker has recently become involved with Marjorie and her daughter Ellie. It is very obvious to the worker that Marjorie is finding it hard to care for her daughter, who has cerebral palsy. Initially when the worker tried to talk to her about her relationship with her daughter and being a carer she said 'everything is fine'. Ellie tells the worker she has to spend most of the time in her bedroom and her mum will not buy her the things she wants. Ellie also discloses that her mum sometimes hits her.

3. A worker has visited Joe, a day care user, on a hospital ward. Joe has schizophrenia and has been sectioned. While the worker was talking to Joe he saw a nurse push a female patient in the centre of her back and say to her in a very loud, cross voice: 'Get in that bed now. I'm fed up with having to tell you to stay in bed.' When the patient bursts into tears the nurse shouts at her: 'Shut up.' Joe tells the worker that same nurse has hit him and that she is 'nasty to all the patients'.

4. Lottie, aged 74, met Keith, aged 35, some years ago when she was attending a day centre where Keith worked. At that time she was perfectly mentally sound but had some health problems. When Lottie started to become confused Keith began to visit her at home. He had left the day centre by this time but kept in touch with other workers at the day centre. As her confusion worsened Keith suggested that Lottie move in with him, because she has no family and friends. As a worker got out of the car today, a neighbour came out and asked whether she knew that Keith had served two prison sentences for abusing children.

© Jacki Pritchard 2007

CONSIDERATIONS FOR A STRATEGY MEETING

- Does the adult abuse policy need to be implemented?

- Is the alleged victim in immediate danger of harm (i.e. carry out a risk assessment)?

- Is a place of safety needed?

- Should there be a joint investigation – if so, which agencies will work together?

- Who will interview the alleged victim; in other words, who will be the investigating officers?

- When and where should the interview take place?

- Does the alleged victim have special needs?

- Are Special Measures required?

 © Jacki Pritchard 2007

ADULT VULNERABLE WITNESSES

The Youth Justice and Criminal Evidence Act 1999 recognises four categories of vulnerability amongst adults:

- learning disabled witnesses

- physically disabled witnesses

- witnesses with mental disorder/illness

- witnesses suffering from fear and distress (intimidated witnesses).

From: Home Office (2002) *Achieving Best Evidence in Criminal Proceedings.* London: Home Office Communication Directorate, p.53.

© Jacki Pritchard 2007

IMPORTANT TERMS FROM
ACHIEVING BEST EVIDENCE

- Vulnerable or intimidated witness

- Supporter

- Intermediary

- Appropriate adult

- Special Measures

- Video interview/recording

- Youth Justice and Criminal Evidence Act 1999

 © Jacki Pritchard 2007

CHECKLIST FOR INVESTIGATIONS

Remember to think about:

- video interview

- appropriate venue

- special facilities

- roles in interviewing – lead and back-up

- supporter

- intermediary

- appropriate adult

- note taking – contemporaneous notes

- going at victim's pace

- taking breaks

- number of interviews

- debriefing

- writing up interviews.

PREPARING FOR INVESTIGATIONS

1. *Initial thoughts*

   Remember about the concept of writing the script.

2. *What do you know already?*

   List facts.

3. *What do you need to find out?*

   Before the interview – is there anyone you need to contact for information?

   During the interview – list facts and information you need to obtain from the victim.

4. *Make a list of questions*

   These do not have to be in any order initially.

   Write each question in sentence form, exactly how you would ask it.

   Cover all the subject areas listed under point 3 above.

   Begin with non-leading questions; you may have to go to closed questions eventually.

   When you have finished, put the questions in order.

© Jacki Pritchard 2007

SUBJECT AREAS FOR INTERVIEW

Victim
- Safety
- Risk now
- Learning disability

Capacity
- Assessment
- Level of functioning
- Understanding

Alleged abuse
- Physical
- Sexual
- Financial

Injuries
- Cuts → Location
- Bruises → Colour, Shape

Clothing
- Wearing at time
- Where now
- Washed

Implements used
- Hands
- Objects

Conversation during incident
- Threats
- Statements

Money
- Accounts
- Management
- Access to

© Jacki Pritchard 2007

COMMON SUBJECT AREAS

- Types of abuse

- Abuser

- Location

- Time of incident

- Duration of incident

- Frequency

- Before incident

- During incident

- After incident

- Witnesses

© Jacki Pritchard 2007

CASE STUDY: LOUISE (AGED 26)

Louise, who has learning disabilities, lives at home with her parents. She attends a day centre three times a week. This has been her routine for a long time. During the past year day centre staff have started to notice a lot of changes in Louise's behaviour. She previously had been very easy going, but nowadays she presents as moody and has a short temper. She has also put on a considerable amount of weight. The day centre regularly organise a lot of activities and outings, which Louise has always enjoyed. Recently, she said she did not want to go out of the centre.

One of the workers in the centre, Clare, took Louise into one of the rooms and directly asked her about the changes everyone had noticed. Louise liked Clare and felt she could tell her what had been happening at home. Louise disclosed her parents had taken in two lodgers because 'Mum and Dad have no money because they had to pay the man'. Louise said she did not like the lodgers because she had had to move out of her bedroom into the attic room and she was not allowed downstairs in the lounge at night. She also said that one of the men, Roger, had hit her once.

Clare told her manager what Louise had disclosed to her. The manager contacted the learning disabilities team. The vulnerable adults policy was implemented and an abuse investigation began.

CASE STUDY: NAOMI (AGED 58)

Naomi had had problems with her eyes for many years; her sight deteriorated over a long period of time and she eventually lost it completely. She was known to the local physical and sensory disability team. One winter she became very ill with flu. Two home carers, Jacquie and Helen, were put in to support her as she lived alone.

Once the home carers became involved they got to know Naomi and her friends who popped in from time to time. There was one particular friend, Travis, who started to call more frequently whilst Naomi was ill and bedbound.

Jacquie and Helen were very observant workers and they started to notice that things went missing from Naomi's house. Naomi had worked in an antiques shop when she was younger and had collected some valuable pieces. Jacquie and Helen did not know this when they mentioned to Naomi that certain things were missing in the lounge and dining room. When they told Naomi what had gone missing she became very distressed because they were things of value.

The home carers told Naomi they would have to report the matter to their own line manager as they did not want to be accused of taking anything. The home care manager contacted Naomi's social worker on the physical and sensory disability team.

© Jacki Pritchard 2007

CASE STUDY: RAVI (AGED 22)

Ravi was an Asian man who had been sectioned under the Mental Health Act 1983 and had been in hospital for several weeks. His family had no contact with him, as they were ashamed that a family member had mental health problems. In the past year he had been diagnosed as having schizophrenia. He kept himself to himself and had little to do with the other patients. He felt very lonely as he did not like most of the staff on the ward and only ever talked to one nurse, Megan.

Because he was already very withdrawn and staff were focusing on Ravi's mental health problems, nobody thought about linking his changes in behaviour to any other possible cause. During one week, Ravi stopped eating completely and became more agitated than he had been. He started chanting about 'Men in suits. Men in bed.'

After a couple of weeks Ravi seemed a little calmer but more fearful of anyone who came near him. Megan spent time talking with Ravi, who eventually told her that he had been raped by one of the other male patients, Andy.

CASE STUDY: MRS ELLIOTT (AGED 82)

Mrs Elliott has had several strokes in recent years. She has lost the use of her right side and it is difficult to understand her speech. Her husband is the main carer. Their children live in other cities so only visit occasionally. Home carers go in twice a day to help Mr Elliott, who has angina, with the care of his wife.

The home carers have never been happy about working in the Elliotts' house, which is very dirty. They have tried to offer help to Mr Elliott regarding cleaning, washing clothes and so on, but he responds by saying 'We have always lived in a tip.'

The home carers help Mrs Elliott with personal care tasks. They have become more concerned recently as several times they have come in during the morning and found Mrs Elliott lying in urine and faeces. When talking to Mr Elliott about this he always says 'She must have just done it.' The home carers have doubted this as they have started noticing sores on Mrs Elliott's bottom and legs. When they reported their concerns to the line manager, they were told to 'monitor it for a while'.

Today the home carers have gone in and found Mrs Elliott with cuts and bruises literally all over her body. On this occasion they contact Mrs Elliott's social worker immediately rather than going to their own line manager.

© Jacki Pritchard 2007

Chapter 7

Case Conferences

Case conferences are a vital part of the investigation process. Unfortunately, far too many workers and managers fail to realise this and consequently case conferences are not convened when they should be. One of the reasons for this inaction is that there is a lack of understanding about the purpose of a case conference and what can be achieved by it. I sometimes think this stems from workers having had bad experiences in the child protection field – maybe many years ago. Things have moved on, and I believe very strongly that we can learn from our mistakes in child protection and that we must also learn from the good practice that does exist. The case conference ultimately should be a way of bringing an investigation to some sort of conclusion and planning ahead for the long-term work through the use of a protection plan.

In this chapter we shall be explaining the purpose of a case conference, but also considering how workers can convene and prepare for such an event. The victim must not be forgotten and thought will be given to how he or she can be helped to participate. Attention must also be given to the role of the chairperson, upon whom so much depends.

Purpose of a case conference

Workers must be clear about what a case conference is trying to achieve. If workers are not clear at the outset why they are attending such a meeting then it is unlikely that they will present the relevant information required. The main purposes of a case conference are to:

- share information in a multi-disciplinary forum
- determine on the balance of probabilities whether abuse has happened
- assess the risk of harm for the future
- make decisions and recommendations in the form of a protection plan.

 Handout 7.1, p.236

When an investigation has taken place the first case conference to be convened will be known as the *initial case conference*. If work is to be ongoing (with either the victim or the abuser) a protection plan will be developed, which will be discussed in full in Chapter 8. This plan needs to be reviewed regularly and this is done by reconvening the case conference; such conferences will be known as *review case conferences*.

Preparation

Preparation is the key to good practice. All too often workers say that they have not got enough time to prepare for certain events because of other pressures at work. The constant complaint is about having 'too much paperwork'. Nevertheless, both workers and managers must manage their workload so that they allocate enough time to prepare for their role and participation in the case conference. If a worker is inexperienced then his or her manager must arrange a special meeting to discuss what is expected of him or her in that particular forum. A case conference is very different to any other meeting. It is vital that *everyone* who is going to attend a conference prepares or receives help to prepare themselves. This will include:

- the chairperson
- the minute-taker
- the investigating officers
- other participants
- the victim (if attending).

Convenors of the case conference

In most cases it is the investigating officers who are responsible for convening the case conference and usually it is social services staff who will be landed with the time-consuming job of making arrangements. Whoever does have responsibility for convening the case conference should meet with the manager of the abuse investigation to discuss:

- inviting participants
- requesting written reports
- inviting the victim and/or advocate
- the date and time
- the venue/meeting rooms
- appointing a chairperson
- appointing a minute-taker
- any special needs of victim
- health and safety issues
- other issues for consideration.

 Handout 7.2, p.237

We shall now look at all these things in turn.

Inviting participants

At the outset convenors of a case conference need to think about numbers of people attending a case conference. In some cases very few people might be involved and therefore this might not be such an issue. In other cases where many agencies are involved there can be a tendency to invite everyone (and their managers!). Convenors need to be realistic and use some common sense. No matter how skilled a chairperson might be, he or she cannot effectively chair a large number of people. Also, it can be very daunting for the victim (and workers, if they are inexperienced) to be part of such a big group. I do not think a case conference should be larger than ten (maximum 12) people. Thought should be given to who could be excluded and they should be asked for a written report instead.

The abuser has no right to attend the case conference and certainly if the police were involved they would say there was a danger of contaminating evidence. Sometimes abusers demand to have their say. It is up to the chairperson what happens in these circumstances. Some will allow the abuser to have a small time slot in the conference purely to present whatever he or she wants to say. There will be circumstances when a degree of flexibility is required, for example where a carer has been under stress and it is crucial that he or she is involved in developing the protection plan which will be developed to support the victim and the carer.

Written reports

Practice is very inconsistent around the UK regarding written reports for case conferences. In some areas it is expected that participants will turn up to the case conference and present their information verbally. In contrast, some policies and procedures have a pro-forma for written reports and it is expected that everyone will provide a written report for the case conference. If you are invited to attend a case conference you should check your local policy and procedure to check what is required of case conference participants. Some policies include pro-formas for written reports; others offer guidance about what should be included (see Appendix 1).

Inviting the victim

A victim has the right to attend his or her own case conference. Obviously in some cases it would not be appropriate – for example, if the person would not be able to understand the proceedings because of capacity issues due to advanced dementia, profound learning disabilities, and so on. Sometimes the victim would find it too upsetting. In these circumstances victims should be asked if they wish to have an advocate attend in their place. An advocate can also attend with the victim to offer support.

Date and time

One of the most time-consuming tasks is trying to find a good time for professionals and workers to meet for a case conference. They all will have commitments – some regular, others which cannot be changed. A lot of time can be lost ringing round trying to find a mutually convenient time for the key people. In some Adult Protection Units there will be administrative people allocated to undertake this onerous task.

Location of venue and meeting rooms

Finding a central venue with easy access for all participants can be difficult for a variety of reasons. One of the main problems is a lack of adequately equipped meeting rooms in general. The main meeting room should be equipped with an alarm system for health and safety reasons. Workers rarely think about violent incidents occurring in an adult protection case conference, but they do happen; usually when you least expect it. If an alarm system is not available, the chairperson should have a personal alarm to hand and people outside the meeting should be alerted to the fact that if the alarm is heard a quick response is needed, and they should dial 999.

More than one main meeting room may be needed. In an ideal world there should always be a second room to house refreshments. It may be necessary to take a break if a victim becomes upset or distressed. Hot drinks should never be located in the main conference room for health and safety reasons – they can be used as a weapon to harm someone. If water is to be provided in the conference room then plastic cups should be available rather than pottery mugs or cups.

Another reason why more than one room may be needed is that this may be one of the rare circumstances in which a chairperson decides to let the alleged abuser in for a short period of time to have his or her say. If the victim does not want to remain in the conference room while the abuser attends then a room is needed to house the victim. To ensure that they do not pass each other when coming in and out of the conference room, yet another room may be needed to house the abuser while he or she is waiting.

Appointing a chairperson

Trying to get someone to chair a case conference is an organisational hazard. There needs to be an independent chairperson. It should never be the line manager of an investigating officer as in some circumstances there could be allegations of collusion. Again the problem stems back to managers being overworked and having few gaps in their busy diaries. It is therefore important that systems are set up so that the convenor does not have to waste even more time ringing round trying to find an available manager.

A simple system which can work very easily is to develop a rota for chairing. The rota can be drawn up for six or twelve months in advance so managers have adequate notice of when they are on duty for chairing. Obviously local areas will differ in physical size and the number of managers in post, but an example of a rota which works well is where two managers are on duty for chairing each day of the week and they chair across the specialisms. This means that every manager has one day a month booked in his or her diary for chairing.

Appointing a minute-taker

Minute-taking is a skilled job and should not be dumped on someone at the last minute. I am aware that this daunting task is sometimes undertaken by a chairperson or one of the investigating officers. This is not acceptable as no one can be expected to manage or contribute to a case conference and in addition take comprehensive minutes. Minutes need to be an accurate account of what is said during the conference, because they can be used as evidence at a later date.

It is my belief that administrative staff should be trained to take case conference minutes in exactly the same way as staff are trained to take minutes at child protection case conferences. Minute-takers need to know what should be recorded and how, but also they need to be prepared emotionally for the awful things they may hear. Training also needs to be given regarding confidentiality, so that minute-takers do not go out of the conference room and discuss what they have heard with colleagues. The chairperson should debrief the minute-taker immediately after the case conference has finished and ensure that he or she is feeling all right.

Special needs

It is also essential to give consideration as to whether a victim may have any special needs or requirements in order to help their participation in the case conference. For example, the victim who has a disability or communication difficulties may need one or more of the following – wheelchair access, loop system, Makaton board. If a victim is from a different ethnic background an interpreter may be needed. Some victims may have health problems, for example if the person has a continence problem a toilet will need to be located near the conference room or if someone has diabetes he or she may need a break in order to eat something.

Health and safety issues

Certain health and safety issues have already been mentioned above but again it is worth noting that a manager should be proactive in asking the convenor whether there are any other health and safety issues which need to be discussed at this stage or with the independent chairperson before the case conference takes place.

Other issues for consideration

The investigating officer may be responsible for convening the case conference and have a great deal on his or her mind. The manager of the investigation should allow time for the worker to vent any anxieties or concerns he or she may have regarding convening but following that the manager should give the investigating officer additional time for personal preparation as discussed below in the section 'Preparation for participants'.

Other practical issues

Handout 7.3 can act as a checklist for convenors:

- date and time
- location of venue
- letter of confirmation
- meeting rooms
- alarm system
- special requirements

- refreshments
- tissues
- place cards
- list of participants
- discussion with independent chairperson.

Handout 7.3, p.238

In addition it is worthwhile expanding on a few points. A convenor may have done a lot of ringing around to get a mutually convenient time for participants to attend. It is worth sending out a letter confirming the date, time and venue and also reminding people that they should leave two hours free for the case conference. It is also worth including a list of participants who are going to attend with the letter. Copies of this list should be made available again on the day of the conference.

Tissues should be available in the event of the victim becoming upset and place cards should be on the table. There may be people in the room whom the victim has never met; or some workers may never have met each other face to face. Identity badges are often hard to read across even a short distance. It is helpful to have place cards clearly showing people's names, job title or relationship to the victim.

The convenor of the case conference should have a discussion/meeting with the independent chairperson before the case conference takes place.

Preparation for participants

It has been said that the manager of the investigation should meet with the person who is going to convene the case conference. It is just as important for any line manager to meet with any of their workers who have been invited to attend a case conference. Very few workers are used to attending adult protection case conferences on a regular basis and consequently they may be very nervous or even dreading the experience. A manager should arrange to address these issues in a pre-booked supervision session or to arrange a special meeting before the conference takes place. Workers must be encouraged to voice their concerns, many of which will be linked to a lack of confidence which in turn may be caused by a fear of the unknown. The most common problems are related to not knowing what is expected of a worker in a case conference and a fear of having to speak in front of other people (especially people who are seen to be in higher status positions). Exercise 7.1 can help workers to express their worst fears.

 Exercise 7.1, p.228

After discussing the worker's general worries and fears, the manager should talk in depth about the information which is required for the case conference and how this can be presented. The manager needs to get the worker to think about the facts they know, their opinion and how this can be evidenced; and finally a worker must be given the opportunity to vent their feelings. Handout 7.4 is a list of questions which can be worked through to help achieve this:

- When and where is the conference?
- Who will be at the case conference?
- What is the agenda?
- What do you know about the service user and his or her situation which is relevant to the conference?
- What information do you need to present?

- How will you present this information?

- Is the case file up to date?

- Have you been using any monitoring tools?

- What do you want to say (your professional opinion)?

- Whose views are you representing (e.g. yours, the service user's, the agency's)?

- Is there anything else you need to do/find out before the conference?

- What are your true feelings about the case (venting)?

- What will you put in a written report?

- In addition what key points (up to ten) do you want to make during the conference which you would put in a trigger list?

 Handout 7.4, p.239

It cannot be emphasised enough that all workers should be encouraged to talk about their feelings; it is only human to feel angry, upset, guilty (e.g. if you feel you have missed something in the past) or frustrated (e.g. if you know that a victim does not want to do anything about the abuse and wishes to remain in the abusive situation).

The manager should endeavour to introduce creative methods of helping in addition to general discussion; for example:

- draft a report and then discuss

- rehearse (present the draft report)

- role play (part of a case conference)

- group work (to work on particular problems)

- provide reading material (e.g. policy and procedure)

- arrange place on a training course (for public speaking, presentation skills).

 Handout 7.5, p.240

Preparing the victim

The victim must not be forgotten in the process of preparation. The investigating officers should explain the purpose in convening a case conference and go through what will happen. At a time of trauma or of feeling stressed (e.g. during an interview), victims may not take in everything that is being said at the time. Consequently, the investigating officers need to check out again (by arranging a visit purely to discuss the case conference) that the victim understands what will happen at a case conference and ask if he or she has any questions. Other workers who may have ongoing or more frequent contact with the victim should also offer support in preparing the victim for the conference.

The chairperson of the case conference should always meet with the victim just before the case conference (at least 20 minutes beforehand) to discuss:

- what the victim wants to be called (whether the victim prefers the use of his or her first name or the more formal use of Mr, Mrs)

- where the victim wants to sit (and next to whom)

- the fact that it is all right to ask for a break at any time

- the location of the toilet and refreshments

- the format of the meeting

- ground rules

- any concerns.

 Handout 7.6, p.241

Preparation for the chairperson

Preparation is a key issue for the chairperson as well as the workers who are going to participate. Ideally, managers who are going to chair adult protection case conferences should attend a training course on how to chair. It is not good enough for a manager to say 'I chair meetings all the time' or 'I've done child protection'. It is possible to transfer some skills from other meetings and specialisms, but adult protection work brings different issues to the table. A crucial difference is, as mentioned before, that adult protection does not have the same legal framework as child protection (there is no equivalent to the Children Act 1989) and therefore information cannot be shared in the same way. Managers need to be trained in regard to such issues as information sharing, using local information-sharing protocols and Section 115 of the Crime and Disorder Act 1998. Exercise 7.2 will help managers think about what skills are needed for chairing.

 Exercise 7.2, p.229

Before the case conference takes place

A chairperson should never just rush in and start chairing; he or she needs to prepare beforehand and there are also a number of tasks to perform before the conference begins. Exercise 7.3 can be a useful way of finding out how much managers know about chairing adult protection case conferences.

 Exercise 7.3, p.230

 Handouts 7.7 and 7.8, pp.242–243

Familiarisation

Although the chairperson is there to be in a neutral position, it can be useful to know something about the case beforehand. The chairperson should be familiar with the facts of the case. This can be achieved by talking to the convenor of the case conference or reading the case file and/or reports which are going to be presented to the conference. It is important for the chairperson to be aware of any particular difficulties that are likely to arise (e.g. any possibility of violent incidents; the extent of the victim's communication difficulties; any special needs of the victim).

Meeting the victim

As discussed above, the investigating officers should have prepared the victim for the case conference but it is helpful for the person to meet with the chairperson about 20 minutes before the conference is due to commence.

Chairing the actual case conference

Chairing a case conference can be extremely difficult and complex, mainly because there are so many tasks to perform. It is not just about 'keeping order' and getting through the agenda. The chairperson needs to continually observe the participants as well as listening to what is being said. All sorts of group dynamics could come into play, which might affect the risk assessment and the decision-making process. It is important that the chairperson does not allow a participant to dominate the conference and encourages shy or reserved participants to make a contribution. At the outset the chairperson should remind participants about the purpose of the case conference and it is helpful if he or she reads out the definitions of *abuse* and *significant harm* (Handouts 7.9 and 7.10), so that everyone is clear about what the conference needs to achieve by its conclusion.

 Handouts 7.9 and 7.10, pp.244–245

It is also important to set clear ground rules so everyone feels comfortable. Most chairs develop their own styles of chairing and many will have a set of ground rules already. However, there are certain rules which must be emphasised so that if problems do arise (someone behaves badly or says something inappropriate) the chair can intervene by referring back to the ground rules. This will be discussed further below. Some chairs have laminated copies of the definitions of abuse and significant harm and the ground rules so that they can be used time and time again for conferences.

The issue of confidentiality can be problematic. Some participants may refuse to share some information. Since people cannot share information in the same way as when working with children, a chairperson needs to be aware of any local information-sharing protocols which exist but also needs to become familiar with Section 115 of the Crime and Disorder Act 1998.

KEY QUESTIONS

Do you know if there is a local information-sharing protocol in place?

Do you know about Section 115 of the Crime and Disorder Act 1998?

Section 115 of the Crime and Disorder Act 1998 says that if a person thinks a crime has been committed or could be committed, he or she has the power to share that information with any personnel in the following agencies:

- local authority

- health authority

- police

- probation.

A person has the *power* to do this but it is *not a duty*. This can be a useful bit of legislation to quote if a participant is refusing to share information in a case conference.

Whilst the chairperson is facilitating the conference, he or she should be making some notes so that at the end of each agenda item a clear summary of the main points can be given. This is why a chairperson should never be expected to take minutes in addition to everything else which needs doing.

A chairperson needs to keep the conference focused; it is very easy for people to digress and go off the point. It is the role of the chairperson to bring people back to give relevant information. After everyone has given their reports/information, the chair opens up the discussion so that the risk assessment can be undertaken. This is where the chairperson needs to have developed specialised skills to get this done. It is often at this point in the conference that things go horribly wrong. The chairperson must ensure that:

- the risk of significant harm is discussed and prediction undertaken; that is, there must be a grading of risk (see Chapter 8)

- decisions and recommendations are made

- a protection plan is developed.

There is a tremendous amount of work for the chairperson to undertake. Participants can behave in all sorts of different ways and it is up to the chairperson to make sure that the conference achieves all its objectives. Anyone who is going to chair must develop specialised skills and present as being confident and assertive.

KEY QUESTIONS

What do you think your weaknesses are in chairing case conferences?

What skills do you need to develop?

Are you lacking knowledge about particular aspects of the adult abuse policy and procedure? If so, how will you rectify this?

What should happen at a case conference – the agenda

The success of a case conference, whether it achieves the objectives as stated in the adult abuse policy, is dependent on a number of factors, namely:

- the chairing skills of the chairperson

- the quality of the information presented by participants

- participants' knowledge and understanding of adult abuse

- participants' skills in risk assessment.

It has already been said that participants and the victim should know what is going to happen at the case conference and know what is expected from them. All chairpersons develop their own style of chairing but the basic agenda needs to include:

- introductions

- clarification that the conference is being convened under the vulnerable adult/adult abuse policy

- details of the subject (the victim's name, address, date of birth)

- expected duration of conference

- minute-taking/circulation of minutes

- issues surrounding information sharing and confidentiality

- ground rules

- reading written reports

- findings of the investigation

- presentation of reports

- open discussion

- risk assessment

- recommendations

- development of a protection plan

- date set for review case conference.

 Handout 7.11, p.246

Introductions

Everyone should state their name and job title or relationship to the victim (and this should include the minute-taker). This is *not* the time for participants to start presenting their information. The chairperson should be sensitive to how the victim is introduced.

Clarification that the conference is being convened under the vulnerable adult/adult abuse policy

It is important for this to be said and minuted for recording purposes. It should be clear what type of meeting it is (i.e. not a strategy meeting but an initial or review case conference) and under which policy it is being convened.

Details of the subject

The chairperson must formally state the name, address and date of birth of the alleged victim. Sometimes it is good to do this when introducing the victim if they are present.

Brief explanation of why the conference is being convened

The investigation officers will explain in full how the investigation started but a brief explanation needs to be given by the chairperson at this point about how the policy and procedure came to be implemented. It is a short chronology of events (e.g. dates of alert, strategy meeting etc.).

Expected duration of conference

Participants should have been asked to keep two hours clear in their diaries but the chairperson should check that no one has to leave early. Not all case conferences will take this long but if breaks are taken then they can last this long.

Minute-taking/circulation of minutes

The purpose of taking minutes should be explained together with an explanation regarding who will receive copies. Some policies state the time limits within which the minutes will be circulated (e.g. ten working days). The chairperson should also explain that any errors or omissions should be reported to the chairperson (again there may be a time limit). It is common practice in some areas for participants to be told that no notes should be taken during the conference or if anyone does take notes they will be collected at the end of the meeting. The written reports are also usually collected at the end of the conference and then circulated with the minutes.

Issues surrounding information sharing and confidentiality

As I have already pointed out, there are many problems surrounding these issues in adult protection work. At the outset the chairperson must ask if anyone has a problem with sharing information and if there are difficulties an explanation should be given regarding any local information-sharing protocols and Section 115 of the Crime and Disorder Act 1998. If anyone continually refuses to share information then they should be asked to leave.

Ground rules

Some basic ground rules should be explained to set the tone of the conference. Again, most chairpersons have their own ways of doing this but things which should be covered are:

- everyone around the table is equal
- everyone has the right to speak and be listened to
- participants' opinions will be respected
- only one person will speak at any one time
- plain language will be used – use of jargon will be avoided
- no one will discriminate in any way
- anyone can ask for a break at any time (a reason does not have to be given publicly but the chairperson will want to know why a break is needed)
- everything which is discussed is confidential.

 Handout 7.12, p.247

Reading written reports

If there has not been time to circulate written reports received from people not present before the case conference, the chairperson should allow 10–15 minutes (i.e. no one should be rushed) for participants to read through the reports. In some cases the victim may need help from a worker to go through the reports if this has not been done before the conference commences.

Findings of the investigation

The two investigating officers should present their report which will include how the referral/ allegation was received (if the alerter is present he or she may present this information), how the investigation has taken place and what has been found. If other people have been involved in the investigation (e.g. a casualty doctor or a GP) they will present their findings next. In some cases the police may have undertaken a criminal investigation separately, so they would present the findings of their investigation.

Each participant will be asked to present their report/information

Some people will be very skilled at presenting reports; other participants will be extremely nervous. The chairperson needs to be sensitive to these situations and act in an encouraging and supportive way. Participants need to check their local policy what is expected of them because there are differences. Some policies require that everyone presents a written report (and there may be a pro-forma for this); others will just expect a verbal report.

Open discussion

Once everyone has presented their report the discussion will be opened up and will include the process of risk assessment.

Risk assessment

Risk assessment is discussed fully in Chapter 8. The main objective in undertaking a risk assessment is to assess the risk of significant harm to the victim in the future. The conference must also consider the risk of harm to the public; that is, workers could be going into an abusive household; care workers could be physically hit or verbally abused by a resident; a professional may be undertaking therapeutic work with an abuser who is potentially violent; an abuser could be placed in a communal setting where other users or visitors could be at risk. The final consideration is risk of harm to property.

Recommendations

Once the risk assessment has been completed, decisions have to be formally made and minuted. It has to be formally minuted whether on the balance of probabilities abuse has happened.

Development of a protection plan

Some policies state that a protection plan should be developed by a core group after the case conference has taken place. However, the usual practice is to develop the plan during the case conference. It is very important that the victim is involved in the development of the plan. Again this is discussed in depth in Chapter 8.

Set date for review case conference

Unless the case conference decides that abuse has definitely not happened, then work will be ongoing – either direct work/intervention with the victim (and maybe the abuser) or there will be plans to monitor situations. The frequency of review case conferences will be dependent on the level/grading of risk assessed. Some policies actually state a definite time limit within which the review case conference should be convened.

KEY QUESTIONS

Are there any parts of the case conference agenda
you are unsure about what might happen?

Are you sure about what is expected of you in the case conference?

What will promote good practice?

In a case conference it is possible to witness many different behaviours and practices, some of which will not be good or professional. Case conferences can be held in highly charged atmospheres which can affect the way in which people behave. We are now going to consider what constitutes good practice in this particular forum.

Preparation

We have already discussed the importance of preparation. Even on the day of the conference more preparation is needed. A worker should never book meetings back to back in his or her diary. A small amount of time should be set aside to psyche up for the conference. It is not good to rush into the conference not having thought about what is about to happen. It is also important to arrive on time. There is nothing worse than a participant coming in late and disrupting the flow of discussion.

Documents

It is always a good idea to take a copy of the vulnerable adult/adult abuse policy to the conference together with the service user's case file/notes. You never know when someone is going to ask you something about a past incident/situation. A worker cannot be expected to have perfect memory recall, so it is useful to have the case notes to hand.

Credibility

It is vital for a worker to maintain their credibility in a conference. Presenting oneself in a professional manner will gain the respect of other participants. A participant's objective should be to be listened to and taken seriously. Credibility will depend on what you say and how you say it.

Presentation

Presentation skills are important (and this is why training is needed in this area). A participant needs to act in a confident manner, without appearing to be arrogant. This involves sitting properly; that is, looking alert and interested. How a participant dresses is important, as is participants not doing anything which might alienate some people because they consider it to be rude/unprofessional (e.g. chewing gum). Many workers who are nervous will talk too quickly or quietly. There is nothing worse than a chairperson or minute-taker asking you to repeat what you have said. Therefore, it is necessary to:

- leave yourself time to psyche up for the conference
- take the vulnerable adult/adult abuse policy
- take the case file
- arrive on time

- be prepared

- know what you want to say

- sit attentively

- speak through the chairperson

- think before you speak

- speak clearly

- project your voice if necessary

- present facts and relevant information

- have the case file in order

- be ready to challenge

- ask for explanation if you do not understand something

- admit if you do not have information/knowledge

- act in a professional manner.

 Handout 7.13, p.248

Do not:

- leave yourself short of time

- slouch

- chew gum

- doodle

- use jargon

- mumble

- waffle to cover up the fact that you do not know something

- get angry

- get upset

- be intimidated.

 Handout 7.14, p.249

Being ineffective

Workers may not function well in a case conference for any of the following reasons:

- they are not prepared

- they do not know what is expected of them

- they are nervous, scared, or feeling inadequate or inferior
- they find working with adult abuse difficult (maybe because they have been abused themselves).

This is why managers should prepare their workers before a conference and not just tell them they have to attend. Frequently, people say that there is no time to do this but again it has to be emphasised that managers have to make time to help their workers prepare in order to promote good practice. Presenting information in meetings is something which should ordinarily be addressed in supervision sessions; that is, it is better to have done some work on this before a situation arises and time has to be found at the last minute.

What makes people behave badly?

Some workers will literally behave badly – maybe because:

- they do not want to be there
- adult protection work makes them feel uncomfortable
- they think adult protection work is a waste of time
- they come with an agenda
- it is a defence mechanism.

Dealing with difficult behaviour

If anyone is not contributing to a case conference or behaves in an unacceptable way, the chairperson should intervene and address that behaviour. However, some chairpersons are ineffectual and do not confront what is going on around the table. In such circumstances, participants should step in and take some action. Unfortunately, what one often sees happen is people looking down at their papers or someone jumping in and moves the discussion along; the end result being the behaviour is not dealt with. Outright confrontation is not what is needed in a case conference; that is it should not become a battleground. However, unacceptable behaviour or comments must be acknowledged and addressed. Exercise 7.4 is designed so that workers anticipate what they might do in such situations if the chairperson does not intervene. The exercise can also be used for managers who are attending a training course on how to chair case conferences.

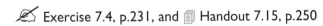 Exercise 7.4, p.231, and 🗐 Handout 7.15, p.250

Jargon

No matter what job a person does, it is very likely that they will use some form of jargon. It is very difficult for anyone to realise that they are doing this because jargon becomes everyday language. It is very easy to forget that some people will not understand the terminology being used. It is vital to avoid jargon in a case conference. Some participants may already be feeling inadequate and the use of jargon may make them feel even worse. Also, the victim must not be forgotten. They may feel totally lost listening to the different 'languages' of professionals. Exercise 7.5 should help identify jargon used in different work settings.

 Exercise 7.5, p.232

Simulation

The best way to learn is to practise and it is quite easy to organise a simulation exercise where participants take on roles and act them out in a simulated case conference. A trainer can take any case study presented in this manual and develop a simulation exercise from it. One example of how to do this is given in Exercise 7.6 and Handouts 7.16.–7.18.

 Exercise 7.6, p.234, and Handouts 7.16–7.18, p.251–255

Alternatively, there is an abundance of prepared simulations in Chapter 12 of *The Abuse of Older People* (Pritchard 1995) and Chapter 6 of *Working with Elder Abuse* (Pritchard 1996).

Key learning points in this chapter

- An initial case conference will consider the findings of an investigation, assess risk of harm and produce a protection plan for long-term work when necessary.

- If the alleged abuser is a vulnerable adult a separate case conference may be convened.

- Case conferences are multi-disciplinary but should not be too large in number (maximum 12 participants).

- Some workers can be asked to send in reports rather than attending.

- Preparation is the key to good practice (for both managers and workers) and it is not acceptable to say that there is not enough time for this.

- Convenors should meet with the investigation manager. Inexperienced participants should meet with their own line manager in order to prepare for their contribution.

- The victim should be invited to the case conference and be prepared for it.

- The victim should be included in the process; support should be provided when required in the form of a supporter or advocate.

- Administrative support is essential to the smooth running of the case conference.

- Administrative workers should be trained to take minutes and be prepared for what they might hear in a conference.

- A case conference should have an independent chairperson.

- Investigating officers should talk to the chairperson before the conference.

- The chairperson should meet with the victim at least 20 minutes before the conference starts.

- A formal agenda should be followed.

- It is preferable for everyone to produce a written report.

- The chairperson should set ground rules.

- Participants need to maintain their credibility; how they present themselves is of vital importance.

- Participants should speak plainly so that everyone understands; avoid using jargon.

- A formal risk assessment should be undertaken and the risk of significant harm graded.

- A protection plan should be developed (with the service user).

- A date should be set for a review case conference.

Suggested reading

The section on case conferences in the local vulnerable adult/adult abuse policy.

Jeary, K. (2004) 'The victim's voice: How is it heard? Issues arising from adult protection case conferences.' *Journal of Adult Protection 6*, 1, April, 12–19.

Manthorpe, J. and Jones, P. (2002) 'Adult protection case conferences: The chair's role.' *Journal of Adult Protection 4*, 4, November, 4–9.

It can also be useful to read old materials on child protection case conferences as the lessons are still valid:

Charles, M. (1993) 'Child protection conferences: Maximising their potential.' In H. Owen and J. Pritchard (eds) *Good Practice in Child Protection*. London: Jessica Kingsley Publishers.

Hallett, C. and Stevenson, O. (1980) *Child Abuse: Aspects of Interprofessional Co-operation*. London: George Allen and Unwin. See Chapters 3 and 4.

Video

WAA4 Case Conferences

This video illustrates the good practice discussed above in convening and conducting case conferences. Five simulations are presented which illustrate parts of case conferences (and which can also be used for minute-takers to practise their skills).

WHAT ARE YOU NERVOUS OR WORRIED ABOUT?

Objective

To encourage workers to be honest about the fears they have about attending a case conference.

Participants

Line manager to undertake this exercise with worker.

Equipment

Paper and pens.

Time

10 minutes' preparation followed by discussion.

Task

1. The worker is asked to think about what in particular worries them about attending a case conference. Ideally the worker would be given time to think about this, for example before a supervision session is due to take place.

2. The worker makes a list of his or her concerns.

Feedback

1. The worker discusses the list with the manager.

2. If some issues can be addressed immediately this will be done. Otherwise a plan will be developed to address the issues before the case conference takes place.

© Jacki Pritchard 2007

WHAT SKILLS AND KNOWLEDGE DOES A CHAIRPERSON NEED?

Objective

To make managers consider what skills and knowledge are needed in order to chair adult protection case conferences effectively.

Participants

Participants will be divided into groups.

Equipment

Flipchart paper and pens.

Time

30 minutes in groups.

Task

1. Each group is asked to write a brief job description for a person who is required to chair case conferences.

2. Participants are asked to detail skills and knowledge.

Feedback

1. Each group will feed back their lists.

2. General discussion.

WHAT DOES A CHAIRPERSON DO?

Objective

To make managers think about the actual tasks a chairperson needs to undertake before, during and after a case conference.

Participants

Participants will be divided into groups.

Equipment

Flipchart paper and pens.

Copies of Handouts 7.7 and 7.8.

Time

15 minutes in groups.

Task

Each group makes a list of tasks to be performed by a chairperson.

Feedback

Each group will feed back their lists.

Participants are given Handouts 7.7 and 7.8 for general discussion.

© Jacki Pritchard 2007

DEALING WITH UNACCEPTABLE BEHAVIOUR

Objective

To make participants think about what action they would take if another participant did or said something unacceptable and the chairperson did not deal with the problem.

Participants

Small groups.

Equipment

The trainer will have prepared flipchart sheets beforehand.

Time

15 minutes.

Task

Each group is given two flipchart sheets. Each sheet has a problematic situation written on it (see Handout 7.15 for some suggestions).

Participants are asked to assume they have an ineffectual chairperson who has not intervened in the situation.

Participants are asked to make suggestions and list what they would:

1. **SAY** in that situation – the exact words/sentence(s) they would use
2. **DO** in that situation – the use of body language.

Feedback

1. Groups feed back their lists.
2. The other groups are asked if they agree with the actions or whether they would do anything differently.

Note for trainer

Do not let participants use global terminology such as 'adopt open position', 'neutral facial expression'. Detail is needed and the trainer must get participants to demonstrate their body language and explain exactly what they would do.

DAILY JARGON

Objective

To make participants think about what jargon would not be understood by a victim at a case conference.

Participants

Individual work.

Equipment

Adhesive notes – two different colours.

Time

10 minutes.

Task

1. Participants are given an adhesive note (all the notes should be the same colour).

2. They will write their profession/job title at the top of the sticker. They then list the jargon they know they use on a daily basis.

3. After five minutes participants are given a different-coloured adhesive note.

4. They write 'Miscellaneous' at the top. They list the jargon they commonly hear from other professionals.

5. Participants then put their adhesive notes around the walls of the room.

DAILY JARGON

 © Jacki Pritchard 2007

DAILY JARGON

6. Participants walk round the room reading the adhesive notes. If a participant does not know the meaning of a word/phrase they will ask the group to identify the writer, who will explain the jargon.

Feedback

Large group discussion about the jargon on the walls and what a victim would not understand.

Note for trainer

1. Participants often find it difficult to identify the jargon they use every day because it is normal language to them. They need to be encouraged to think about abbreviations, forms they use, computer systems, and so on.

2. If participants have struggled to identify their own jargon and the training course is being run over a couple of days, the trainer can set a piece of homework. Participants are asked to identify a family member or friend who does *not* work in the same profession/job. The participant asks that person to make a list of words/phrases which the participant uses at home/out socially and which could be considered to be jargon. The list is brought into the course the next day and shared with the group.

© Jacki Pritchard 2007

CASE CONFERENCE SIMULATION

Objective

To simulate a case conference in order to give participants the opportunity to practise and learn through role play.

Participants

Large group.

Equipment

Large table and chairs.

Information sheet – Handout 7.16.

Attendance list – Handout 7.17.

Role play briefs – Handout 7.18.

Name labels for participants to wear.

Time

20 minutes for preparation.

Simulation of case conference – one hour.

Task

1. Participants will be given their roles and will have 20 minutes to prepare. Participants are *not* allowed to read each other's roles. They can ask the trainer for clarification and meet other participants but *cannot* discuss the information they have.

2. Participants role play as best they can.

© Jacki Pritchard 2007

CASE CONFERENCE SIMULATION

Feedback

1. Each participant must formally come out of role and debrief.

2. Group discussion about what was learnt from participating in the simulation.

Note for trainer

1. Prepare and photocopy the materials needed beforehand.

2. Explain how the simulation will be conducted.

3. State that participants must not discuss the case or what is on their briefing sheets during the preparation time.

4. During the preparation time speak to each participant and make sure they understand their roles.

5. Introduce the victim to the chairperson and relevant workers.

6. Allow enough time for debriefing and full discussion regarding:

    - how it felt being in role

    - what was learnt about the process of case conferencing

    - what went well/badly

    - who was powerful/dominant/influential

    - body language

    - key issues in the case study

    - key lessons learnt for adult protection work in general.

© Jacki Pritchard 2007

PURPOSE OF CASE CONFERENCES

- To exchange information in a multi-disciplinary forum

- To determine on the balance of probabilities whether abuse has happened

- To assess the level of risk of harm

- To make decisions and recommendations in the form of a protection plan

Tasks for participants

- Give and share information

- Assess the level of risk

- Develop a protection plan to co-ordinate future intervention

© Jacki Pritchard 2007

PREPARATION FOR CONVENORS

The investigating officer should meet with the manager of the investigation to discuss:

- inviting participants

- requesting written reports

- inviting the victim and/or advocate

- the date and time

- the venue/meeting rooms

- appointing a chairperson

- appointing a minute-taker

- any special needs of victim

- health and safety issues

- other issues for consideration.

© Jacki Pritchard 2007

PRACTICAL ISSUES

- Date and time

- Location of venue

- Letter of confirmation

- Meeting rooms

- Alarm system

- Special requirements

- Refreshments

- Tissues

- Place cards

- List of participants

- Discussion with independent chairperson

© Jacki Pritchard 2007

PREPARATION FOR PARTICIPANTS

- When and where is the conference?

- Who will be at the case conference?

- What is the agenda?

- What do you know about the service user and his or her situation which is relevant to the conference?

- What information do you need to present?

- How will you present this information?

- Is the case file up to date?

- Have you been using any monitoring tools?

- What do you want to say (your professional opinion)?

- Whose views are you representing (e.g. yours, the service user's, the agency's)?

- Is there anything else you need to do/find out before the conference?

- What are your true feelings about the case (venting)?

- What will you put in a written report?

CREATIVE WAYS OF PREPARING A WORKER FOR A CASE CONFERENCE

- Draft a report and then discuss

- Rehearse (present the draft report)

- Role play (part of a case conference)

- Group work (to work on particular problems)

- Provide reading material (e.g. policy and procedure)

- Arrange place on a training course (for public speaking, presentation skills)

© Jacki Pritchard 2007

PREPARING THE VICTIM

The chairperson should meet with the victim immediately before the case conference to discuss:

- what the victim wants to be called (whether the victim prefers the use of his or her first name or the more formal use of Mr, Mrs)

- where the victim wants to sit (and next to whom)

- the fact that it is all right to ask for a break at any time

- the location of the toilet and refreshments

- the format of the meeting

- ground rules

- any concerns.

© Jacki Pritchard 2007

PREPARATION FOR CHAIRING

- Talk to the convenor to get some background information

- Are there any health and safety issues?

- Is there an alarm system located in the conference room or is a personal alarm needed?

- Are there likely to be any difficulties?

- Are any special facilities needed?

- Check details of victim/abuser

- Obtain list of participants

- Check the date, time and venue

- Check whether a minute-taker has been appointed

- Read reports which may have been prepared

- Meet with the victim just before the case conference

- Do you need to know anything else?

© Jacki Pritchard 2007

BEING A CHAIRPERSON MEANS

- Being clear and assertive

- Setting clear ground rules

- Reading out the definitions of 'abuse' and 'significant harm'

- Making sure the agenda is followed

- Ensuring confidentiality

- Involving the subject of the case conference

- Making sure everyone has their say

- Encouraging individuals to contribute

- Not letting individuals take over

- Not letting the discussion digress

- Facilitating decision-making

- Developing a protection plan

- Checking that the minute-taker has correctly recorded the decisions and recommendations

- Setting a date for a review case conference

© Jacki Pritchard 2007

DEFINITION OF ABUSE

Abuse may consist of a single act or repeated acts. It may be physical, verbal or psychological, it may be an act of neglect or an omission to act, or it may occur when a vulnerable person is persuaded to enter into a financial or sexual transaction to which he or she has not consented, or cannot consent. Abuse can occur in any relationship and may result in significant harm to, or exploitation of, the person subjected to it.

From: Department of Health (2000) *No Secrets: Guidance on Developing and Implementing Multi- Agency Policies and Procedures to Protect Vulnerable Adults from Abuse.* London: Department of Health, p.9.

 © Department of Health 2000

DEFINITION OF SIGNIFICANT HARM

…not only ill treatment (including sexual abuse and forms of ill treatment which are not physical), but also the impairment of, or an avoidable deterioration in, physical or mental health; and the impairment of physical, intellectual, emotional, social or behavioural development.

From: Lord Chancellor's Department (1997) *Who Decides? Making Decisions on Behalf of Mentally Incapacitated Adults.* London: The Stationery Office, p.68.

CASE CONFERENCE AGENDA

- Introductions

- Clarification that the conference is being convened under the vulnerable adult/adult abuse policy

- Details of the subject (the victim's name, address, date of birth)

- Expected duration of conference

- Minute-taking/circulation of minutes

- Issues surrounding information sharing and confidentiality

- Ground rules

- Reading written reports

- Findings of the investigation

- Presentation of reports

- Open discussion

- Risk assessment

- Recommendations

- Development of a protection plan

- Date set for review case conference

© Jacki Pritchard 2007

GROUND RULES

- Everyone around the table is equal.

- Everyone has the right to speak and be listened to.

- Participants' opinions will be respected.

- Only one person will speak at any one time.

- Plain language will be used – use of jargon will be avoided.

- No one will discriminate in any way.

- Anyone can ask for a break at any time.

- Everything which is discussed is confidential.

© Jacki Pritchard 2007

GOOD PRACTICE: DOS

- Leave yourself time to psyche up for the conference

- Take the vulnerable adult/adult abuse policy

- Take the case file

- Arrive on time

- Be prepared

- Know what you want to say

- Sit attentively

- Speak through the chairperson

- Think before you speak

- Speak clearly

- Project your voice if necessary

- Present facts and relevant information

- Have the case file in order

- Be ready to challenge

- Ask for explanation if you do not understand something

- Admit if you do not have information/knowledge

- Act in a professional manner

   © Jacki Pritchard 2007

GOOD PRACTICE: DON'TS

- Leave yourself short of time

- Slouch

- Chew gum

- Doodle

- Use jargon

- Mumble

- Waffle to cover up the fact that you do not know something

- Get angry

- Get upset

- Be intimidated

© Jacki Pritchard 2007

PROBLEMATIC BEHAVIOUR

1. A participant keeps repeating the same thing over and over again.

2. You know a colleague has crucial information about a past incident which is relevant, but he or she is not contributing to the discussion.

3. Two participants keep whispering to each other.

4. A GP says: 'She's suffering from dementia. How can you believe anything she says?'

5. One participant is dominating the conference so much that people are not voicing their own opinions and they are visibly 'switching off'.

6. The victim is not being included in the discussion.

7. Another participant says to you aggressively: 'You're talking a load of rubbish.'

8. The chairperson is ignoring a participant who is trying to speak.

9. A policeman says in front of the victim: 'It's a waste of time being here. Adults with learning disabilities are useless at giving statements and evidence.'

10. The victim starts to cry after a participant has made a discriminatory comment.

11. A consultant uses medical terminology you do not understand.

12. Two participants are passing notes to each other.

© Jacki Pritchard 2007

CASE CONFERENCE SIMULATION
DON MAYFIELD (AGED 30) PART I

Subject: Don Mayfield (aged 30)

Information Sheet

Don is 30 years old and has lived in supported accommodation for a number of years. He currently lives with nine other adults (males and females) in a project which is run within a voluntary organisation. He has no contact with his family.

Don has learning disabilities. He can communicate but tends to do so in short sentences; this makes him seem rather abrupt. He sometimes misunderstands what is said to him if he is anxious. He becomes very withdrawn when frustrated, for example when people do not understand what he is trying to say. In general, Don is able to function very well. He works a few hours a day in a local greengrocer's shop, moving boxes of fruit and veg, stacking shelves, and so on. He enjoys going out for a drink to the local working men's club; other service users also go to the club and are usually welcomed by the people there.

In the last few years some work has been carried out with Don regarding his sexuality. He is homosexual, but has never been involved in a long-term relationship. He did see a counsellor regularly for a year to discuss various issues, including safe sex.

Three weeks ago, Don returned home early from the club, very upset, and disclosed to his key worker that he had 'been made to have sex' (his own words) in the toilets by a man, named Gordon, who works behind the bar. Don said Gordon 'hurt' him.

An adult abuse investigation has taken place, but it has not proceeded exactly as the local policy states. Today the case conference is about to be convened. Don has *not* been medically examined by the police surgeon, but he has been to see his GP. Since he made the disclosure he has been barred from the working men's club, which has upset him greatly.

© Jacki Pritchard 2007

CASE CONFERENCE SIMULATION
DON MAYFIELD (AGED 30) PART 2

Subject: Don Mayfield (aged 30)

Attendance Sheet

Independent chairperson

Minute-taker

Don Mayfield

Don's social worker

Don's key worker from the project

Manager of the project

General practitioner

Police officer 1

Police officer 2

Counsellor

© Jacki Pritchard 2007

CASE CONFERENCE SIMULATION
DON MAYFIELD (AGED 30) PART 3

Subject: Don Mayfield (aged 30)

Role play briefs for participants

Role: Independent chairperson

You have been asked to chair the case conference today.

Role: Minute-taker

You are to take the minutes. Interrupt if you cannot hear or do not understand any of the participants.

Role: Don Mayfield

You definitely were raped by Gordon, the barman, but you are at the stage now where you feel no one believes you and you are fed up with answering the same questions. You get very embarrassed when asked about sexual matters and become very withdrawn. Gordon did rape you in the toilets; he approached you while you were standing at the urinals. He also hit you on the bottom with a belt which resulted in some bruises. You are not sure what time it was when it happened but you can remember that you went to the toilet after someone had sung 'Agadoo' in the karaoke competition. Since the incident you have been interviewed several times by the police and social worker. You have always wanted your key worker present at these times. You have also visited the GP, because you cannot sleep properly (you have nightmares when you do drop off) and you feel sick all the time. You have shown the GP the bruises on your bottom.

Role: Don's social worker

Don is well settled in the project where he lives and has no problems in his job at the greengrocer's shop. Consequently, you do not see Don very often; it tends to be at reviews. However, you were brought in to do the adult abuse investigation with the police. You think Don *is* telling the truth. You feel angry with the lead police officer because he is openly homophobic and has no time for people with learning disabilities. You feel the police have not carried out the investigation properly (there was no video interview or medical examination by the police surgeon), but feel powerless to do anything about it.

CASE CONFERENCE SIMULATION
DON MAYFIELD (AGED 30) PART 3

Role: Don's key worker from the project

You are feeling angry because you feel that no one has really listened to what Don has said. You have sat in with Don during the interviews (with police and social worker), but felt very intimidated by them. You are feeling guilty that maybe you did not support Don enough during the interviews; you wonder if you could have done something to help so he would have been believed. Today you are going to try to be more forceful.

Role: Manager of the project

You have not really had much involvement in the abuse investigation. When the incident was reported to you, you immediately involved social services and the police. You are attending today to support your worker (and obviously Don as well).

Role: General practitioner

You have not been around very long in your current GP practice, so you do not know Don very well. However, he came to the surgery with his key worker a week after the alleged incident, because he could not sleep properly (and when he did sleep he was having nightmares) and he was feeling sick all the time. Don told you about the incident and you believed him. You gave him a general examination and found some old bruises on his buttocks.

Role: Counsellor

You have not had contact with Don recently, but you were involved with him for a year when he needed to work on issues regarding his sexuality and later on other issues such as safe sex. Don was assessed by a clinical psychologist before he was referred to you; it was felt then that Don has a good level of understanding and knows the difference between the truth and a lie. You believe that Don would know the difference between consenting sex in a relationship and being forced to do something he did not want to do.

© Jacki Pritchard 2007

CASE CONFERENCE SIMULATION
DON MAYFIELD (AGED 30) PART 3

Role: Police officer 1

You are homophobic and have no time for adults with learning disabilities. You think this investigation is a waste of your precious time; these cases never get to court anyway! You are thinking even if Don was raped he deserved everything he got. You have not followed procedures correctly and have told other people involved that Don would not make a credible witness so it is wasting everyone's time. You deliberately did not get the police surgeon involved. You will say that there was not enough evidence to warrant a medical examination. You have interviewed the alleged perpetrator Gordon, who seemed 'a good bloke'. He has strongly denied that he had sexual intercourse with Don and said that Don had 'come on' to him.

Role: Police officer 2

You have only just come into this particular job. You do not get on with your colleague, who has many years of experience, because he is openly homophobic and has no time for adults with learning disabilities. You, on the other hand, are keen to find out what has really happened and are very aware that adults with learning disability are often victims of abuse. You tried to get your colleague to contact the police surgeon, but he said there was not enough evidence to warrant a medical examination.

Chapter 8

Risk Assessment and Developing Protection Plans

Risk assessment is integral to all adult protection work. From the point where any worker has concerns about someone's safety, a risk assessment is required. If an alert is passed through as a referral for an adult abuse investigation, immediately a risk assessment should begin. Risk assessment is a crucial part of the adult abuse investigation process. The investigating officers should be assessing the risk of significant harm when they are involved in interviewing victims and liaising with other people during the investigation. That liaison is part of the risk assessment process. The investigating officers' assessment should then be presented to a case conference where the assessment is taken further. The development of a protection plan is a stage within the investigation process whereby goals are set to minimise the risk of harm occurring. This whole process will be discussed in detail in this chapter.

Unfortunately, workers across the sectors will view risk assessment differently. For example, many grassroots workers will automatically think of health and safety issues when the term 'risk assessment' is used. Risk assessment encompasses all aspects of life, not just the practical issues. A simple example will illustrate the broadness of risk assessment.

Case Example

A home carer is involved with an older person, Mabel, who is slightly confused. Bare electric wires are visible both on the toaster and the kettle. Mabel and the home carer could be at risk of electrocution. A social worker is also involved with Mabel because there has been a disclosure from her that her grandson physically and financially abuses her. Mabel does want to do anything about it because of the possible repercussions; for example, her grandson may be prosecuted and sent to prison, and then she would have no one to visit her.

In this example of Mabel's situation, there could be many different types of harm which need to be assessed.

Some workers will never have had formal training on risk assessment and risk management; despite this fact they will be expected to complete risk assessments during the course of their day-to-day work. Others will have received training but will be using different models of risk. It is rare to find one common risk form in many organisations; usually different teams or sections are using various risk tools. Where adult abuse procedures are concerned there should be a common risk tool so that anyone who becomes involved in an investigation will assess risk in the same way. Sadly, this is not always found within a policy.

What is being assessed?

When somebody has been abused they will have suffered some form of harm. The objective in assessing risk in an abuse investigation is to assess the risk of *significant harm*. Abuse can have both short-term and long-term effects. Part of abuse work which is not always given enough consideration is the long-term work which needs to be undertaken with the victim regarding the healing process. We shall discuss this further below.

The circumstances surrounding a risk assessment may be complicated. Even after the investigation it is not always clear whether abuse has happened or not. A risk assessment has to predict the possible likelihood of harm occurring in the future; the decision in the case conference may be to monitor the situation and this should be done through a protection plan. Another common situation is the victim choosing to remain in an abusive situation even when it might be obvious to the workers involved that harm is going to occur. This has to be acknowledged and ways of minimising the risk of harm must be considered.

Significant harm

Let us just remind ourselves about the definition of significant harm again:

> …not only ill treatment (including sexual abuse and forms of ill treatment which are not physical), but also the impairment of, or an avoidable deterioration in, physical or mental health; and the impairment of physical, intellectual, emotional, social or behavioural development. (Lord Chancellor's Department 1997, p.68)

 Handout 8.1, p.269

Something which is often not considered in great depth within adult protection work is the concept of *dangerousness*. A risk assessment should be considering how dangerous the abuser is and what risks he or she poses to the victim in the future. The probation and prison services carry out numerous assessments regarding the likelihood of re-offending. We can learn a great deal from the literature which exists regarding this (e.g. Kemshall 1997, 1998). Simply, dangerousness is the risk of harming others. It is interesting that at the same time geriatricians were highlighting the abuse of older people by their carers the Butler Committee broadened the definition of harm from physical to include lasting psychological harm (Butler Committee, Home Office and Department of Health and Social Security 1975). More recently the Criminal Justice Act 1991 has used the principle of harm reduction or prevention as a key objective for the imposition of preventative sentencing under Section 2(2)(b).

Workers must think about harm in relation to public protection; it is not just about assessing risk of harm to the victim in an abuse case, but also assessing risk of harm to the general public and to property. Therefore, anyone contributing to a risk assessment should understand the following terms and be thinking about them during the process of assessing risk:

- risk assessment
- risk management
- significant harm
- likelihood/probability
- public protection
- dangerousness.

 Handout 8.2, p.270

Brearley's model of risk

Paul Brearley wrote extensively about risk many years ago (Brearley 1982a and 1982b). Even though there have been many developments in health and social care since then, his works are still very useful to read and his model of risk is sound. I have adapted his work into the tool shown in Handout 8.3.

 Handout 8.3, p.271

The terminology

The terms in risk assessment work need to be explained. Often the terminology is used incorrectly; workers tend to mix up the words 'risk' and 'danger'. It is important that everyone contributing to a risk assessment is using the correct terminology with the same meanings.

Risk-taking action

Rather than starting with the word 'risk', it is better to start with the following question:

> ### KEY QUESTION
>
> What is the risk-taking action?

We all take risks – every day of our lives – and many of us will not give a second thought to it at all (e.g. getting in the car to drive). Risk is a part of life, and some people will be greater risk-takers than others. Workers, who should be encouraging service users to take risks, often feel in a Catch 22 situation because they also have the duty to care which they will interpret as a duty to protect.

Case Example

Bethan is very cruel to her father, Dorian. She is verbally abusive to him at home and humiliates him in public when she takes him out in a wheelchair. Dorian tells the home carer that Bethan takes his money without asking and she often forgets to pay the bills. Dorian refuses to do anything about the abuse and wants to remain living with his daughter.

A fundamental starting point is to consider whether the service user has the full mental capacity to make an informed decision about risk-taking and whether the person's actions will affect anyone else.

KEY QUESTIONS

Does the service user have mental capacity?

Will his or her risk-taking action affect anyone else?

Benefits

We all take risks in order to get something out of doing so – a buzz, some excitement – it results in some sort of benefit to us. When assessing risk workers often do not spend enough time finding out why the person wants to take the risk and what he or she will get out of it. Very often it is important for victims to maintain their relationship with abusers because they love them dearly. It is necessary to explain this in detail; that is, to understand the victim's thoughts, beliefs, value base, and so on.

Hazards

A 'hazard' can be absolutely anything – a person (e.g. the abuser), an object (e.g. worn carpet), a situation (e.g. the environment (e.g. no running water), a medical condition (e.g. Alzheimer's disease) or a disability (e.g. hearing impairment). A hazard can stop someone achieving the benefit or it may also directly cause the danger. Workers may struggle with the concept of hazard.

Dangers

A 'danger' is the worst possible feared outcome of a situation or action. In a risk assessment, workers have to predict what dangers *could* happen and how *likely* they are to happen. This is where risk assessment can become very subjective rather than being a scientific process. It is important to look at past behaviour and incidents (evidence) as well as the current situation and capabilities of the person in order to predict what might occur in the future.

Let us now consider this tool in relation to adult protection work.

Risk assessment and adult protection

I feel very strongly that a proper risk tool should be developed specifically for the local vulnerable adult/adult abuse policy and procedures. Sometimes one is included in the policy and procedures but workers are not given specific guidance or training on how to use it. I developed such a tool and guidance for the *North Wales Policy and Procedure for the Protection of Vulnerable Adults* (North Wales Vulnerable Adults Form 2005). The tool itself is reproduced in Appendix 3.

In day-to-day practice workers should be assessing risk and liaising with other people to reach an agreement about how they can support a service user in taking risks. A care plan will be developed in order to do this; that is, to minimise the level of possible harm in the future. The same methods of working and assessing will be utilised as we progress through an adult abuse investigation. Let us now consider the different stages of the process.

Meeting with the service user

It is absolutely imperative to involve the service user in the risk assessment process. It is not something a worker can impose on a service user, it is something which they should do *with* him or her. Relating this to adult protection work, the risk assessment will be undertaken whilst the victim is being interviewed by the two investigating officers.

It is important to find out *why* the person wants to take the risk and to get their views. If the worker thinks other people may have an opinion about the risk-taking action, then permission must be sought to contact those people. If the service user refuses to give permission, the only occasions a worker could override the self-determination principle is if the service user lacks capacity or there is a risk to public protection (e.g. a crime has been committed or could be committed in the future) or if it was thought the person lacked capacity. It is important to come back to the point which has been made several times in this manual. A worker should regularly revisit with the service user the limits of confidentiality, and should stress that if a service user is at risk of harm a worker has to report this to his or her line manager. Investigating officers must be upfront and honest with the victims they interview that information will be shared with other people; for example, via the case conference.

If a worker does decide to override self-determination or break confidentiality, he or she must record and explain the reasons for doing this on the case file. For example, a worker might be acting under Section 115 of the Crime and Disorder Act 1998 (the information-sharing principle) to prevent a crime being committed. Or if it is thought a service user may lack capacity the worker should write on the file that he or she is acting in that person's best interests as defined in *Making Decisions* (Lord Chancellor's Department 1999).

Gathering information

During an abuse investigation, the investigating officers may have to liaise with other workers or professionals who know the victim and/or abuser. The main objective of the investigation and the liaison work may be to find out if abuse has happened, but in addition information may be gathered to contribute to the risk assessment.

Case Example

It was thought that Karla had a personality disorder; she was known to the community mental health team. She had lived with her boyfriend, Nick, for six months when it became apparent to her support worker that she was being physically abused. One day Karla was admitted to hospital with severe head injuries. She did recover and was determined to return home to live with Nick. A risk assessment was undertaken. An important part of the process was to gain information about Nick's violent behaviour. He had served several prison sentences for violence and, therefore, both the probation and prison services had already undertaken risk assessments before in regard to the likelihood of him re-offending.

Writing the risk assessment

The investigating officers will usually have written a report for the case conference to present the findings of the investigation, but it is useful to write the risk assessment as a separate document. As was stated above, some abuse policies will have a risk assessment tool and a pro-forma will be included which will be presented to the case conference. If specific guidance is not given regarding the format of the risk assessment report, workers can use the headings shown in Handout 8.3.

 Handout 8.3, p.271

Presenting the risk assessment

In the case conference, after all participants have presented their individual reports, the chairperson should open up the discussion so that the formal risk assessment can be undertaken. This is when it is helpful to have a specific risk tool, which the investigating officers will have started to complete; other participants will contribute to the completion of the assessment. Everyone should have copies of the risk form which has been completed. Consequently, risk assessment is being undertaken in a multi-disciplinary way. The investigating officers will talk through their assessment and then other participants will contribute to the process; they must predict the likelihood of harm occurring. The dangers will have been listed. Each one of them in turn has to be considered and the likelihood of occurrence graded. The chairperson has to ask the following key question for each danger:

KEY QUESTION

How likely is it this will happen?

The process of risk assessment fails when workers are not prepared. Prediction can only be undertaken by considering the 'evidence'. Workers need to know what is expected of them, what information is needed at the case conference. A simple example (not related to abuse) can illustrate this point.

Everyone is worried about an older woman, Jane, falling because she has poor mobility. In order to predict how likely it is that she will fall in the future it is necessary to have information about Jane's current physical condition and mobility, and the environment in which Jane lives. Also needed is the record of any previous falls – their frequency and the circumstances in which they occurred. Therefore, it is crucial to look at:

- current circumstances

- environment

- past behaviours/incidents

- frequency

- duration.

Risk assessment requires some sort of grading. To answer the question 'How likely is it this will happen?' it can be useful to use the simple gradings:

- very likely

- quite likely

- not very likely

- not at all likely.

A consensus of opinion has to be reached regarding a grading for each danger stated on the risk assessment form. Having gone through this process for each danger, the chairperson should formally ask the participants at the case conference if they support the person in taking the risks. This will lead on to discussion about how the risk of harm occurring can be minimised and a protection plan developed. There should be a final grading regarding the overall level of risk; that is, how likely it is that this person will be a victim of significant harm in the future. There are many methods of grading risk but currently in adult protection work it is not done in a very sophisticated way. In general, people tend to use the terms *low-*, *moderate-* or *high-*risk case.

Throughout this process the victim should be included in the discussion (especially if he or she is present at the case conference). It is important to repeat the point: risk assessment is something you undertake *with* the service user.

Exercise 8.1 can be used to help workers think about risk assessment in general, but Exercise 8.2 will take them on to think about risk in adult abuse cases.

✍ Exercise 8.1, p.267

✍ Exercise 8.2, p.268 and 📄 Handouts 8.4 and 8.5, pp.272–273

Developing a protection plan

Some policies will require that the protection plan is developed during the case conference; others will state that this work is done within a certain time limit after the case conference. It is imperative that a protection plan is written up clearly and in detail. It must be clear *who* is going to do *what* and *when*. Handout 8.6 outlines a pro-forma for the development of protection plans.

 Handout 8.6, p.274

A protection plan needs to be detailed but not full of irrelevant information. Very often a care plan will be in place alongside the protection plan so the latter does not need to include the same information unless it is directly related to protection issues. It should be remembered that a protection plan's purpose is to inform us how agencies are doing their best to protect a victim of abuse. If there is still uncertainty about whether a vulnerable adult has been abused, the protection plan should show how agencies are monitoring a situation. A protection should be written in such a way that someone (e.g. a solicitor in the Crown Prosecution Service) could pick it up and know exactly what was being done to protect the adult. This is why there should be a section which details workers' specific roles and responsibilities.

Objectives

This section of a protection plan should give a brief summary of the situation: who is being abused by whom and specifically which categories of abuse are suspected or have been proven. Also, it should be stated clearly what agencies hope to achieve within the time limit set for the next case conference.

KEY QUESTION

What are you trying to achieve in the protection plan
before the next case conference?

People involved

All sorts of people could be involved in a protection plan. It is not just professionals and workers; a neighbour or friend could be visiting the vulnerable person on a daily basis just to see that he or she is all right. It can be useful to have a named worker who will be known as the *key worker*. This term is not used in the sense of a key worker in a residential setting; in a protection plan, the key worker is a person who is named to take responsibility for coordinating the plan (e.g. a social worker or a community psychiatric nurse). If the plan is not working once it has been implemented, then the key worker should be informed and the review case conference reconvened earlier than planned. A primary worker is someone who may have more face-to-face contact with the victim than the key worker (for example, home carer, day care worker).

Everyone who has an active role in the plan should be named and it is useful to have their information in table form stating:

- name

- job title/relationship to victim (or abuser)

- address

- telephone/fax number, e-mail address, and so on.

Responsibilities and tasks

Detailing what is actually going to be done to protect a vulnerable adult is the crucial part of a protection plan. It is not good enough to write 'Social worker will visit regularly' or 'Home care service will provide support'. This way of recording does not inform us. What are these people doing exactly? A plan needs to explain what responsibilities have been given to an agency and its workers and what tasks are actually being carried out and how often.

KEY QUESTION

Who is going to do *what* and *when?*

Monitoring

We hear time and time again in case conferences a worker offering 'to monitor a situation'. The following key questions need to be asked of that worker:

KEY QUESTIONS

What are you going to monitor?

How and where will you record this?

If an agency is not willing to share their written records, it is pointless a worker being designated to monitor a situation. If a particular monitoring tool is going to be used by certain workers (e.g. home carers or day care staff may use bodymaps) this should be recorded in the plan. Bodymaps are an excellent way of monitoring and collecting evidence. Examples are given in Appendix 2.

Review

A grading of risk should have been undertaken and recorded in the case conference minutes and in the protection plan, which should be reviewed at the next case conference. The timing of this should be dependent on the level of risk. If it is a high-risk case the review case conference should occur fairly quickly (e.g. within a month); if it is a low-risk case the conference may meet within three months.

Again it is important to emphasise that the protection plan should be developed *with* service users; it should not be something which is imposed on them. Also, if a separate case conference has been convened on the alleged abuser because he or she is a vulnerable adult, a separate protection plan will be developed for that person.

TASK

Think of a victim you have worked with in the past. Write a protection plan for them using the pro-forma shown on Handout 8.3.

Two case studies are presented in Handouts 8.7 and 8.8 which can be used in training sessions to help groups develop and write protection plans.

Case studies are presented in the following handouts:

 Handouts 8.7 and 8.8, pp.275–276

Key learning points from this chapter

- A vulnerable adult/adult abuse policy should include a risk tool.

- Risk assessment is an integral part of the investigation process.

- In adult protection work workers are assessing the risk of *significant harm.*

- Workers need to understand the terms *risk-taking action, benefits, hazards* and *dangers.*

- Lack of capacity can be a major issue in risk assessment.

- If a worker needs to override self-determination and break confidentiality in order to gain/share information, the reasons for doing so must be explained and recorded.

- Workers need to consider the concept of *dangerousness.*

- Public protection has to be a major consideration in risk assessment and adult protection work.

- Workers must assess risk of harm to the victim, the general public and to property.

- The risk assessment should be presented to a case conference.

- The likelihood of significant harm occurring (as a result of each danger which is considered) should be graded.

- A protection plan should be developed *with* the service user – not imposed on him or her.

- If a vulnerable adult is the alleged abuser, it may be necessary to develop a separate protection plan for that person.

- Protection plans must be reviewed regularly by reconvening a case conference.

Suggested reading

Brearley, C.P. (1982a) *Risk and Ageing.* London: Routledge and Kegan Paul.

Brearley, C.P. (1982b) *Risk in Social Work.* London: Routledge and Kegan Paul.

Kemshall, H. and Pritchard, J. (eds) (1996) *Good Practice in Risk Assessment and Risk Management.* London: Jessica Kingsley Publishers.

Kemshall, H. and Pritchard, J. (eds) (1997) *Good Practice in Risk Assessment and Risk Management 2: Protection, Rights and Responsibilities.* London: Jessica Kingsley Publishers.

 Videos

WAA1, WAA2, WAA3, WAA4, WAA5, WAA6

All the case studies in each video can be used by trainers to work on the subject of risk assessment and the development of protection plans. Participants can watch a case study and then exercises can be set, for example for participants to identify the hazards and dangers, discuss the level of harm or write a protection plan.

WHO COULD BE INVOLVED IN A RISK ASSESSMENT?

Objective

To encourage workers to be more creative in risk assessment.

Participants

Work individually initially, then in pairs.

Equipment

Paper and pens.

Time

10 minutes for individual work; 20 minutes in pairs.

Task

1. Each participant will think of an abuse situation they have been involved in/known about.

2. The participant will then list the people who might be involved in the risk assessment.

3. The participant will list the hazards and dangers involved in this case.

4. Participants will then work in pairs. They will have 10 minutes each to share and discuss their case and risk assessment.

5. Participants help each other by making suggestions about how the risk assessment can be improved upon.

Feedback

1. General discussion about what participants have learnt about assessing risk.

2. Participants help each other by making suggestions about how the risk assessment can be improved upon.

RISKY SITUATIONS

Objective

To help participants to use risk assessment methods in adult abuse cases.

Participants

Small groups.

Equipment

Flipchart paper and pens.

Copies of Handouts 8.4 and 8.5.

Time

30 minutes.

Task

1. Each group will be asked to work on just one scenario from the cases listed on Handout 8.5.

2. Each participant will be given a copy of Handout 8.4 and asked to discuss the questions in their group.

Feedback

1. One scenario will be taken at a time. The group will feed back from their flipchart sheets.

2. Other groups will comment on what has been presented and add their own ideas.

© Jacki Pritchard 2007

DEFINITION OF SIGNIFICANT HARM

…not only ill treatment (including sexual abuse and forms of ill treatment which are not physical), but also the impairment of, or an avoidable deterioration in, physical or mental health; and the impairment of physical, intellectual, emotional, social or behavioural development.

From: Lord Chancellor's Department (1997) *Who Decides? Making Decisions on Behalf of Mentally Incapacitated Adults.* London: The Stationery Office, p.68.

© Crown copyright 1997

CRUCIAL TERMINOLOGY

- Risk assessment

- Risk management

- Significant harm

- Likelihood/probability

- Public protection

- Dangerousness

© Jacki Pritchard 2007

ASSESSING RISK TOOL

Records need to show *how* you have assessed the degree of risk. Sometimes it is useful to write a report in addition to the risk assessment form. Any record should include information under the headings of:

- **Define the risk(s)**
  (What is the risk-taking?)

- **Benefits**
  (What does the service user get out of taking the risk(s)?)

- **Hazards**
  (those things which hinder positive outcomes (benefits)/cause dangers.)

- **Dangers**
  (state the worst possible outcomes.)

- **Probability and likelihood**
  (How likely is it that the danger(s) will occur? Include other people's opinions/reports. What criteria have been used to make these predictions? Think about current circumstances, environment, past behaviours/incidents and their frequency/duration.)

- **Actions to be taken**
  (goal setting)

- **Monitoring tools**
  (How and who is going to monitor? Where will this be recorded?)

- **Review procedures**
  (set date for review.)

- **Signatures**
  (all those involved including service user if mentally sound)

- **Date**

© Jacki Pritchard 2007

EXERCISE: RISKY SITUATIONS

In your group discuss the following questions:

1. What is the risk-taking action(s)?

2. What are the (a) hazards and (b) dangers?

3. Who might be invited to the case conference?

4. What evidence would be needed in order to predict the likelihood of the dangers occurring?

5. What resources might be put into a protection plan?

© Jacki Pritchard 2007

EXERCISE: RISKY SITUATIONS

1. Sam, who has learning disabilities, lives in a supported accommodation project. Staff describe him as having 'challenging behaviour and always kicking off'. It is known that he was sexually abused by his mother in childhood. Sam is verbally and physically aggressive to female staff and service users, but staff see it as 'the way he is'. In recent months his behaviour has got worse; several service users have been hit and sustained injuries. One member of staff was knocked unconscious by a blow to her head.

2. Ruth is blind and physically disabled after being attacked by a burglar 20 years ago. She is agoraphobic, has no family and relies on home care services to help her. Ruth gets very depressed at certain times of the year and drinks when she is feeling low. A group of teenagers heard about Ruth and her situation, and started calling round and offering to help her. Ruth gives them money to go to the local off-licence. The home carers have become aware that things have started going missing.

3. Beth is 49 years old and it is thought she has early onset dementia. Her daughter, Karen, tells the social worker that she is worried about her mother's safety because her father Jack, who 'has little patience', has always been physically violent towards Beth and the three children. None of the children visit their parents. Karen keeps in touch by telephone. Home care services are involved because Jack works during the daytime. He often goes out at night.

4. Reg Hunter is 89 years old. He is well known in the local community as being a Schedule 1 offender and having murdered his next door neighbour 30 years ago. He went to prison and served 15 years. Since his release it is known that he has continued to present violent behaviour towards both men and women in public places. He has been arrested for being drunk and disorderly on several occasions. Reg has now had a stroke which has affected his left side. He is admitted to a care home. The social worker has not told the care home about Reg's history of offending.

5. When Alan (age 25) was sectioned under the Mental Health Act 1983 he was cared for by Steve (age 50), who was a nurse on the hospital ward. Alan had been admitted into the care system when he was ten years old and has always formed inappropriate attachments as he craves affection. After discharge, Steve kept in touch and then suggested Alan move in with him. Steve is violent towards Alan and forces him into sexual activity. Alan tells his community psychiatric nurse about this but says he wants to remain living with Steve.

DEVELOPING PROTECTION PLANS

Protection plans must be *specific* and *detailed*. They should be developed and agreed in case conferences, but more detail can be added after the conference has taken place. A suggested pro-forma follows.

Objectives of the plan

What are you trying to achieve?

List of people involved

- Key worker – person who will coordinate the plan.

- Primary worker – person who has most face-to-face contact with the victim.

- Professionals, volunteers, advocates, other important people (family, neighbours, friends) – people who are contributing.

Responsibilities and tasks

Remember to include work being done with victim and abuser.

State for each person involved:

- name, job/relationship with victim/abuser

- objectives – what he or she is trying to achieve

- how he or she will do this (tasks)

- when this will be done – contact frequency/day/time/duration.

Monitoring

- How each person is going to record what he or she is doing, what has been achieved, problems, and so on.

- Specific tools to be used, for example bodymaps, checklists.

- Where the record will be kept.

- How the information will be presented for review.

Review

A date must be set for review.

 © Jacki Pritchard 2007

CASE STUDY: LILIAN (AGED 73)

Background information

Lilian is in her seventies. She has been a victim of domestic violence from various partners throughout her adult life and in recent years has been physically and financially abused by her son. Lilian has had 17 children; only five are living. One son (not the alleged abuser) has served a prison sentence for murder but is now living in the community, and one daughter has been on remand for manslaughter. The family have been known to various local social services departments and probation services since the 1960s.

Lilian was previously living alone and received home care support. One morning she gave a note to the home care workers asking them to get her out of the house because her son was 'hurting' her. A social worker visited Lilian later in the day and admitted her to a care home on the other side of the city.

The presenting problems on admission

- Lilian has few clothes. The ones she has brought with her are torn, dirty and soiled. She does not possess any knickers at all.

- She is grossly underweight.

- She has a drink problem.

- She will only write about the abuse, not talk about it.

- She is scared her son and other family members will find her.

Task for group work

1. Consider the issues surrounding Lilian's care and development of a protection plan.

2. Consider other protection issues (e.g. for staff).

3. Consider the long-term work which needs to be undertaken with Lilian.

© Jacki Pritchard 2007

CASE STUDY: JEANETTE (AGED 28)

Jeanette was diagnosed as having schizophrenia when she was 21 years old and has been known to the local mental health services since then. She spent most of her childhood in the care system, being placed in a large number of children's homes and with foster families. She has always welcomed support and been willing to work with the various social workers and community psychiatric nurses she has been allocated. Jeanette has no living family and never maintains friendships for very long.

Jeanette had a baby, Alice, two months ago. The father is Gary, who is a Schedule 1 offender. She met him a few days after he had been released from prison. About six months later she decided to stop taking her medication because she wanted to get pregnant. Gary is 40 years old and has served several prison sentences for physically and sexually abusing children. Prior to his last imprisonment, he had had some contact with a community mental health team. It has been recorded that he 'may' have a personality disorder. Various case conferences were convened while Jeanette was pregnant and it was made clear to her that the situation would have to be monitored very carefully when the baby was born and that Gary should not live in the same household as the baby.

Jeanette receives regular visits from her social worker and health visitor. Two home carers, Cath and Val, also go in to give some support; they have become very concerned during the last two weeks. Jeanette has been very bad tempered, which is very out of character for her. She has also had a black eye and several bruises on both her arms. She said she had walked into the door when she had got up to feed Alice in the night. Cath and Val are worried that Jeanette may have stopped taking her medication. There have been occasions when they thought Jeanette was talking to Alice, but then they realised she was talking to the wall. Also, Gary has been in the house every morning when the home carers have called.

Task for group work

1. List the main hazards and dangers in this case.

2. Assume a review case conference has been convened because of the concerns raised by the home carers. Consider what should be written in a protection plan for Jeanette.

 © Jacki Pritchard 2007

Chapter 9

The Importance of Recording

It would probably not be an exaggeration to say that the majority of workers, no matter what job they do, do not like having to do paperwork. This can be for all sorts of reasons. A major problem can be lack of time to do it properly. It cannot be emphasised enough how crucial it is to record properly and in depth for adult protection work. It concerns me that I meet a vast number of workers who have never been taught how to record properly. So, in this chapter I am going to go back to some fundamental principles of good recording practices and consider what sort of records need to be kept when dealing with abuse cases.

Forms

The majority of vulnerable adult/adult abuse policies do include forms; for example:

- a form to record an alert
- a form to monitor the stages of an investigation
- a pro-forma for the investigating officers' report
- a risk assessment tool
- a pro-forma for a protection plan.

Workers *must* familiarise themselves with the forms in their local policy. If a worker does not follow policy and procedures then they can be totally liable for their actions (or inaction) if something goes wrong. Some examples of alerting and monitoring forms are given in Appendix 1.

Records as evidence

All sorts of written documents can be produced as evidence in a court of law. The Crown Prosecution Service have to carry out the evidential test when considering whether a case should proceed to court. Written documents have to go through this test, which is not just about assessing whether someone will be a credible witness. This is why it is so vital that workers record properly. During a training course on recording workers must be made aware of all the things they record that could be used as evidence:

- referrals
- assessments
- summaries
- agreements/contracts
- care plans/protection plans
- letters and memos
- forms
- bodymaps
- monitoring protocols
- reports
- review documents
- minutes of strategy meetings/case conferences
- running records
- process records
- notes
- messages
- diaries
- notebooks.

 Handout 9.1, p.297

Contemporaneous notes

I still come across a number of workers working with vulnerable adults who have never been told about the importance of contemporaneous notes. Even experienced social workers tell me how they have taken a disclosure or conducted an interview, gone back to the office to write up the record and then binned their original notes. It is absolutely imperative that these notes are kept. This is because if the police pass a case to the Crown Prosecution Service any original notes are needed for the evidential test to be carried out:

> This is the first stage in the decision to prosecute. Crown Prosecutors must be satisfied that there is enough evidence to provide a 'realistic prospect of conviction' against each defendant on each charge. They must consider whether the evidence can be used and is reliable. They must also consider what the defence case may be and how that is likely to affect the prosecution case. A 're-alistic prospect of conviction' is an objective test. It means that a jury or a bench of magistrates, properly directed in accordance with the law, will be more likely than not to convict the defendant of the charge alleged. (This is a separate test from the one that criminal courts themselves must apply. A jury or magistrates' court should only convict if it is sure of a defendant's guilt.) If the case does not pass the evidential test, it must not go ahead, no matter how important or serious it may be… If the case does pass the evidential test, Crown Prosecutors must then decide whether a prosecution is needed in the public interest. They must balance factors for and against prosecution carefully and fairly. Some factors may increase the need to prosecute but others may suggest that another course of action would be better. A prosecution will usually take place however, unless there are public interest factors tending against prosecution which clearly outweigh those tending in favour. The CPS will only start or continue a prosecution if a case has passed both tests. (Crown Prosecution Service 2006)

It is also important for workers to be aware that if they do take notes during a disclosure these should not be written verbatim. This is because these notes could be deemed to be the first statement, which really should be carried out by the police.

Minute-taking

Minutes which are taken during a strategy meeting or case conference need to be comprehensive and accurate. They will evidence how decisions have been reached. It is problematic in many areas that trained minute-takers for adult protection case conferences are often not available. I believe very strongly that minute-takers for adult protection meetings should be trained in exactly the same way as minute-takers for child protection case conferences. It is no use sending in any administrative person who is available; the minute-taker needs to know how and what to record. Also it is abusive to put an administrative person into a case conference where they might hear the most distressing and upsetting things. Training administrative people how to take minutes also involves covering issues such as confidentiality and support before, during and after the meeting has taken place. Some areas have developed pro-formas for the minutes of strategy meetings and case conferences, so minute-takers need to be trained to use these.

Why it is necessary to keep records

It helps if people know exactly why they are being asked to do something, because then they might produce a better piece of work. Therefore, a trainer should always go into detail about the legalities of record keeping. Few workers know which statutes require them to document their activity. Sometimes workers believe it is their organisation which is just being bureaucratic or that managers get pleasure out of checking up on them. One of the main reasons why workers need to record is because they are accountable to their manager and to the organisation which employs them, but there are many other reasons and benefits:

- it is a legal requirement
- for accountability
- to explain and justify actions
- to give reasons for decisions made
- it acts as an aid to memory
- it safeguards against allegations
- it is a tool for monitoring, reviewing and evaluating work with the service user
- it is a tool for the worker to help him or her learn and be objective
- it is the basis for risk assessment and care planning
- records may be needed in a court of law.

 Handout 9.2, p.298

Written records are a way of communicating:

- what work is being undertaken (objectives)

- how work is being done (methods)

- what work has been done (monitor, review, evaluate)

- needs

- incidents/events

- opinions

- the reasons underpinning decision-making.

 Handout 9.3, p.299

Most organisations will have a policy or guidance regarding recording and archiving; this should be introduced to a worker when they are inducted. If you are reading this now and have never seen such a document then it would be wise to seek it out. When workers are dealing with abuse of children, guidance is made very clear because of the existence of the Children Act 1989. When working with adults guidance is not always so clear, so time limits can differ between agencies. Files may be kept for five, seven or ten years. Guidance may also differ regarding keeping diaries. My own personal view is you should *never* throw away your old work diaries. I believe that sometimes it can take years to prove abuse is happening or for a victim to make a decision to leave. Therefore, diaries may be needed at any time in the future. Guidance should also advise workers about keeping notes, notebooks, messages, and so on. Another problem which is occurring is workers' use of the internet and e-mails; some print off everything, others just delete. There needs to be consistency in record keeping within organisations.

Explaining to the service user

I want to go back to the point I have made several times in previous chapters about being honest and upfront with service users regarding the limits of confidentiality. When a worker first becomes involved explanation is needed about the limits of confidentiality. It is equally important to explain the fact that the organisation keeps written records. Good practice involves giving some examples so it makes sense. For example, a worker should explain that files are kept and who might have access to them. It is also good to point out that there are various forms which have to be completed. If bodymaps have to be used to monitor injuries in cases where adult abuse is suspected, it is not going to come as such a shock to the service user if they have regularly been reminded about records which are kept. A worker should also explain that a service user has the right to apply to see their record but some information (e.g. from a third party) has to be kept confidential.

Content

I am frequently asked on recording courses 'How much detail should I put in?' Some workers say their managers criticise them because they 'write too much'. I always suggest that the starting point should be to ask the following questions:

KEY QUESTIONS

Who am I writing this record for?

Who might read this?

In adult protection work all sorts of people could gain access to records:

- colleagues
- a manager
- senior management
- legal department
- other agencies (e.g. police, Crown Prosecution Service).

The content of a record and the way it is laid out will depend on its purpose. Writing a report for a panel to obtain a resource (e.g. day care) will be very different to writing a court report. Exercise 9.1 can be used at the beginning of a training course to get participants writing a written record; it will give the trainer insight into how workers record. When the task is set it is highly unlikely that anyone in the group will ask why they have to do this. Consequently, the trainer will usually read very different accounts – detail and styles will vary. Later in the course the trainer will point out that no one did ask what was the purpose in writing the record so how did they know what to write, how much detail was needed, and so on?

✍ Exercise 9.1, p.293

After undertaking this first exercise, a trainer will normally present information about the purpose of recording (as discussed above). Exercises 9.2 and 9.3 can be used to think about good practice in relation to content and layout, after which this can be related to adult protection work.

✍ Exercise 9.2, p.294 and 📄 Handout 9.4, p.300

✍ Exercise 9.3, p.295 and 📄 Handout 9.5, p.301

Good content needs to be:

- relevant
- objective
- factual
- clear
- concise
- accurate
- non-judgemental
- non-discriminatory.

 Handout 9.4, p.300

Visually, records need to be easy to read. They should be set out neatly and clearly. This can be done by using:

- legible handwriting
- a black pen
- paragraphs
- headings/sub-headings
- numbering/lettering, e.g. 1, 2, 3; (i) (ii) (iii); a) b) c)
- bullet points
- asterisks

- capitals
- bold
- italics
- underlining
- punctuation
- quotation marks.

 Handout 9.5, p.301

Abbreviations

Earlier in this manual the avoidance of using jargon has been mentioned. We use a form of jargon in written records when we use abbreviations. Really workers should avoid using abbreviations, but so many are in the habit of doing it for quickness' sake it is hard to change and write in full. Unfortunately, other professionals reading the record may not understand what an abbreviation means or it may have two meanings (e.g. SW – support worker or social worker? HV – home visit or health visitor? NFA – no further action or no fixed abode?). Workers also abbreviate places which are well known to them (e.g. RHH – Royal Hallamshire Hospital; 'Saw Mrs X at Waterton' rather than Waterton Day Centre). If workers know they regularly use abbreviations and feel they cannot stop (although they should!), then a glossary should be developed and placed on the service user's file. Exercise 9.4 can be used on a training course to identify abbreviations which are used frequently, but it can also be used in a team meeting to develop a glossary.

 Exercise 9.4, p.296

Some other good practice points are:

Do

- use black pen
- cross out mistakes with just one black line and initial
- check what you have written
- record regularly
- record as soon as possible after the event (no more than 48 hours after the event)
- re-read and check what you have written.

Don't

- use correction fluid
- write long sentences
- be vague
- waffle
- use jargon
- use clichés
- use shorthand
- use abbreviations.

 Handout 9.6, p.302

Explanation

I read many case files and what is very common is that workers record an action or decision, but they fail to explain *how* a decision was reached. There could be all sorts of situations where a worker could be questioned years later about something they did.

KEY QUESTION

Are your records good enough to trigger your memory months
or years later about why you did something?

Preparation

Lack of time to do things thoroughly is a constant complaint from workers and is often the reason for recording not being made a priority in the working day. The necessary forms may be filled in as and when required, but general day-to-day recording is often put on the back burner. This is very dangerous practice. In order to achieve a high standard in recording preparation is needed. A worker must:

- sit and think
- plan
- draft
- write (and maybe rewrite)

in order to:

- describe
- explain
- inform
- argue for.

Handout 9.7, p.303

Certain issues should be considered before writing any written record and should act as a prompt for structuring what is to be recorded:

- facts
- opinion
- hearsay
- confidentiality
- access.

 Handout 9.8, p.304

During a training course on recording these terms need to be explained very clearly to workers.

Facts

Records need to relate the facts of a case. Facts are what we know has definitely happened. A fact is not based on feelings, guesses, assumptions or our own conclusions.

Opinions

It worries me greatly when workers tell me they have been told they must not include their opinion in a record. It is absolutely fine to give an opinion if you are qualified or have the relevant experience to do so. Workers should not undermine themselves by thinking or saying 'I am only a [home carer, care worker etc.]'. Such grassroots workers often know a service user better than anybody. Because they have regular contact and know the person well, they are able to notice any changes in the person which could be crucial in identifying abuse. Of course it would not be appropriate for say a home carer to see a blue/purple bruise and write in the service user's file that he or she thought the bruise was seven days old – because he or she is not a medical expert. However, it would be good for the home carer to write about what he or she observed – the colour of the bruise, its shape and location on the body – and complete a bodymap.

> ### KEY QUESTIONS
>
> Whose opinion is this?
>
> Is the person qualified to assess/give an opinion?

Opinions can be given in the body of the text you are writing but it can also be helpful to use headings to make different people's opinions stand out; the reader can then easily distinguish who is saying what. This method can be used in day-to-day recording or in reports.

Hearsay

Hearsay is information which cannot be adequately substantiated. It could be something which you are told by someone else – really second- or third-hand information. For example, a neighbour living across the road tells the social worker that another neighbour who lives next door to the alleged victim 'is always hearing shouting and banging in the house'.

Confidentiality

Workers should record that they have explained about the limits of confidentiality and that they have to share information with their manager. This could come under one heading in the record or, if writing chronologically, every time the service user was reminded of this issue it should be recorded in the process record again.

Access

This has been mentioned already but it is important that a worker when planning to write a record asks themselves the following questions:

KEY QUESTIONS

Who might read this record?

Will they understand what I am saying?

This takes us back to the point that records should be clear and should not include jargon and abbreviations which another professional might not understand.

Running and process records

There is still great variation between agencies and organisations regarding how information is kept. Some organisations are very advanced in their use of technology and each worker records using a computer; elsewhere workers do not have access to a computer and keep paper files. Then there is the ongoing debate and struggle within some organisations that want to become paperless! Whatever methods of recording are being used it is helpful for workers to be aware of some useful terminology – a process record and a running record. Even when certain software packages are being used, a worker should still think back to what are good recording principles.

So what is the difference between a running and a process record? Simply, think in terms of the short and long versions of recording. A running record is the short version. These can often be referred to as contact sheets and are an excellent way of developing a chronology, which solicitors require and work from. Chronologies are also helpful to workers who inherit cases from colleagues.

A running record literally records the action (remembering that it is vital to include both the date and time). For example:

14 August 2006

12.45 – 13.50	Home visit to Mr Williamson – disclosure about physical abuse.
14.10 – 14.45	Alerted and discussed alert with Richard Bentley, manager, Community Learning Disability Team.
15.04	Rang Family Support Unit, Churchtown Police – left message on answer machine.
16.15	Rang Family Support Unit again – left message on answer machine.
16.50	Rang Family Support Unit – spoke to PC Nuttall.

15 August 2006

11.30 – 12.30	Strategy meeting convened under Churchtown vulnerable adult protection policy and procedures (see minutes on file).

A process record goes into detail about what happened; that is, it is the full version. In the example above we read that Mr Williamson gave a disclosure about physical abuse on 14 August 2006. The process record would give the full details of that disclosure. Below we shall consider how to structure a process record.

What needs to be included – disclosure/investigation

We are back to the dilemma which has been raised above – how much detail is needed? The answer is as much detail as possible but the key word is *relevance*. At any stage in working with a case of adult abuse anything which is going to help us prove that abuse has happened (or is continuing) must be included. Workers often find it difficult to switch their minds to thinking they should be gathering evidence. Every case is different but it is useful to follow a simple framework for all recording; think simply in terms of beginning, middle and end – like one does when writing an essay. Again it is important to stress the need for planning. Below is a comprehensive list of subject areas a worker needs to think about when planning to write up a record:

- date, time, duration, location, people present at disclosure/interview

- the alleged victim's basic details

- the alleged abuser's basic details (including relationship, if any, to the victim)

- alleged/possible types of abuse

- relevant background information/social history

- confidentiality – explanation to victim

- victim's capacity

- consent

- sharing information – agreement of victim

- people involved with victim/abuser – agencies, family, friends, and so on.

- liaison with other professionals, workers, agencies

- victim's account

- incident(s) – date, time, frequency, duration, location, triggers, detail of what happened

- before, during, after incident(s) – what was said/done

- victim's feelings/wishes – at time of abuse and at disclosure/interview

- use of quotes

- observations

- recording of injuries, for example bodymaps

- medical examination

- use of monitoring tools/protocols

- assessment of risk of significant harm

- actions taken

- agreements made with victim

- decision-making (including explanation of reasons for decisions taken)

- professional opinion

- work to be done

- name, job title, signature, date and time written record completed.

 Handout 9.9, p.305

After using this checklist to plan the worker then needs to make a decision about whether he or she will record chronologically (that is, exactly as the disclosure or interview took place) or by dividing the subject matter into headings (which is the most useful format for report writing). It does not matter which the worker chooses as long as the record is clear and easy to read. Handout 9.10 gives an idea of a format for process recording:

- Beginning:
  - name of service user and date of birth
  - date and time (of meeting, incident)
  - who was present (name of person and their job, role)
  - purpose of meeting/contact.

- Middle:
  - what you want to record

- o facts

- o opinions

- o service user's wishes/feelings.

- End:

  - o summary of key points

  - o conclusions

  - o action agreed with service user

  - o name and job title of person writing the record

  - o signature

  - o date and time record written.

 Handout 9.10, p.307

It has been said before that many workers will be using computers and will have to write as the software package requires. However, they can use the handouts in this chapter to guide them about what should be within the content of the record even if it may be laid out differently because of the computer software.

While preparing and during the process of writing, the following is a useful question to keep the worker on track regarding purpose:

KEY QUESTION

WHO did WHAT and WHEN?

When a worker has finished writing a record they should always re-read what they have written. It is all too easy to rush on to the next task. Simple mistakes can be made in haste and it should be remembered that just missing out one word of a sentence can completely change the meaning.

Monitoring tools

Elsewhere in this manual I have repeatedly talked about the importance of monitoring and being specific. If monitoring tools or protocols are going to be used then in the service user file it must be explained exactly what tool is being used and why. In the previous chapter it was said this should be written up in the form of a protection plan, but it is important to reiterate what tools are being used in the file as well. A bodymap can be used to evidence injuries. It is crucial that certain data is written on the bodymap and examples are given in Appendix 2. I have seen bodymaps in files where workers have drawn the injuries but not put the name of the service user and his or her details on the form; nor have they put their own details and signature. It is also important for workers to be trained to complete a bodymap for each new injury they see. Injuries should not be added and dated onto an existing bodymap. If protocols are being used to monitor changes in behaviour or appearance the same details are needed. If monitoring tools or protocols have been completed then they must be cross-referenced in a service user file. They should be completed as soon as possible and not done from memory. The same applies when reports (e.g. incident reports, psychiatrist's assessment of mental capacity) are received and placed in the file.

Managers reading records

Finally something needs to be said about managers reading their workers' records. It is not good enough for a manager to just look at files when they are about to 'sign off cases'. A manager has a responsibility for managing and ensuring that workers are recording properly. If a worker is poor at recording how is a manager going to know this if he or she does not regularly read records? Through a written record a manager should know what a worker is doing and not doing. It is the manager's responsibility to check that a worker is implementing policies when necessary and following procedures correctly. If paper files are kept, then they should be brought into a supervision session. A manager should countersign a worker's signature to show they have read the record. In adult protection work this should be done on a regular basis. Any decisions made during debriefing sessions (e.g. what is going to be done next) should be recorded on a service user file. When a worker vents about their feelings in a debriefing session this should be recorded separately in the same way that supervision notes are kept. Again I must refer to computers. Most software packages which are being used nowadays have the facility for a manager to record on the file that they have read the record.

Disagreements

Finally, something has to be said about disagreements which occur between managers and workers. It is not uncommon. If a worker does disagree with a manager, it is very important that this is recorded on the file. I know many workers refuse to do this because they say the manager 'will make life hell for me'. However, workers should record what they really think for their own protection. A common example of this sort of conflict is that a worker thinks that the adult abuse policy should be implemented but a manager says that the situation can be monitored for a while under normal assessment procedures.

Victims' recording

When we are thinking about recording we must not forget the victim. There is no reason at all why service users should not contribute to their own record. This is something workers rarely think about. Assessments and care plans are shown to the service user, so why shouldn't a service user write his or her own version of events? I have worked with many victims of abuse and over the years have learnt that a lot of women in domestic violence situations have kept diaries of what has happened to them. Others have written poetry. Creative writing is a method of working I use to help victims through the healing process (Pritchard 2003a; Pritchard and Sainsbury 2004), but we should be mindful that a victim's personal writing could be evidence of what has happened to them. It can be copied and kept on file. It can also give a very clear insight into their emotions and how they feel from day to day. Two examples are given below.

Denise, aged 40, wrote regularly in her journal about the abuse she experienced in childhood but also the current domestic violence she experienced from her partner. Denise regularly went into the local psychiatric hospital on a voluntary basis. She also was a frequent visitor to the accident and emergency department when she overdosed. She was supported by the local community mental health team.

 Excerpts from Denise's journal

I wasn't allowed to talk to guys and if I did, I was beaten bad. He gave me black eyes, broken bones in my ankle and my nose was broken, I had cracked ribs. I was beaten once so badly. I crawled to a police station, but dared not go in, as he found me outside the police station he said if I told anyone he would kill my son and nothing or no one was worth my son's life.

21 February 2003

Well world I got up this morning and felt really sad so I went for a walk down Station Lane and did some shopping. I was crying and feeling very very low. I felt so hurt and went to sleep for an hour. I felt a little tired but when I woke about an hour later I felt much better. I went to see the doctor at 3 p.m. and he put me on some medication. I took my first pill around 4 p.m. and within two hours I didn't feel down at all. I have done my housework again.

22 February 2003

When I got up this morning I felt down and hurt. A bit later I feel OK, a bit better than when I got up. Two of my daughters come to see me today. It was nice to see them.

23 February 2003

I got up this morning and I am feeling fine. I still hurt a lot but will get over it. I always do. I don't know how I do it but I get there. I am keeping contact with some of the people I met in hospital.

The following poem is one of many written by Betty Burns whilst she was living in a domestic violence situation. Betty was a victim of elder abuse but had been abused by her husband for the previous 43 years. Betty kept diaries throughout her marriage.

A poem

What can life offer me but strife,
No devotion as a mother no love as a wife.
An object of abuse whose life has no meaning,
Cook and bottle washer doing washing and cleaning.
Someone living on borrowed time without care,
Caught like a timid animal in a deathly snare.
Man is my killer being thoughtless and cruel,
Measuring my life the one they would rule.

Fetch bring and carry do as they say,
Makes me a servant in every way.
Tired and ill a fact they ignore,
Treat me as an object a perpetual bore.
I feel I must travel and go on my way,
Leave this place and go astray.
Pain and heartache all suffered in vain,
A feeling of loss and resentment remain.

My needs are ignored not part of life,
Still voices tell me that is rife.
What I gave is thought of as just right,
Not their worry but my own plight.
Misery surrounds me life hard to bear,
Alone in my suffering of this I'm aware.
Wrapped in depression not wanted I'm sure,
Life has nothing but death is a cure.

By Betty Burns

Key learning points from this chapter

- Workers should know what documentation they should produce if they are following the vulnerable adult/adult abuse policy and procedures.

- Written records can be used as evidence in a court of law.

- Workers should keep any original notes they make during a disclosure or in an investigation interview (these are known as contemporaneous notes).

- Prepare before writing a record: sit, think, plan, draft.

- Think about the purpose of the record.

- Ask yourself who could have access to and read the record.

- A record should explain what you did and why you did it.

- Explain the reasons for decision-making; do not just write down action taken.

- Think about good content and layout.

- Structure your recording.

- Cross reference to monitoring tools, protocols.

- Do not use abbreviations – develop a glossary which lists abbreviations if you must use them.

- Re-read and check what you have written.

- Remember victims can write accounts of events and how they feel.

Suggested reading

Department of Health (1999) *Recording with Care: Inspection of Case Recording in Social Services Departments.* London: Department of Health.

Department of Health (2006) *Records Management: NHS Code of Practice.* London: Department of Health.

Hilton, C. and Hyder, M. (1998) *Getting to Grips with Punctuation and Grammar.* London: Letts Educational.

Hopkins, G. (1998a) *Plain English for Social Services: A Guide to Better Communication.* Lyme Regis: Russell House Publishing.

Hopkins, G. (1998b) *The Write Stuff: A Guide to Effective Writing in Social Care and Related Services.* Lyme Regis: Russell House Publishing.

Nursing Midwifery Council (2004) *Guidelines for Records and Record Keeping.* London: NMC.

WHAT DID YOU DO THIS MORNING?

Objective

To see how participants currently record.

Participants

Individual.

Equipment

Paper and pens.

Time

10 minutes.

Task

1. Participants are given a blank A4 sheet of paper and asked to imagine that it is either the computer screen on which they normally write records or the form they use to record if they keep paper files.

2. Participants are asked to write a true written record of what they have done from the time they woke up on that day until they walked into the training room.

Feedback

1. The trainer will read the records during a breaktime.

2. When participants have done Exercises 9.2 and 9.3 they will be given their records back and be asked to evaluate their earlier record.

3. The trainer will also give verbal comments to individuals on their records.

© Jacki Pritchard 2007

WHAT MAKES GOOD CONTENT?

Objective

To make workers think about what makes a good written record.

Participants

Large-group exercise.

Equipment

Flipchart stand, paper and pens for the trainer.

Copies of Handout 9.4.

Time

15 minutes.

Task

1. The trainer asks the large group to think about what makes good content and lists their comments on flipchart paper.

2. The trainer facilitates open discussion.

3. The trainer pins sheets onto a wall after the exercise is completed.

4. The trainer gives out Handout 9.4 and discusses it with the group.

© Jacki Pritchard 2007

WHAT MAKES A GOOD LAYOUT?

Objective

To make care workers think how to present a written record.

Participants

Large-group exercise.

Equipment

Flipchart stand, paper and pens for the trainer.

Copies of Handout 9.5.

Time

15 minutes.

Task

1. The trainer asks the large group to think about what makes a written record look good and lists their comments on flipchart paper.

2. The trainer facilitates open discussion.

3. The trainer pins sheets onto a wall after the exercise is completed.

4. The trainer gives out Handout 9.5 and discusses it with the group.

ABBREVIATIONS

Objective

To make workers realise how many abbreviations they use in their written records.

Participants

Small groups.

Equipment

Flipchart paper and pens.

Time

10 minutes.

Task

1. Participants are asked to think about the abbreviations they use when they write any document for recording purposes. This will include the shortening of names and titles of institutions, and so on.

2. Each group will list the abbreviations on the flipchart sheet.

Feedback

The trainer will ask a person in each group to read down the list (without translating/explaining the term), but pausing after each abbreviation. Others are asked to be honest and shout out if they do not know the meaning of something. Participants are also asked to shout out if the abbreviations could have two meanings (e.g. HV = home visit or health visitor; NFA = no further action or no fixed abode).

© Jacki Pritchard 2007

TYPES OF WRITTEN RECORDS

Remember all types of written records can be used as evidence

- Referrals

- Assessments

- Summaries

- Agreements/contracts

- Care plans/protection plans

- Letters and memos

- Forms

- Bodymaps

- Monitoring protocols

- Reports

- Review documents

- Minutes of strategy meetings/case conferences

- Running records

- Process records

- Notes

- Messages

- Diaries

- Notebooks

WHY WE NEED TO RECORD

- Legal requirement

- Accountability

- To explain and justify actions

- To give reasons for decisions made

- Acts as an aid to memory

- Safeguards against allegations

- Tool for monitoring, reviewing and evaluating work with the service user

- Tool for the worker to learn and be objective

- Basis for risk assessment and care planning

- Records may be needed in a court of law

© Jacki Pritchard 2007

WRITTEN RECORDS CAN COMMUNICATE

- What work is being undertaken (objectives)

- How work is being done (methods)

- What work has been done (monitor, review, evaluate)

- Needs

- Incidents/events

- Opinions

- The reasons underpinning decision-making

GOOD CONTENT

- Relevant

- Objective

- Factual

- Clear

- Concise

- Accurate

- Non-judgemental

- Non-discriminatory

 © Jacki Pritchard 2007

GOOD LAYOUT

Use a variety of things to make a document look user friendly:

- Legible handwriting

- A black pen

- Paragraphs

- Headings/sub-headings

- Numbering/lettering e.g. 1, 2, 3; (i) (ii) (iii); a) b) c)

- Bullet points

- Asterisks

- Capitals

- Bold

- Italics

- Underlining

- Punctuation

- Quotation marks

© Jacki Pritchard 2007

DOS AND DON'TS FOR WRITTEN RECORDS

Do

- use black pen

- cross out mistakes with just one black line and initial

- check what you have written

- record regularly

- record as soon as possible after the event (no more than 48 hours after the event)

- re-read and check what you have written.

Don't

- use correction fluid

- write long sentences

- be vague

- waffle

- use jargon

- use clichés

- use shorthand

- use abbreviations.

© Jacki Pritchard 2007

PREPARATION

You communicate in writing to:

- describe

- explain

- inform

- argue for.

Therefore, a worker must:

- sit and think

- plan

- draft

- write (and maybe rewrite).

© Jacki Pritchard 2007

ISSUES YOU MUST THINK ABOUT WHEN RECORDING ADULT ABUSE WORK

- Facts

- Opinion

- Hearsay

- Confidentiality

- Access

© Jacki Pritchard 2007

CHECKLIST: SUBJECTS FOR RECORDING

- Date, time, duration, location, people present at disclosure/interview

- The alleged victim's basic details

- The alleged abuser's basic details (including relationship, if any, to the victim)

- Alleged/possible types of abuse

- Relevant background information/social history

- Confidentiality – explanation to victim

- Victim's capacity

- Consent

- Sharing information – agreement of victim

- People involved with victim/abuser – agencies, family, friends, and so on

- Liaison with other professionals, workers, agencies

- Victim's account

- Incident(s) – date, time, frequency, duration, location, triggers, detail of what happened

- Before, during, after incident(s) – what was said/done

© Jacki Pritchard 2007

CHECKLIST: SUBJECTS FOR RECORDING

- Victim's feelings/wishes – at time of abuse and at disclosure/interview

- Use of quotes

- Observations

- Recording of injuries, for example bodymaps

- Medical examination

- Use of monitoring tools/protocols

- Assessment of risk of significant harm

- Actions taken

- Agreements made with victim

- Decision-making (including explanation of reasons for decisions taken)

- Professional opinion

- Work to be done

- Name, job title, signature, date and time written record completed

© Jacki Pritchard 2007

STRUCTURING A PROCESS RECORD

Beginning:

- name of service user and date of birth

- date and time (of meeting, incident)

- who was present (name of person and their job, role)

- purpose of meeting/contact.

Middle:

- what you want to record

- facts

- opinions

- service user's wishes/feelings.

End:

- summary of key points

- conclusions

- action agreed with service user

- name and job title of person writing the record

- signature

- date and time record written.

© Jacki Pritchard 2007

Chapter 10

The Abuse of Older People

It will be helpful in this chapter to first understand how elder abuse has been recognised in the UK. We need to be clear about definitions; I shall be referring to any adult aged over 65 years as an *older adult.*

It has already been said that members of our society are rarely aware of the fact that older people can be victims of abuse. Part of the reason for this is probably due to the fact that child abuse and domestic violence have gained recognition since the 1980s. The media tend to feature stories about children and younger adults rather than older people. When the word 'abuse' is used people rarely think of an older man or older woman. The fact is that older people *are* abused.

How long have we known about elder abuse?

The reality is that the abuse of older people has been occurring for hundreds of years. Authors over the centuries have written about it in plays and novels. Shakespeare's *King Lear* is a classic example of how a man can be a victim of abuse. But coming more up to date, elder abuse was first acknowledged by professionals in the 1970s. Two geriatricians wrote in medical journals about their 'elderly patients' who were abused by family members (Baker 1975; Burston 1975 and 1977). Eastman then wrote about older people being abused by their carers in the 1980s (Eastman 1984). Later in that decade the British Geriatrics Society convened a major conference about the abuse of older people, out of which came the publication *Abuse of Elderly People: An Unnecessary and Preventable Problem* (Tomlin 1989).

At the beginning of the 1990s the Social Services Inspectorate undertook research in two London boroughs, the findings of which were published in *Confronting Elder Abuse* (Department of Health 1992). As a result of that research, practice guidelines were produced in the following year entitled *No Longer Afraid: The Safeguard of Older People in Domestic Settings* (Department of Health 1993).

Terminology

So let's just be clear about terminology that has been used over the years in relation to the abuse of older adults:

- pensioner
- senior citizen
- elderly
- older person
- granny bashing (battering)
- old age abuse
- elder abuse
- mistreatment
- abuse
- adult abuse.

 Handout 10.1, p.320

Nowadays we refer to 'older people' where we would have previously referred to: 'pensioners', 'senior citizens', or 'the elderly'. In the early 1970s people used the awful term 'granny bashing' (or 'battering') to refer to older people who were physically abused. The term 'old age abuse' was used in the 1980s and finally we moved on to use the term 'elder abuse'. There was also a lot of debate in the 1990s about whether the term 'mistreatment' should be used instead of 'abuse'. I personally feel that abuse is abuse and we should not shy away from that fact. Perhaps the debate should be around the following question:

KEY QUESTION

Is mistreatment a form of abuse?

There is nothing wrong with using the term 'elder abuse' to refer to the abuse of older people. However, because attention is now given to the abuse of vulnerable adults (that is, anyone over 18 years of age), the term 'adult abuse' is used, which includes the abuse of older people.

How much elder abuse is there?

One always has to be wary of statistics produced by researchers regarding abuse. Statistics will depend on many things; for example, how abuse is defined and from where data have been obtained. As a researcher myself, I am only too conscious of the fact that data are usually retrieved from agencies (e.g. social services, police) but there are going to be thousands of victims and abusers who are not known to any agency. Over the past 20 years estimates of prevalence have varied stating that between 4 and 10 per cent of older people experience some form of abuse. More recently campaigns supported by Action on Elder Abuse and Help the Aged have stated that about half a million older people are abused in the UK.

I undertook a research project which was funded by the Joseph Rowntree Foundation and the objective was to look at the needs of older women who had been abused (Pritchard 2000). The project was carried out in three social services departments in the UK, where I monitored all the vulnerable adult (aged 18+) referrals regarding abuse. The findings clearly illustrated that older people were the largest group of victims. Over an 18-month period there were 186 vulnerable adult cases, 126 of which were older people (that is, 68%). I continued to monitor cases in two departments after the project finished and again statistics showed that older people formed the largest group of victims:

Table 10.1: Monitoring period: March 1999 to March 2002

	Vulnerable adults	Older people	%
Stage 1	186	126	68
Stage 2	258	171	66
Stage 3	430	269	63

Stage 1 – March 1999; Stage 2 – March 2000; Stage 3 – March 2002

As was discussed in Chapter 4 it is very wrong to stereotype but we all do it at some time or other. People tend to think of a victim as being female and an abuser as being male. This was not always the case. In the 1970s and 1980s elder abuse gained more recognition in North America than it did here in the UK. Much research focused on family violence, which included elder abuse. Murray Straus and Richard Gelles have written extensively on all aspects of family violence and it is very useful to read their works (Gelles 1997; Gelles and Straus 1988; Straus and Gelles 1986; Straus, Gelles and Steinmetz 1980).

Over the years literature on elder abuse has focused on carers' stress with victims being stereotyped thus: 'The majority are female, over 80 and are dependent as a result of physical and mental capacity' (Eastman 1984, p.41). So the image that was created around the abuse of older adults was one of dependency and causing stress for the carer.

The reality is that the stress of the carer can contribute to abuse situations, but there are many other causes of elder abuse and workers must develop an understanding of why abuse happens. It is dangerous practice to assume that elder abuse is only about the carer's stress. This is why so many cases of abuse have been missed over the years. Older people are frequently dismissed because they are confused, have short-term memory loss and consequently they are considered to be 'unreliable witnesses'. Abusers know that many older people may not be listened to or taken seriously and consequently target such victims. This goes back to the point made in earlier chapters that much abuse is premeditated and deliberate.

It is vital that workers realise that both men and women can be victims of abuse. Many victims worry about disclosing about abuse; they are often fearful that they will not be believed or are anxious about the possible repercussions. For male victims it is even harder because society generally does not acknowledge that men are abused. This brings us back to stereotyping; that is, that men are supposed to be strong and unlikely to be harmed by anyone. As far back as 1978, Suzanne Steinmetz highlighted the fact that men were battered (Steinmetz 1978). The idea of the battered husband syndrome was developed and other academics have pursued research in this area (Gelles 1997; Straus 1999; Straus and Gelles 1986).

When I was undertaking the research project on older female victims of abuse, older men started disclosing to me about the abuse they had experienced. Consequently, it was agreed that the research project should be expanded to include older men and the research reports were written up separately (Pritchard 2000, 2001b, 2002). During the three-year period which was monitored, 15 per cent of vulnerable adult cases were concerned with older male victims.

Table 10.2: Male and female victims

Type of service user	Number of referrals	
Vulnerable adults (over 18 years)	430	
Older people (over 60 years)	269	(63% of vulnerable adults)
Older females	202	(47% of vulnerable adults)
Older males	67	(15% of vulnerable adults)

We need to consider who abuses older people. Once again we have to look back at what has been said in the past; because of the emphasis on the carer's stress: 'The abuser is typically identified as being female, middle-aged and usually the offspring of the abused' (Gelles and Cornell 1985, p.104). It was thought that women in their caring roles might become stressed and lash out in a fit of temper. Of course this did happen and still does. However, nowadays people tend to stereotype the abuser as male, but again it is wrong to do so. People must understand that women can abuse and there is a growing amount of literature about this (Elliot 1993; Saradjian 1996).

Case Examples

- Grace reluctantly agreed to have her mother to live with her after her father died. Grace had never really got on with her mother because she thought she had always favoured her older brother. Grace neglected her mother both physically and emotionally.

- Mr and Mrs Gregg became housebound because their health was deteriorating. Their children lived in other parts of the country. They had known their next-door neighbour, Tina, for years and welcomed her suggestion that she helped them with shopping, cashing pensions, banking. Tina took amounts of money for herself and told the Greggs that the shopping cost more than it did.

- Sue and Glenda worked together as home carers. When they went shopping to the supermarket for service users they took it in turns to put the reward points on their own cards.

- Tanya used to get to the end of her tether with her grandmother, who had Alzheimer's disease. She kept asking the same questions, which really got on her nerves. She started to give her grandmother extra medication to make Tanya's sleep during the daytime.

It is important to remember that elder abuse can occur because of things which have happened in the past or that the abuser (rather than the victim) has problems currently.

Case Examples

- Nina had never forgiven her sister, Lily, for 'stealing' her boyfriend and then marrying him. The sisters had not spoken for years. When they were in their seventies, Lily had a severe stroke. Nina was her only living relative. She agreed to care for Lily, so she could seek revenge. She kept Lily locked in a small bedroom, physically abused her and neglected her.

- Debbie was 24 years old and had four children under the age of six. Her partner insisted that his parents, who were in their sixties, came to live with them when his mother had a stroke. They lived in a three-bedroomed council house. Debbie was exhausted with having to look after the children and her mother-in-law, whom she regularly verbally abused. Her husband did little to help even though he was unemployed. One day Debbie threw a vase at her mother-in-law.

- Tim was 16 years old and was obsessed with the fruit machines in amusement arcades. He started borrowing money from his friends and stealing from his parents. As things got worse and the money he owed grew into vast amounts, he started breaking into homes where he knew older people lived and stole their money and possessions. He also mugged older people on the streets.

- Jean and Mick were in their mid sixties and had been married for 24 years. Everyone thought Jean was a 'lovely', 'really friendly' person; whereas Mick was considered to be 'miserable'. At home, Jean was a different person. All through their marriage she had been extremely violent to Mick, who suffered from severe depression.

- Everyone knew that Edna and Jim, who were both aged 74, liked to have a drink. For years, every weekend they went down to the working men's club and drank a great deal. No one knew just how much they drank during the week when they were at home. The reality was that they were both alcoholics and this was one of the reasons none of their four children had anything to do with them. The children had had enough of their parents physically fighting and being verbally abusive to each other. The eldest son said: 'They're both as bad as each other.' Edna and Jim were well known to the police, who were called out frequently by the neighbours when the couple were fighting.

- Sarah applied for a job in the care home which was located around the corner from where she lived. She wanted to work nights, so her husband could look after the children. She had an interview one afternoon and was asked to cover the night shift that same night because someone had rung in sick. Sarah had never worked in the care sector before. On her first shift she rough-handled service users and failed to check on some service users who needed attention during the night. She had not been told to read the files or care plans.

It is important for workers to keep an open mind about who can be an abuser and Handout 10.2 can be given to participants as a reminder that anyone can be an abuser:

- a family member
- a friend
- a neighbour
- a worker
- a professional
- a volunteer
- an advocate
- a stranger.

 Handout 10.2, p.321

The rest of this chapter contains extra training materials focusing on the abuse of older people:

✍ Exercise 10.1, p.315, and 📄 Handout 3.6, p.78

How can an older person be harmed? – to help participants think about ways in which an older person may be harmed either physically or emotionally and focus on the definition of significant harm.

✍ Exercise 10.2, p.316, and 📄 Handout 10.3, p.322

Abuse or not abuse? – to make participants think about what constitutes abuse in relation to older people.

✍ Exercise 10.3, p.317, and 📄 Handout 10.4, p.323

Abuse or bad practice? – to make participants think further about what constitutes abuse in an institution.

✍ Exercise 10.4, p.318, and 📄 Handout 10.5, p.324

What would you say and do? – to get participants to think how they would respond in certain situations.

✍ Exercise 10.5, p.319, and 📄 Handout 10.6, p.325

Alert or not to alert? – to get participants to think about whether they would alert in certain situations.

〜 Case studies are presented in the following handouts:

📄 Handouts 10.7, 10.8, 10.9, 10.10, pp.326–329

Suggested reading

Aitken, L. and Griffin, G. (1996) *Gender Issues in Elder Abuse.* London: Sage.

Bennett, G. and Kingston, P. (1993) *Elder Abuse: Concepts, Theories and Interventions.* London: Chapman and Hall.

Decalmer, P. and Glendenning, F.J. (eds) (1997) *The Mistreatment of Elderly People.* Second edition. London: Sage.

McCreadie, C. (1996) *Elder Abuse: Update on Research.* London: Institute of Gerontology, King's College.

Pritchard, J. (2000) *The Needs of Older Women: Services for Victims of Elder Abuse and Other Abuse.* Bristol: The Policy Press.

Pritchard, J. (2001) *Male Victims of Elder Abuse: Their Experiences and Needs.* London: Jessica Kingsley Publishers.

Slater, P. and Eastman, M. (eds) (1999) *Elder Abuse: Critical Issues in Policy and Practice.* London: Age Concern.

Video

WAA5: The Abuse of Older People (two-video set)

This is a two-video set because Video 1 addresses abuse of older people in the community and Video 2 focuses on institutional abuse. No matter where a worker is based, he or she needs to know about elder abuse in both the community and in communal settings.

HOW CAN AN OLDER PERSON BE HARMED?

Objective

Being 'harmed' will mean different things to different people. This exercise will help participants think about ways in which an older person may be harmed either physically or emotionally.

Participants

Participants are split into two or four small groups.

Equipment

Flipchart paper and pens.

Copies of Handout 3.6.

Time

10 minutes in groups.

Task

1. Each group will be asked to focus on one aspect of harm. The trainer will tell the groups whether they will focus on *physical* or *emotional* harm.

2. The groups list ways in which an older person can be harmed.

Feedback

1. Each group will feed back their list.

2. The trainer will facilitate a general discussion on the meaning of harm.

3. Participants are given the definition of 'significant harm' (Handout 3.6) to promote further discussion.

ABUSE OR NOT ABUSE? (OLDER PEOPLE)

Objective

To make participants think about what constitutes abuse in relation to older people.

Participants

In small groups.

Equipment

Copies of Handout 10.3.

Time

Groups spend 30 minutes undertaking the exercise.

Task

1. Groups will consider each scenario in turn. They have to reach a consensus regarding whether this is a case of abuse or not.

2. If the consensus of opinion is that it *is* abuse, the group has to consider which categories of abuse are taking place.

Feedback

1. Participants remain sitting in their groups. The trainer takes one scenario at a time and goes around asking each group what their consensus of opinion was.

2. If there was a disagreement *within* the group, the trainer will ask participants to explain what they discussed. Where there are differences *between* the groups, the trainer will ask the groups to debate; that is, put forward their arguments.

Note for trainer

This exercise is suitable for all workers across the disciplines and will get participants to think about the abuse of older adults.

 © Jacki Pritchard 2007

ABUSE OR BAD PRACTICE? (OLDER PEOPLE)

Objective

To make participants think further about what constitutes abuse in an institution.

Participants

In small groups.

Equipment

Copies of Handout 10.4.

Time

Groups spend 30 minutes undertaking the exercise.

Task

1. Groups will consider each scenario in turn. They have to reach a consensus regarding whether this is a case of abuse *or* bad practice.

2. If the consensus of opinion is that it *is* abuse, the group has to decide into which category or categories of abuse they would put the action/behaviour(s).

Feedback

1. Participants remain sitting in their groups. The trainer takes one scenario at a time and goes around asking each group what their consensus of opinion was.

2. If there was a disagreement *within* the group, the trainer will ask participants to explain what they discussed. Where there are differences *between* the groups, the trainer will ask the groups to debate; that is, put forward their arguments.

Note for trainer

It must be made clear when explaining the purpose of the exercise that the groups cannot say the scenario is both abuse and bad practice. The main purpose of the exercise is to get participants thinking about when bad practice crosses that fine line to become abuse.

WHAT WOULD YOU SAY AND DO?

Objective

To get participants to think about how they would respond in certain situations and to ensure that they would not contaminate evidence.

Participants

Small groups.

Equipment

Flipchart paper and pens.

Copies of Handout 10.5.

Time

45 minutes.

Task

1. The groups are asked to consider each scenario in turn on Handout 10.5.

2. Participants write down the exact words they would say if they were the worker in that situation.

3. Participants write down what they would do next.

Feedback

1. The trainer takes in each scenario in turn and asks the groups to feed back their verbal responses and actions.

2. General discussion about the dilemmas involved in alerting.

3. Clarification from the trainer about local policy and procedures.

Note for trainer

When explaining the exercise, the trainer should encourage the groups to write down more than one verbal response as participants may have different views about how to deal with situations and it is important that all views are expressed.

 © Jacki Pritchard 2007

ALERT OR NOT TO ALERT? (OLDER PEOPLE)

Objective

To get participants to think about whether to make an alert.

Participants

Individual work; work in pairs.

Equipment

Pens.

Copies of Handout 10.6.

Time

5 minutes' individual work; 10 minutes' discussion in pairs.

Task

1.   Each participant is given a copy of Handout 10.6.

2.   Participants answer the questionnaire.

3.   Participants work in pairs and discuss their answers.

Feedback

1.   Participants talk about the scenarios where they were not sure what they would do.

2.   Pairs feed back if they have had disagreements about what they would do.

3.   General discussion about alerting.

KEY TERMS USED NOW AND IN THE PAST TO REFER TO THOSE AGED 65 YEARS + AND THE ABUSE OF THEM

- Pensioner

- Senior citizen

- Elderly

- Older person

- Granny bashing (battering)

- Old age abuse

- Elder abuse

- Mistreatment

- Abuse

- Adult abuse

 © Jacki Pritchard 2007

WHO CAN ABUSE?

Anyone can be an abuser – male or female.

- A family member

- A friend

- A neighbour

- A worker

- A professional

- A volunteer

- An advocate

- A stranger

ABUSE OR NOT ABUSE? (OLDER PEOPLE)

1. A husband is caring for his wife who has Alzheimer's disease. He gets very tired and sometimes shouts and swears at her in frustration.

2. A home carer goes to the local supermarket to shop for her service users. She takes advantage of the special offer – buy two get one free. She gives the service users the two products she has purchased but takes the free one home.

3. A nurse says she will be back in a minute with Betty's medication for pain relief. She comes back in an hour.

4. Arnold touches a home carer's bottom. She turns round and slaps him across the face.

5. Two care workers take some residents into a pub when they are out on a day trip. The barman refuses to serve them saying 'it is a young person's pub'.

6. Two residents who are slightly confused enjoy each other's company and are openly affectionate in public. Their respective families say they must be kept apart.

7. Mike tells his mother she must pay something towards her grand-daughter's university fees or she will not visit her any more.

8. Suzanne refuses to buy her mum, who is housebound, any new clothes because she says: 'You don't go anywhere. Who is going to see you?'

9. Nettie's daughter and son in law go out to work. Nettie is immobile and is often left lying in urine and faeces for hours because the couple refuse to have services coming into their home.

10. Duncan enjoys watching pornographic videos. His wife finds them embarrassing, but he says she has to watch them.

© Jacki Pritchard 2007

ABUSE OR BAD PRACTICE? (OLDER PEOPLE)

1. As a care worker is pushing Ned along the corridor in his wheelchair, she says: 'You have a bath now or else there's no cigarettes for you tonight.'

2. All residents are toileted before mealtimes, whether they want to go or not.

3. Older people in a care home are referred to as the 'resis' by the manager of the home.

4. Beattie has Alzheimer's disease; she is physically very fit and likes to wander around the home. During the summer months chairs and tables with parasols are put outside. Beattie is told she cannot go out because she might wander off and 'staff haven't got eyes in the back of their heads'.

5. Larry likes to go to the toilet quite often during the course of the day. Staff think he does it to get attention. So they tell him that when he goes they are going to leave him there for 30 minutes so they do not have to keep taking him.

6. Ezra is African Caribbean. When he comes into the home he says he wants to buy a bottle of white rum every week to keep in his room. He is told that it is a waste of his allowance to spend money on drink which is so expensive.

7. Keeley is a young care worker who wears a lot of jewellery. She keeps scratching service users with her large rings and bracelets and her long necklaces keep hitting their heads and going into their eyes.

8. Lily is confused. Every morning she tells the care workers a man has come into her bedroom and got in her bed. They do not take her seriously and laugh it off.

9. Saul has had a stroke. After being in hospital, he has returned to the care home where he lived before. Because he dribbles from his mouth staff now put a towel over his chest all day long.

10. Bob has a continence problem which he is very embarrassed about. This afternoon he is sitting in the lounge when he has an accident. He asks for help from a care worker. When she helps him get out of the chair she says in a very loud voice so everyone else can hear: 'You've wet yourself again, Bob. There's a right puddle there.'

© Jacki Pritchard 2007

WHAT WOULD YOU SAY AND DO?

1. One morning a home carer walks into Mabel's bedroom (as she does every morning) to get her up and dressed. This morning she finds Mabel in bed with the man from next door. Mabel has Alzheimer's disease.

2. You hear a care worker say to a service user: 'You're a bloody nuisance. I'll make you sorry for what you've just done.'

3. A nurse tells a care worker that she will have to stay on the ward to help with the care of Mrs Biggs, who is 99 years old, because nursing staff 'haven't got the time to cope with her'.

4. Mr and Mrs Green tell the community psychiatric nurse that their son hits them and swears at them regularly. They do not want her to do anything because he has schizophrenia.

5. Frances tells the home carer that she thinks another home carer has taken money from the sideboard.

6. The manager of a care home tells an agency worker that all service users have to be in bed by 10.00 p.m.

7. The home carer finds blood on Jane's nightdress and the bed sheets. Jane lives with her husband, Peter.

8. A care worker refers to black service users as 'the foreigners'.

9. Phyllis is mentally sound but very frail physically. She still likes to try to do things for herself and hates being stuck in the house. In the summer months she would like to sit in the garden. Her daughter tells the home carers that she must remain in the house at all times.

10. You are bathing Esther when you notice she has very large bruises on the inside of her thighs.

11. Mr Harris tells the hospital social worker that his son financially abuses him and he has no savings left. In the past year, the son has regularly taken his cash card (without Mr Harris' permission) and drawn money out. £10,000 has gone from Mr Harris' bank account. He does not want the social worker to tell anyone else about this.

12. Mrs Udin tells the district nurse that she is frightened of her grandson, who is aged 16. He threatens her if she does not give him money. Mrs Udin is Asian and lives with her eldest son and his family.

 © Jacki Pritchard 2007

ALERT OR NOT TO ALERT? (OLDER PEOPLE)

1. A worker went to use the toilet upstairs. When she came back down into the lounge she saw Mrs Haydock (primary carer) slap her husband (who has Alzheimer's disease) across the face.

   Yes ☐ **No** ☐ **Don't know** ☐

2. Mr Green lives alone as he has no living relatives; he is slightly confused. When he goes to the day centre he always says that his neighbour manages his money but she will not buy the things he wants. He complains there is never any food in the house and he is always hungry. Mr Green consistently asks for second helpings at lunchtime.

   Yes ☐ **No** ☐ **Don't know** ☐

3. Ethel is in the advanced stages of Alzheimer's disease. She frequently talks about 'him' getting into her bed at night and 'doing naughty things'. Ethel lives with her brother and his wife.

   Yes ☐ **No** ☐ **Don't know** ☐

4. When a worker visits a son who cares for his mother, he admits that he lost his temper last night and hit his mother. The worker saw red marks and bruising on the mother's face. The son says this is not the first time he has done this and it is because he is finding it very hard to cope with her since she developed dementia.

   Yes ☐ **No** ☐ **Don't know** ☐

5. Mrs Yates openly talks about the violence she has experienced from her husband during their marriage. Since he has started having a form of dementia he has changed and become much calmer. However, she tells the worker that her son, who has never left home, has begun to hit her regularly, which he has never done before. She does not want to do anything about it.

   Yes ☐ **No** ☐ **Don't know** ☐

6. Fred, who has dementia, has just come out of hospital, having been in there for four weeks. He tells a worker that one of the nurses was 'cruel' to him and that he was 'frightened'. He cannot remember the name of the nurse.

   Yes ☐ **No** ☐ **Don't know** ☐

CASE STUDY: OSCAR (AGED 81)

Oscar had lived on his own for years. Very few people knew much about him. It was thought he had been married many years ago but no one remembered anything about his wife. He had no living family. He liked to keep himself to himself; the only visitor he had was his next-door neighbour, Liz Barrow.

Oscar had always been a strong man physically and had 'never had a day off work in 50 years'. However, when he was 80 his health suddenly started to deteriorate. His GP referred him to social services and home care services were provided. Oscar disliked the thought of having people come into his house. Kate and Meryl were experienced home carers and little shocked them. However, they were taken aback when they saw the state of Oscar's house. They thought that Oscar must have been self-neglecting.

Oscar liked the home carers once he got to know them and looked forward to them coming in. Oscar still liked to live with a lot of mess around him – piles of newspapers, old bottles, and so on; and he did not like to have a bath very often. When Kate and Meryl tried to encourage him to take an interest in himself and his surroundings he said: 'What's the point? I can't change anything. I've made too many mistakes already.'

In the year before services became involved, Oscar's mobility had deteriorated a great deal and he had not been out of the house for over a year. Mrs Barrow had done the shopping and paid the bills. She was not pleased when it was suggested that the home carers would take on these tasks. Oscar said he had a savings account: 'I've a fair bit in it. Mrs Barrow puts anything that's left over in there.' This turned out to be a joint account and when Oscar asked Mrs Barrow to give the home carers some money from the account she refused.

 © Jacki Pritchard 2007

CASE STUDY: VIV (AGED 88)

Viv was diagnosed as having Alzheimer's disease eight years ago. She lives with her son, Daniel, who is 50 years old and works for a firm of accountants. He is determined to keep caring for his mother and says he will never consider residential care. Home carers come in to help Viv get up in the mornings. She attends a day centre four days a week when Daniel is at work; he does not work Fridays.

During the past three months the home carers began to notice some changes in Viv's behaviour. She was becoming very aggressive towards them and she also tried to injure herself on several occasions. When they mentioned this to Daniel, he said he had not noticed anything different about his mother. The home carers reported their concerns to their home care manager, who did nothing with this information.

A support worker, Barbara, has been involved with Viv and Daniel for the past two years. She visits once a month on a Friday mainly to give some time to Daniel. She has been concerned that he seems very isolated. He does not have any friends; his time is equally divided between going to work and caring for his mother. It is Friday afternoon and Barbara is going on her summer holidays that evening. Her last visit is to Viv and Daniel. When she arrives she can see that Daniel is very upset. He says Viv is in bed asleep and he does not want to disturb her. Barbara asked what was wrong. She was very open about the fact that she could see he had been crying. Daniel immediately burst into tears. Barbara insisted on seeing Viv and went upstairs. When she went into her bedroom she saw that Viv was lying on the bed. Her feet were tied together with the belt from her dressing gown and her face was red and swollen.

CASE STUDY: MR GRIFFIN (AGED 66)

Mr Griffin became resident in a care home after he had had a stroke and lost the use of his left side. Soon after admission the social worker and members of his family noticed that Mr Griffin was getting bruises on his face and arms. When asked about it he said he did not know how he had got the bruises. The bruising became more and more obvious and Mr Griffin became very weepy when asked about the bruising. Eventually he disclosed that two care workers who worked nights were regularly hitting him. Mr Griffin said he had been too frightened to talk about what was happening to him because the care workers had threatened him.

The social worker went to speak to the manager of the home who said that Mr Griffin was a 'very awkward man' who had 'taken a real dislike to the night staff and is probably making it up'. The social worker went to her manager who said 'see how things go over the next couple of weeks'.

Other residents in the home told Mr Griffin's family that they were frightened of the night staff as well and had heard them shouting at Mr Griffin. The family were very distressed. They told the social worker what the other residents had said and said they wanted Mr Griffin moved to another home. When the social worker talked to other residents they denied having said anything to the family. The manager of the home became very angry and said her staff would never hurt anyone. The social worker checked Mr Griffin's file in the home; there was no record of any incidents and bodymaps had not been completed.

© Jacki Pritchard 2007

CASE STUDY: GERT WILDER (AGED 66)

Gert Wilder has lived in her home for the past 55 years. She has three children, two of whom live in other parts of the country. Her youngest daughter, Sandra, has never left the local area. Sandra is in her forties and is currently unemployed. She has a council flat which is located a mile from her mother's house.

Gert was admitted to hospital having taken an overdose. Initially as she was recovering she admitted that she had wanted to kill herself because 'life is so hard and miserable'. After Sandra had visited her in hospital, Gert told the nursing staff that it had 'been a mistake taking too many pills. Just my memory. I didn't mean to kill myself.' A referral was made to the community mental health team for older people because of Gert's anxiety and depression. After she was discharged a community psychiatric nurse, Tim, became involved and home care support was put in. Gert's mobility is poor and she has various health problems including angina and diabetes.

Gert liked the home carers and began to tell them about how Sandra frightened her. She admitted that this was the reason why she had attempted suicide: 'I just felt that night I couldn't take any more of her threats. I was so frightened.' Gert explained that Sandra had always had financial difficulties, because of a gambling problem. Throughout her adult life she had borrowed money from her parents. After Gert's husband died, Sandra became more threatening and eventually started being physically violent towards her mother. Gert admitted that neighbours had called the police on several occasions when they heard shouting.

One day when Vanessa, one of the home carers, visited Gert she saw that she had numerous bruises on her face and Gert was obviously experiencing pain elsewhere on her body. She admitted that Sandra had battered her the night before when she had refused to agree to sell the house to pay off Sandra's extensive debts. Vanessa explained that she would have to report the incident to her manager, but she also asked Gert what she wanted to do about her situation. Gert said she did not want Vanessa to tell her manager and that she did not want anyone else involved – especially the police. She felt she might have to sell the house to help Sandra, who had borrowed large amounts of money from loan sharks.

Chapter 11

The Abuse of Younger Adults

Within health and social care there are many different specialisms which work with and provide services for younger adults. You might immediately think of the obvious ones – adults with physical disabilities, learning disabilities or sensory impairment, and adults who have mental health problems. Then there are also all those very specialist teams (within specialisms if you like): homeless, forensic social work, substance misuse, alcohol misuse, and so on. Because of their behaviours a lot of service users within these specialisms often get labelled in some way (e.g. attention-seeker, storyteller) and if they make an allegation of abuse they may not be taken seriously. It would be impossible to discuss each specialism within this chapter. Therefore, it must be stated at the very beginning that my main objective is to highlight the fact that the issue of abuse of younger vulnerable adults, like elder abuse previously, is not given enough attention by society in general, within organisations or on training courses. Extra training materials are included in this chapter to help raise awareness about the particular issues and dilemmas which arise for younger vulnerable adults. The reader should then take on the responsibility to seek out more information from the references and organisations cited.

In Chapter 10 we looked at the abuse of older people. You might be wondering why I chose to put older adults before younger ones. It seemed logical to consider elder abuse first because it was older adults rather than younger adults who got the attention first of all. It was not until the 1990s that the abuse of younger adults was given attention publicly. Of course, organisations who deal with younger adults have been aware for a very long time that they are abused but, as is the case with older people, society and the media do not give them much attention. This is ironic really when it was the death of a younger adult with learning disabilities, Beverley Lewis, which led to the first Adult Protection Unit being set up in the country within Gloucestershire County Council.

Chapter 2 gave an overview of developments and guidance for adult abuse work and for a long time the abuse of older people had more attention than abuse of younger vulnerable adults. The Department of Health's guidance *No Secrets* is clear that we should be looking at *all* vulnerable adults; that is, anyone over the age of 18 years. Research nationally has been limited so we have to rely on 'local' statistics, that is the annual reports which Adult Protection Committees produce, to inform us. It is important to repeat the point made in other chapters that research statistics will only indicate the tip of the iceberg. There will be thousands of victims who will not be known to any agency. For a long time it has concerned me that particular groups of vulnerable adults have not been given enough attention; in particular younger adults with physical or sensory impairment, learning disabilities or mental health problems. These adults are extremely vulnerable and often the abuse remains well hidden. One of the reasons for this is that even if an adult with communication difficulties does disclose, sometimes he or she is not taken seriously.

It is also worrying that the Department of Health produced practice guidelines on elder abuse, *No Longer Afraid*, in 1993 but it took another seven years to produce guidance for all vulnerable adults; that is, *No Secrets* (Department of Health 2000a). Despite the length of time in which *No Secrets* has been in place, the number of referrals regarding younger adults is much lower than it is for older people. This is a common pattern when you look at statistics produced in different parts of the country. Adult Protection Committees produce annual reports and many of these are accessible via the internet. For the purpose of this manual I randomly selected statistics from five areas to show that referrals regarding younger adults is consistently lower than for people over the age of 65. To illustrate the point I am making in Table 11.1 I have used the percentage figures of referrals for each specialism rather than actual figures, because all sorts of factors can affect the number of referrals made within an area.

The same trend was picked up in the data returns from the nine pilot authorities involved in the project funded by the Department of Health, the Adult Protection Analysis Project, for the period 6 June 2005 to 2 December 2005 (Table 11.2; Action on Elder Abuse 2006).

In order to raise awareness about important social issues it is helpful to have the backing of the media. Unfortunately, media attention is not always positive. Over the years there have been some useful documentaries which have highlighted the abuse of younger adults (e.g. BBC Panorama's *Perfect Victims*, 1995; *McIntyre Undercover*). But people forget too easily. I mentioned the death of Beverley Lewis in 1989; very few people remember her name or even know about her, yet they do remember the child deaths and inquiries (and rightly so) – Jasmine Beckford, Kimberley Carlisle, Victoria Climbié, to name but a few. People have been shocked recently to learn of the abuses in Cornwall (Healthcare Commission and Commission for Social Care Inspection 2006), but why do so few remember the horrors which happened in the Longcare Homes (for younger adults with learning disabilities) in the 1990s? If you are reading this and do not know about Longcare then I suggest that you read the original inquiry (Burgner 1998) and John Pring's *Silent Victims* (Pring 2003).

Younger adults with disabilities or mental health problems just do not get the attention they deserve and this is why I felt it was imperative that I should include a chapter with extra training materials related to these people. Trainers need to ensure that these service user groups get adequate attention on training courses.

Table 11.1: Percentage of referrals by service users group

Local area	OP	LD	MH	PD	Other
Brent	52	29	12	7	0
Croyden	46	32	16	6	0
Devon	47	42	3	8	0
Lincolnshire	57	25	17	1	0
Newport	48	33	6	10	3

Key: OP, Older People; LD, Learning Disabilities; MH, Mental Health; PD, Physical Disability and Sensory Impairment. Statistics compiled from the Adult Protection Committee annual reports 2005–2006 from the five areas: Brent Multi-Agency Adult Protection Committee 2006; Croydon Multi Agency Adult Protection Committee 2006; Devon Adult Protection Committee 2006; Lincolnshire Adult Protection Committee 2006; Newport Area Adult Protection Committee 2006

Table 11.2: Percentage of referrals (639 in total)

Type of referral	%
Older people	36
Learning disabilities	25
Physical disabilities	12
Mental health	8
Other/not known	19

From: Action on Elder Abuse (2006) *Adult Protection Data Collection and Reporting Requirements.* London: AEA, pp.58–9

Adults with disabilities

I keep making the point that we shall never really know how much abuse there is and not to rely too heavily on statistics – although they make interesting reading. Literature on abuse of adults with disabilities is limited, so if you are seeking information then it is necessary to find articles from years back as well as trying to find out what has been written recently (a good source being the *Journal of Adult Protection*). Hilary Brown has been prolific in her writing (e.g. Brown 1994; Brown *et al.* 1999a and 1999b; Brown, Stein and Turk 1995; Brown and Turk 1992) and continues to highlight the abuse of adults with learning disabilities. It is also helpful to keep in touch with the organisations (and their websites) who specialise in working with adults with disabilities. In relation to learning disabilities the British Institute of Learning Disabilities (BILD), the Ann Craft Trust (ACT) and Voice UK are particularly useful. There are often useful commentaries on recent events. The following example is from the BILD website:

Investigation finds widespread institutional abuse of people with learning disabilities at an NHS trust in Cornwall

Commissions recommend special measures to protect people who use services after findings show significant failings in local procedures

BILD COMMENT

Widespread institutional abuse of people with learning disabilities at an NHS Trust in Cornwall is revealed in a report published by the Healthcare Commission and the Commission for Social Care Inspection (CSCI).

The report details the findings of a joint investigation into services for people with learning disabilities at Cornwall Partnership NHS Trust. The services investigated were the Budock Hospital near Falmouth, which is a treatment centre for 18 inpatients. The investigation also looked at two other treatment centres, 4 children's units and 46 houses occupied by groups of up to four people with learning disabilities.

The report describes many years of abusive practices at the trust and the failure of senior trust executives to tackle this. Examples of abuse included physical abuse and misuse of people's money. (BILD 2007)

Or you can get factual information; for example: '23 per cent of adults with learning disabilities have experienced physical abuse and 47 per cent have experienced verbal abuse and bullying' (Foundation for People with Learning Disabilities 2003).

Some key issues I would expect a trainer to raise on a basic awareness course in relation to younger vulnerable adults with disabilities would be:

- difficulties in communicating

- having to rely on family members or carers for practical and emotional support

- isolation

- financial abuse

- being befriended.

Adults with mental health problems

A major problem is that adults with mental health problems are stigmatised. People do still stereotype, thinking that someone with a mental health problem is more likely to be an abuser than a victim – which is definitely not the case. The dilemma for workers is if someone does have episodes of being ill (for example, they become delusional) it is very difficult to know when they make allegations of abuse whether this is the true situation. I also have concerns that there is an abundance of literature which focuses on the concept of dangerousness and the offender with mental health problems. This can lead us totally down the wrong track.

My experience both through my research projects and training is that historically people working in the field of mental health have been reluctant to implement adult abuse procedures and have had the attitude that abuse can be dealt with through the care programming approach. This is gradually changing, but I am still hearing constantly that a high percentage of people with mental health problems will have experienced abuse and workers have not got enough time to deal with all the issues this raises (from the past or in the present). Sometimes comments made imply that it is not out of the ordinary for a person with mental health problems to have experienced abuse.

This leads me to a key point I persistently make on training courses. Many vulnerable adults will have been abused in the past, either in childhood or earlier in adulthood. The problem for workers is trying to find out whether the adult is being abused currently or whether issues from the past need to be dealt with now. Many adults with mental health problems (like those with learning disabilities) will have been in institutions where they may well have been abused. We know that abuse in institutions still goes on and the scary thing is – how can victims secure help? Will they be believed?

> During my time in hospital, the brutality I witnessed and experienced only compounded my distress: being raped by a male patient, being dragged by nurses and locked in a small room for 'playing up'.

> I was distraught. I didn't have the confidence to complain – I couldn't believe it, so who'd believe me? He was a nice, amiable nurse that everyone liked. I suppose that wouldn't happen if I wasn't mentally ill. (ReSisters 2002, p.31)

Adults with mental health problems are labelled, so not taken seriously:

> That's just one of the things that happens when you're mentally ill. You're dismissed, seen as wrong or not well.

> Disbelieved. I was raped again at 19 and I didn't tell anybody. There wasn't any point. It's down to being labelled. (ReSisters 2002, p.55)

Or they are taken advantage of by people in positions of trust:

> I had taken an overdose…and my GP came to my home. He asked me to get undressed… It was sexual assault and attempted rape. I fought him and shouted, 'you're a doctor!'… It was so confusing as he had been one of the only ones to help. This had a profound effect on me. They are getting away with it. (ReSisters 2002, p.31)

So, again, key issues to be raised by trainers are:

- Adults with mental health problems can be victims. It is wrong to stereotype them and see them as perpetrators of abuse.

- When there is a suspicion or allegation that a person with mental health problems is being abused, it must be investigated.

- The vulnerable adult/adult abuse policy and procedures should be followed and the manager must not hide behind the care programming approach.

- Just because the number of abuse referrals regarding younger adults with mental health problems is small does not mean it is not happening.

People with physical disabilities and sensory impairment

This group of people are vulnerable in exactly the same way as adults with learning disabilities or mental health problems. Everything I have said applies to them. I am concerned that literature is scarce regarding abuse of these people. I have certainly come across cases in my own practice and therefore case examples are included in this chapter.

The rest of this chapter contains extra training materials focusing on the abuse of younger people:

✍ Exercise 11.1, p.336, and 📄 Handout 3.1, p.73

What makes a younger adult vulnerable? – to make participants think about how a younger person with disabilities or a mental health problem can be vulnerable and susceptible to abuse.

✍ Exercise 11.2, p.337, and 📄 Handout 11.1, p.340

Abuse or not abuse? – to make participants think about what constitutes abuse in relation to younger adults.

✍ Exercise 11.3, p.338, and 📄 Handout 11.2, p.341

Abuse or bad practice? – to make participants think further about what constitutes abuse in an institution.

✍ Exercise 11.4, p.339, and 📄 Handout 11.3, p.342

Alert or not to alert? – to get participants to think about whether they would alert in certain situations.

〰 Case studies are presented in the following handouts:

📄 Handouts 11.4, 11.5, 11.6, 11.7, 11.8, 11.9, 11.10, 11.11, 11.12, pp.344–352

Suggested reading

Journal of Adult Protection is an excellent resource for finding articles relating to younger adults. It is worth noting that there was a special edition in September 2003, Volume 5, Issue 3: 'The Sexual Abuse of People with Learning Difficulties', and in December 2005, Volume 7, Issue 4 there was a special issue on mental health.

Henderson, J. (2002) 'Experiences of "care" in mental health.' *Journal of Adult Protection 4*, 3, September, 34–45.

Williams, C. (1995) *Invisible Victims: Crime and Abuse Against People with Learning Difficulties.* London: Jessica Kingsley Publishers.

Williams, J. and Keating, F. (2000) 'Abuse in mental health services: Some theoretical considerations.' *Journal of Adult Protection 2*, 3, September, 32–9.

Videos

WAA1, WAA2, WAA3, WAA4, WAA5 and WAA6

All the videos contain specific case studies about younger adults.

WHAT MAKES A YOUNGER ADULT VULNERABLE?

Objective

To make participants think about how a younger person with disabilities, a mental health problem or other problems can be vulnerable and susceptible to abuse.

Participants

In small groups.

Equipment

Flipchart paper and pens.

Copies of Handout 3.1.

Time

15 minutes.

Task

1. Participants are asked to think about younger service users who may have disabilities, mental health problems or other problems (e.g. substance misuse, homelessness).

2. Participants list examples of how and why they think these service users could be vulnerable.

3. Participants list any examples of where younger vulnerable adults have been abused as a direct result of their vulnerability.

Feedback

1. Each group feeds back their work.

2. General discussion about vulnerability.

3. Trainer gives out the definition of vulnerable adult (Handout 3.1) and discusses its relevance to younger adults.

Note for trainer

1. The trainer is advised to have to hand examples of younger adults who have been abused in case participants have no examples themselves.

2. The exercise should bring out how vulnerability can make younger adults susceptible to abuse and it is important to emphasise that vulnerable adults can be targeted and groomed.

 © Jacki Pritchard 2007

ABUSE OR NOT ABUSE? (YOUNGER ADULTS)

Objective

To make participants think about what constitutes abuse in relation to younger adults.

Participants

In small groups.

Equipment

Copies of Handout 11.1.

Time

Groups spend 30 minutes undertaking the exercise.

Task

1. Groups will consider each scenario in turn. They have to reach a consensus regarding whether this is a case of abuse or not.

2. If the consensus of opinion is that it *is* abuse, the group has to consider which categories of abuse are taking place.

Feedback

1. Participants remain sitting in their groups. The trainer takes one scenario at a time and goes around asking each group what their consensus of opinion was.

2. If there was a disagreement *within* the group, the trainer will ask participants to explain what they discussed. Where there are differences *between* the groups, the trainer will ask the groups to debate; that is, put forward their arguments.

Note for trainer

This exercise is suitable for all workers across the disciplines and will get participants to think about the abuse of younger adults.

© Jacki Pritchard 2007

ABUSE OR BAD PRACTICE? (YOUNGER ADULTS)

Objective

To make participants think further about what constitutes abuse in an institution.

Participants

In small groups.

Equipment

Copies of Handout 11.2.

Time

Groups spend 30 minutes undertaking the exercise.

Task

1. Groups will consider each scenario in turn. They have to reach a consensus regarding whether this is a case of abuse *or* bad practice.

2. If the consensus of opinion is that it *is* abuse, the group has to decide into which category or categories of abuse they would put each action/behaviour.

Feedback

1. Participants remain sitting in their groups. The trainer takes one scenario at a time and goes around asking each group what their consensus of opinion was.

2. If there was a disagreement *within* the group, the trainer will ask participants to explain what they discussed. Where there are differences *between* the groups, the trainer will ask the groups to debate; that is, put forward their arguments.

Note for trainer

It must be made clear when explaining the purpose of the exercise that the groups cannot say the scenario is both abuse and bad practice. The main purpose of the exercise is to get participants thinking about when bad practice crosses that fine line to become abuse.

 © Jacki Pritchard 2007

ALERT OR NOT TO ALERT? (YOUNGER ADULTS)

Objective

To get participants to think about whether to make an alert.

Participants

Individual work; work in pairs.

Equipment

Pens.

Copies of Handout 11.3.

Time

5 minutes' individual work; 10 minutes' discussion in pairs.

Task

1. Each participant is given a copy of Handout 11.3.

2. Participants answer the questionnaire.

3. Participants work in pairs and discuss their answers.

Feedback

1. Participants talk about the scenarios where they were not sure what they would do.

2. Pairs feed back if they have had disagreements about what they would do.

3. General discussion about alerting.

© Jacki Pritchard 2007

ABUSE OR NOT ABUSE? (YOUNGER ADULTS)

1. Martin has profound learning disabilities. He takes food from other service users' plates and eats with his fingers. The care worker taps his hand when she sees him do this.

2. Sarah is five foot three inches tall and weighs 14 stone. Staff say that she is overweight and have put her on a diet. She used to like to have three sugars in her tea, but now is not allowed any.

3. Marion works extra shifts to boost her low income. This means sometimes working an early shift, having a few hours off and then returning for a late shift. She has started falling asleep on duty.

4. Simon goes home every weekend. He complains he gets bored because his parents will not take him out in the car. The car was obtained through Simon's mobility allowance.

5. A Jewish service user is given pork to eat. It is not considered to be important to follow his religious beliefs because 'he has profound learning disabilities and won't know'.

6. Every time a worker talks to Alice she mimics her Welsh accent.

7. Most evenings a gang of teenagers shout 'retards' at adults with learning disabilities who are living in supported accommodation.

8. A manager has called a service user a 'dirty sod' ever since she found him masturbating in the bathroom.

9. Rachel attends a day centre and likes to touch Jed, who is a day centre worker, on his bottom.

10. One service user calls another service user 'Schizo boy'.

11. When Zoe's father visits her in the project she always wants to go out into town, which is eight miles away. Mr Grey insists on using taxis and says Zoe has to use her own money for the taxis.

12. Staff are regularly hit, bitten and shouted at by one service user. The manager says 'nothing can be done'.

© Jacki Pritchard 2007

ABUSE OR BAD PRACTICE? (YOUNGER ADULTS)

1. Four people who have learning disabilities and live in supported accommodation go out walking every Wednesday afternoon. Avril, who has some physical disabilities, comes to live in the house and says she would like to go out as well. The support workers tell her she cannot go because 'you would slow us down too much'.

2. Service users with mental health problems who are living in a halfway house keep telling the support workers that money is going missing. They all say they think it is the agency member of staff who is taking it. The support workers say they will keep an eye on the situation but they do not tell their line manager about the allegations.

3. Workers constantly talk about service users 'kicking off' and they use this term in written records.

4. Alicia has mental health problems and can present with different identities. A nurse on the hospital ward asks: 'Who are we today then?'

5. Workers have been told they must give their service users structure and routine. In the care plan it is written that Don should have a sleep after lunch between 1.00 and 2.00. Today, Don wants to watch the television programme *Neighbours* at 1.35 p.m. and refuses to go to bed. The workers say he must go to bed and take him up to his room (where there is no television).

6. Aaron frequently masturbates in public. The manager and staff have agreed that the shed at the bottom of the garden can be 'his personal place' and have told Aaron when he wants to masturbate he should go down there.

7. Delia has Tourette's syndrome. One worker, who has very strong religious beliefs, refers to her as the 'one with the dirty mouth'.

8. Max has attempted suicide again. His key worker says to him: 'Do you realise how much stress you cause for me and your family every time you do this? You really are very selfish. In fact suicide is a totally selfish act.'

9. Amie is blind and physically disabled. She attends a day centre once a week to give her mum a break. One of the day care workers insists on cutting up Amie's food for her even though Amie explains she can do it herself. The worker says: 'I like to look after you properly. It gives me pleasure to help.'

10. Sue has worked with the service users in the house since they were children. They are all in their twenties now. She says, 'They are like family to me.' She never knocks on their bedroom doors; she just goes straight in.

ALERT OR NOT TO ALERT? (YOUNGER ADULTS)

1. Kieran is 21 years old and profoundly deaf. He had always lived with his mother until she died eight months ago. The social worker from the sensory impairment team has been involved with Kieran and visits fairly regularly. Two months ago Kieran met a young lad called Rob in the newsagent and became friendly with him. Kieran is a very open and honest young man and it becomes clear to the social worker that Rob is suggesting that Kieran gets involved in certain activities, for example growing cannabis in the house. When she goes to the bathroom she notices on the landing that there are 20 boxes containing DVD players. When asked about this, Kieran says he is 'just storing them for Rob until he knows what he is going to do with them'.

    Yes ☐   **No** ☐   **Don't know** ☐

2. Janice is 51 years old. She has had severe mental health problems in the past. She had ECT treatment on her last admission to hospital; her memory has been affected and is now very poor. She has no recall at all about the fact that her son, Ed, who is a drug user, has physically and financially abused her in the past. Janice presents as being well at the current time. She tells her community psychiatric nurse that Ed is visiting on a daily basis wanting money, which she does give him. Janice says she is 'a little frightened of him', but does not want anything done about it.

    Yes ☐   **No** ☐   **Don't know** ☐

3. Suzy is 22 years old and has moderate learning disabilities. Before coming to live in supported accommodation, she lived at home with her mother, stepfather and four younger siblings (ages 4 to 16). She settled well into the house and seemed very reluctant to have any contact with home. Today it is her birthday and her step-father is coming this afternoon to take her home for a party. She tells her key worker that she does not want to go because her stepfather 'used to touch me where he shouldn't and he does it to the others too'.

    Yes ☐   **No** ☐   **Don't know** ☐

   © Jacki Pritchard 2007

ALERT OR NOT TO ALERT? (YOUNGER ADULTS)

4. David has profound learning disabilities and lives in a care home. A worker hears David making very loud noises and when she comes in she finds that he has cuts on his face and is bleeding from his lips. Another service user, Joe (who, according to staff, has a tendency to make things up), comes in and tells the worker he saw another service user, Lee, hit David. Joe says he does not want her to tell anyone because he is frightened of Lee.

   Yes ☐ **No** ☐ **Don't know** ☐

5. Gerry is 35 years old and lives alone. He sustained some brain injury as a result of being run over and is physically disabled. He has support workers coming in to help him. He has formed a relationship with Meryl, whom he met via a chat room on the internet. At first he seemed really happy, but during the last few weeks workers have noticed that he seems very depressed. This morning a worker comes in to help Gerry get up. She sees lacerations down both arms. Gerry admits that Meryl is violent but he does not want to do anything about it.

   Yes ☐ **No** ☐ **Don't know** ☐

6. Lana has been working nights as a relief worker with adults with learning disabilities. Whilst having a cup of coffee with a colleague they talk about their previous jobs. Lana says she used to work in a care home for older people with mental health problems. She says she was suspended for hitting two of the residents: 'They never proved anything. There were no witnesses. It wasn't anything serious. Working with old nutters like that drove me mad.'

   Yes ☐ **No** ☐ **Don't know** ☐

© Jacki Pritchard 2007

CASE STUDY: SASHA (AGED 25)

Sasha was blind and physically disabled; she had always been cared for by her parents, Mr and Mrs MacKenzie, and brother, Mike. She met Liz, who was a nurse, when she was in hospital. Liz kept in touch with Sasha after discharge and they became friends. After about six months Liz asked Sasha to move into her flat. Sasha's parents were not happy about this, but thought that they should try to let Sasha lead her life as she wished to do. During the first month after she left home, Sasha came back to her parents' house for Sunday dinner every week. Liz did not come with her.

Mr and Mrs McKenzie went to see Sasha at the flat a couple of times, but they were never made to feel welcome by Liz. Sasha then said she was not coming for Sunday dinner any more. Mike did visit his sister regularly in the flat. Over the next few months he became concerned that she was losing a lot of weight and she did not seem like her usual self. She was reluctant to talk and spent most of the time listening to the radio when Mike visited. He did not see much of Liz, but when she was there she was very abrupt with both Mike and Sasha.

Mike thought that maybe Sasha wanted to return home, but could not admit that she had made a mistake. When he discussed this with her, she said she was 'fine and enjoying my independence'. During the next few weeks other things began to worry Mike. Sasha had always liked to be taken out, but suddenly she did not want to go anywhere. She used to enjoy being taken for a drive, but seemed to have lost interest in everything including herself.

Finally, Mike called round early one morning because he was going on holiday. He found the front door ajar and went in. He found Sasha lying on the bed crying. He noticed blood on the sheets.

 © Jacki Pritchard 2007

CASE STUDY: APRIL WINTERS (AGED 43)

April was born with a lot of physical disabilities and throughout her life has had to deal with many health problems. She uses a wheelchair and needs help with all her personal care. Her father left home when she was a baby. Since then she has been cared for by her mother, who has always been supported by professionals within health and social services.

In recent months, April has had frequent admissions to hospital due to hydrocephalus and problems with the shunt which had been inserted. She is always admitted to the same ward and has got to know the staff really well. April likes to talk a lot and has few inhibitions. Nurses on the ward have become concerned because on each admission they have noticed that April has lost a lot of weight and her skin seems very rough and dry. She also seems generally unkempt and smells of urine.

When nurses have been chatting to April, she has talked about her mother and what her life is like at home. It becomes clear to the staff on the ward that April is being neglected both physically and emotionally. April says that her mum is 'getting old' and 'finding it hard to look after me'. Mrs Winters is now 87 years old and 'sleeps a lot'. April spends most of the day watching television and there are no visitors coming to the house apart from professionals. She says she is 'bored'. A hospital social worker came to talk to April and offered her various options. April said: 'I must go home. I can't leave my mum.'

CASE STUDY: DOROTHY (AGED 55)

Dorothy has been physically disabled for most of her life. Her primary carer had been her husband, John, until he died suddenly three years ago at the age of 62. Her youngest daughter, Melanie, who is a schoolteacher, lives a few miles away. Her other children live in different parts of the country. Dorothy has always been an activist – fighting for the rights of disabled people, being involved in local groups and so on.

After the death of her father, Melanie reluctantly agreed to help with the care of her mother. However, as she works full-time and has children herself, home care services came in during the morning to check on Dorothy and to help with personal care tasks. Dorothy welcomed the company as she did not get out as much since John died; he had driven her around wherever she wanted to go.

Dorothy had always been a very proud woman. She liked her house and herself to 'look nice and respectable'. However, the home carers noticed gradual changes in Dorothy. She became very bad tempered and used to shout at the home carers. She had always been an avid reader of romance novels, but now she could not be bothered to read or watch the television programmes she used to enjoy. She also seemed to lose interest in herself; she did not put on her make-up any more. When the home carers tried to talk to Dorothy about the changes they had noticed she told them to mind their own business. They thought she was probably still grieving for John.

The home carers did not see much of Melanie because she worked. However, during one of the school holidays she did come round and was there when the home carers came in. They saw Melanie slap Dorothy across the face. As she did so she said: 'I hate you. You're ruining my life.'

© Jacki Pritchard 2007

CASE STUDY: MALCOLM BROWN (AGED 30)

Mrs Brown cares for her son, Malcolm, who experiences various problems due to having physical and learning disabilities. Mr Brown left the family home after Malcolm was born, from which time Mrs Brown has been the primary carer for Malcolm. She has always refused to let Malcolm have any form of respite care. She frequently seeks advice from professionals, but then rejects it as she says 'I know what is best for my son'.

Various social workers and nurses have been involved with Malcolm and his mother over the years. Currently, two social workers are involved. Chester Grey, social worker on the learning disabilities team, supports Malcolm. Anna Mason, from the older persons' team, has been involved in assessing the needs of Mrs Brown.

Anna has become very worried after hearing detailed descriptions about how Mrs Brown has been caring for Malcolm. Mrs Brown openly talks about her and Malcolm sleeping in the same bed: 'I have to be with him at all times in case he has an epileptic fit.' She evacuates his bowels manually because 'it is very necessary and we have always done it this way'. Mrs Brown has also talked about their frequent visits to the GP's surgery and to the accident and emergency department in the local hospital. Anna has talked in supervision with her manager about the possibility of this being a case of Munchausen's Syndrome by Proxy. She has been told 'to monitor the situation'.

Anna has also discussed her concerns with Chester Grey, who has different concerns. He is worried about Malcolm's violent outbursts and feels that Mrs Brown could be at risk of physical harm from her son.

CASE STUDY: LEROY JACKSON (AGED 22)

Leroy is African Caribbean and has moderate learning disabilities. When he was six years old he was run over by a car and lost his right leg. He lives with his mother, father and four younger siblings. His parents are very protective towards Leroy and do not like him to have contact with people outside the family. They have always resented involvement from any of the statutory services. They see teachers, social workers, and so on as 'interfering busy bodies, who should mind their own business'.

However, in recent months, Leroy has been going to a day centre which he really enjoys. The staff have helped him to develop a lot of skills and they believe that he would be capable of having a simple job; for example, helping in a shop. His parents have rejected this idea. Leroy was very upset when his parents said he could not apply for a job collecting trolleys in a local supermarket. He told the day centre workers his family regularly call him 'stupid' and 'useless'. After this he was not at all motivated when he attended the centre; he became very lethargic and seemed to have lost confidence in himself.

Day centre staff then became concerned about Leroy's finances and alerted the learning disabilities team. An adult abuse investigation is now taking place regarding his parents' management of his finances – they take and manage all his benefit. They also have a car through mobility allowance, but Leroy complains he is not allowed to go in the car. He is not allowed to go on day trips with the day centre; his parents say they cannot afford it. He brings enough money to the centre to pay for his lunch but never has any extra to buy anything else. Staff know from what Leroy has told them that he got a lot of compensation as a child after the road traffic accident. Since the abuse investigation has started, Mr and Mrs Jackson have withdrawn Leroy from the day centre.

© Jacki Pritchard 2007

CASE STUDY: HELEN GRANGE (AGED 26)

Helen Grange has Down's syndrome; she can communicate very well and likes to be actively involved in 'doing things'. She has always lived with her mother; her father left home soon after Helen was born.

Five days a week Helen attends a centre from which various activities are organised for her. She attends adult education classes and also helps out in the local community. One of her projects is to help at a luncheon club, which is run in a sheltered accommodation complex for older people. In the morning Helen works in the kitchen preparing the food, then at midday she serves the meals in the dining area.

The luncheon club is organised by Henry Sharp, who is a 70-year-old volunteer. Part of the funding for the luncheon club comes from social services. Henry is responsible for managing the grant which is allocated to run the luncheon club.

The week before Christmas the luncheon club was having its Christmas party. Helen had gone to help out as usual. At around 11.30 a.m. Marion, one of the home carers who works in the complex, was walking down one of the corridors when she saw Henry kissing Helen and fondling her breasts. She did not approach them, but walked away in the other direction.

Marion's line manager, Mrs Grey, attended the Christmas party as did the home carers who worked in the complex. During the party Marion told Mrs Grey what she had seen in the corridor. Mrs Grey immediately rang the area social services office to report an allegation of sexual abuse. Helen's social worker was on leave so the referral went to the duty social worker.

CASE STUDY: GRAHAM (AGED 39)

Graham was diagnosed as having schizophrenia many years ago. He has no living family and has always seen any professional or worker as 'my family'. He has never made friends easily because 'everyone thinks I'm a freak'. His self-esteem is extremely low and he totally lacks confidence in everything he tries to do.

He recently had to move to a new flat because his old place was being demolished. He found having to move to a new area again very unsettling. He did not like having to find new places to shop and it also meant he had to change to a different community mental health team and have a new community psychiatric nurse allocated.

One day Graham got lost on the new estate and he was crying when three teenagers saw him. When he said he was lost the boys offered to take him home. Graham invited them in for a cup of tea. The boys saw that Graham had a lot of 'quality stuff'. Graham did like to play CDs a lot and watch DVDs. The boys picked up very quickly that Graham was very lonely and would welcome company, so they said they would call round again. This developed into a regular pattern.

Graham had never drunk alcohol before. The boys brought round cans of beer and would get Graham drunk. When he woke up in the morning he could remember little about the night before. He felt he was becoming very forgetful in general. Graham started to find that he had less money in his 'money box' than he thought he had. He also lost CDs and DVDs. Then one day he came home from the shops and found that he had been burgled.

   © Jacki Pritchard 2007

CASE STUDY: NANCY (AGED 44)

Nancy has been known to mental health services all through adulthood. She experiences depression and severe anxiety attacks. In the past she has also been agoraphobic but this has not been a problem in recent years. She has been under the care of numerous psychiatrists, and seen countless counsellors and therapists. She has also attended any support group she has heard of in the county.

She has now found a new support group for people who self-harm. It is facilitated by a social worker and a community psychiatric nurse. During the first meeting she attended she told group members that she had been sexually abused by her mother in childhood but no one had believed her at the time. She said professionals throughout childhood and adulthood called her attention-seeking. Her aim was to lead what she called 'a normal life and get rid of all my ghosts and demons'.

During the next six months Nancy attended the group regularly and disclosed more details about the abuse she had experienced through her life. She talked about her mother sexually abusing her from an early age and then involving her in a satanic ring when she was a teenager. It was at this time she met her first husband who was also in the group. She was vague about how she left her first husband but went on to say that she currently lives with her second husband who physically abuses her. She was adamant that she loves her husband and does not want to leave the situation.

After this particular meeting, Nancy became ill and was sectioned. Six months later she returned to the group and immediately disclosed that a male nurse had raped her whilst she had been in hospital. She said she had been too frightened to tell anyone and said no one would believe her anyway.

© Jacki Pritchard 2007

CASE STUDY: FRANCESCA (AGED 30)

Francesca has known her husband, Matt, since they were in their teens; they married when she was 18 years old. They have one child, Chantelle, aged eight years old. Francesca got pregnant when they were first married but the baby died when it was a few days old.

Francesca comes from a close-knit family who spend a lot of time with each other. However, the family have become very concerned during the past few years because Francesca seems to have distanced herself from them. She has told her sisters that she is very busy working full-time and having to look after Matt and Chantelle. On the few occasions her family have visited, Francesca has seemed on edge and obsessional about being tidy and keeping things clean. As soon as cups were empty Francesca would take them out to wash and dry them. When her sister dropped a biscuit on the carpet Francesca screamed at her.

Francesca had several visits to her GP, Dr Lawrence, when she was experiencing some gynaecological problems. Dr Lawrence picked up on the fact that Francesca was very nervous and had lost her confidence; previously she had been very extrovert. During one appointment he also noticed some bruising on Francesca's back; she said she had fallen down the stairs.

One Monday morning Francesca did not turn up for work and did not ring in. Her friend, Lucy, thought this was really odd so at lunchtime she went round to Francesca's house. All the curtains were drawn but Lucy could not get any response when she knocked. She also rang the house phone and Francesca's mobile. Eventually she called the police who broke in. Francesca had taken an overdose; she had been very badly beaten.

Later in hospital she disclosed that Matt had left taking Chantelle with him. He said he was going to work in Italy. She gave a limited account of the violence she had been experiencing and how he had nearly drowned her on several occasions. When the police spoke to members of Matt's family they confirmed that he had got a job in Rome and that he had taken Chantelle with him because Francesca was 'an unfit mother because she has mental health problems'.

 © Jacki Pritchard 2007

Chapter 12

The Abuse of Black and Minority Ethnic People

It is extremely important that attention is given to the subject of abuse of black and minority ethnic people even though our knowledge regarding this subject may be limited. We know that health and social care services may not be accessed by many minority ethnic groups. We also know that any victim of adult abuse may find it extremely difficult to disclose about abuse. So it is not surprising that the number of referrals about adult victims from minority ethnic groups is low. Yet they are there. We have to accept that abuse will occur in different groups and therefore we must think about it. Workers have to be made aware that they may come across such cases. According to the 2001 Census, 7.9 per cent (4,635,296) of the population are from minority ethnic groups.

We are living in an era when everyone is expected to be politically correct – quite rightly so. However, sometimes things move on so quickly that people are not aware of the correct terminology they should be using. A person may say something which offends another person quite unintentionally. In 1993 the Department of Health's definition of elder abuse made the point that abuse can be inflicted without intent; that is, because of lack of knowledge, education, training etc.:

> Abuse may be described as physical, sexual, psychological, or financial. It may be intentional or unintentional, or the result of neglect. It causes harm to the older person, either temporarily or over a period of time. (Department of Health 1993, p.3)

We have already discussed earlier in the manual terminology, but it would seem appropriate to give special attention to the terminology which will be used in relation to issues related to black and minority ethnic people. Below, key terms will be considered using definitions from a variety of sources – dictionaries, websites, and so on – which can be used by trainers to start a group discussion. Trainers need to find out just how much training workers have had (if any) on race awareness before tackling the subject of abuse. So let us start with the word *race*.

Race

- A group of people of common ancestry, distinguished from others by physical characteristics such as hair type, colour of skin, stature, and so on.

- A group, especially of people, with particular similar physical characteristics, who are considered as belonging to the same type, or the fact of belonging to such a group.

- A group of people who share the same culture, language, history, characteristics.

KEY QUESTION

How many different races can you name?

Ethnic

- Of or relating to a human group having racial, religious, linguistic and other traits in common.

- Relating to the classification of mankind into groups, especially on the basis of racial characteristics.

- Denoting or deriving from the cultural traditions of a group of people.

Ethnic group

- Relating to a group of people having a common national or cultural tradition.

- A national or racial group living in a country or area which contains a larger group of people of a different race or nationality.

KEY QUESTION

How many different ethnic groups can you name?

Typical terms used on monitoring forms within organisations are:

- Asian or Asian British – Indian
- Asian or Asian British – Bangladeshi
- Asian or Asian British – Pakistani
- Other Asian background
- Black or black British – African
- Black or black British – Caribbean

- Other black background
- Chinese or other ethnic background
- Mixed – white and black African
- Mixed – white and black Caribbean
- Mixed – white and Asian
- Other mixed background.

Minority ethnic people

The title of this chapter includes the terms 'black' and 'minority ethnic' and one of the objectives in writing the chapter is to raise awareness about the possibility of abuse occurring in *all* minority ethnic groups. If the term 'black' people was used, some people would immediately think of African Caribbean or Asian people; but Asian people might not see themselves as black. We need to include people from all races – hence the term *minority ethnic people* will be used to include many different cultural backgrounds.

KEY QUESTIONS

How many minority ethnic people have you
come into contact with through work?

How many minority ethnic people do you know in your private life?

Culture

KEY QUESTION

What does the word 'culture' mean to you?

Culture is a very difficult term to define. Some definitions might include:

- the total of the inherited ideas, beliefs, values and knowledge, which constitute the shared bases of social action
- the total range of activities and ideas of a people
- a particular civilisation at a particular period
- the customs, institutions, and achievements of a particular nation, people or group
- the way of life, especially the general customs and beliefs, of a particular group of people at a particular time.

UNESCO has said:

> In its wildest sense culture may now be said to be the whole complex of distinctive spiritual, material, intellectual and emotional features that characterise a society or group. It includes not only the arts and letters, but also modes of life, the fundamental rights of human beings, value systems, traditions and beliefs. (UNESCO 2002)

In other words, 'culture' includes spiritual beliefs, actual physical property, and people's thoughts and emotions. It includes ways of life, basic human rights, and people's values, beliefs and traditions.

KEY QUESTIONS

Do you know about many different cultures?

Where would you go to find out more information?

Equal opportunities

Everyone should be treated equally regardless of age, gender, race, culture, religion, disability and sexuality.

Discrimination

Some general dictionary definitions are:

- unfair treatment of a person, racial group, minority

- action based on prejudice, bias

- to treat a person or particular group of people differently, especially in a worse way from the way in which you treat other people, because of their skin colour, religion, sex, and so on.

After working on definitions it is important for a trainer to get workers thinking about how much they actually know about different minority ethnic groups.

Knowing about different groups

None of us can know everything and most of what we know is either from what we have been taught or what we have gained from personal experience. In some parts of the UK there may be very few minority ethnic people living in particular areas; consequently, people's knowledge about different races, cultures, and so on can be very limited. Unfortunately stereotypes can develop because of assumptions which are made. Therefore, on a training course it is important to find out about workers' degree of knowledge and level of experience. Exercise 12.1 can be used during this introductory part of a course to get workers to explore how many people from different minority ethnic groups they know well, have met briefly or worked with. This exercise also gets them to start thinking about differences.

✍ Exercise 12.1, p.361

It is also important to explore values and attitudes. Exercise 12.2 could be used as a way of assessing workers' knowledge and experience.

 Exercise 12.2, p.362

Defining abuse in different cultures

Dilemmas will arise for workers when they feel that a certain action or behaviour is abusive but it may be acceptable within that culture. It is at this point that workers need to refer to the definitions within their local policy and procedures relating to vulnerable adults/adult abuse. I am not going to say it will always be straightforward; life is just not like that – there will always be grey areas. However, a worker must be clear in his or her own mind about what constitutes abuse and be able to express this verbally. Professionals and workers then need to work together closely to manage these allegations of abuse.

It has already been said in Chapter 3 that at the beginning of any training session there needs to be a participative exercise to get workers thinking about what abuse means to them. On basic awareness training courses workers are often surprised to learn that there are so many categories of abuse. Exercise 12.3 is designed to help workers think about how people from minority ethnic groups might be abused based on their own knowledge and experiences.

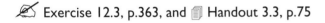 Exercise 12.3, p.363, and ▤ Handout 3.3, p.75

Discriminatory abuse

Discriminatory abuse is a 'new' category of abuse in that it became the sixth category of abuse when *No Secrets* came into being in the year 2000 (Department of Health 2000a). Formerly, many abuse policies had statements about principles underpinning adult protection work and this usually included something about equal opportunities and anti-discriminatory practice. Having discriminatory abuse as a category in its own right gives more recognition to the issue. However, many policies are not detailed enough about this type of abuse. Many state the obvious that no person should be discriminated on the grounds of:

- age
- gender
- race
- culture
- religion
- sexuality
- disability.

 Handout 12.1, p.371

It is important on a training course to try to get workers to think around discrimination in general and then to link this to discriminatory abuse. If Exercises 12.4, 12.5 and 12.6 are used on a course then workers should by the end be very clear about the actual actions or behaviours which could constitute discriminatory abuse.

✍ Exercise 12.4, p.364, and 📄 Handout 12.2, p.372

Initial exercise to encourage workers to think about the different forms of discrimination.

✍ Exercise 12.5, p.365, and 📄 Handout 12.3, p.373

Takes workers a step further to think about defining the term discriminatory abuse.

✍ Exercise 12.6, p.366

Encourages workers to be specific about what constitutes discriminatory abuse.

Human rights

It has been said frequently through this manual that every person has human rights and workers need to become familiar with the Human Rights Act 1998. Two useful study guides have been produced by the Home Office (2001a and 2001b), but updated guides are available on the internet. Handout 12.4 summarises the articles within the Act:

Article 2:	Right to life
Article 3:	Prohibition of torture
Article 4:	Prohibition of slavery and forced labour
Article 5:	Right to liberty and security
Article 6:	Right to a fair trial
Article 7:	No punishment without law
Article 8:	Right to respect for private and family life
Article 9:	Freedom of thought, conscience and religion
Article 10:	Freedom of expression
Article 11:	Freedom of assembly and association
Article 12:	Right to marry
Article 14:	Prohibition of discrimination
Article 16:	Restrictions on political activity of aliens
Article 17:	Prohibition of abuse of rights
Article 18:	Limitation on use of restrictions on rights.

 Handout 12.4, p.374

Exercise 12.7 can be used in several ways to focus workers on what actually constitutes discriminatory abuse. It can be introduced when a trainer wants participants to focus on categorising abuse, but it can also be used as a follow-on exercise when there has been some discussion or work undertaken on discriminatory abuse in particular. The scenarios illustrate the point that actions or behaviours can constitute different categories of abuse.

✍ Exercise 12.7, p.367, and ▤ Handout 12.5, p.375

Exercise 12.8 takes participants further, that is, to obtain their views on what distinguishes the fine line between abuse and bad practice in institutions.

✍ Exercise 12.8, p.368, and ▤ Handout 12.6, p.376

Systemic abuse

Some mention must be made of systemic abuse. This is where the system rather than a person abuses someone or a need is not met. For example, maybe someone from a different minority ethnic group may require someone from the same minority ethnic group to work with them. However, the organisation cannot provide such a person. There are many facets to this form of abuse. Exercise 12.9 should help workers think of other examples.

✍ Exercise 12.9, p.369

Would you alert?

Many workers, whether experienced or not, may feel uncomfortable when they suspect that abuse is happening. They may feel unsure and are 'scared of getting it wrong'. This is why a lot of workers keep things to themselves when in fact they should alert their manager immediately. When working with service users from different ethnic backgrounds a worker may feel even more uncertain. This could be because they know little about the culture and traditions, but sometimes it is because the worker is worried about being accused of being racist. The main objective of Exercise 12.10 is to get workers thinking about whether they would report certain situations.

✍ Exercise 12.10, p.370, and ▤ Handout 12.7, p.377

Key things to think about

It was said at the beginning of this chapter that our knowledge about the abuse of black and minority ethnic people is very limited but it *is* a very important subject. Therefore, to conclude I would suggest that trainers and workers need to think specifically about the following issues:

- The prevalence and incidence of the abuse of black and minority ethnic people are really unknown; abuse is going to be well hidden because minority ethnic groups do not access services in the same way other groups do.

- The six categories of abuse as defined in *No Secrets* will happen in all communities but workers must be aware of cultural differences, traditions and practices.

- Discriminatory abuse – is it really being addressed by the implementation of abuse policies?

- Neglect and systemic abuse – are we failing minority ethnic groups?

- Abuse of asylum seekers.

- Forced marriages.

 Case studies are presented in the following handouts:

 Handouts 12.8, 12.9, 12.10, 12.11, 12.12, 12.13, pp.378–383

Suggested reading

George, J. (1994) 'Racial aspects of elder abuse.' In M. Eastman (ed.) *Old Age Abuse: A New Perspective.* London: Chapman and Hall.

Williams, L. (2004) 'Refugee and asylum seekers as a group at risk of adult abuse.' *Journal of Adult Protection 6*, 4, December, 4–15.

 Video

WAA6: The Abuse of Black and Minority Ethnic People

This video includes seven case studies which look at abuse across service user groups and within different minority ethnic groups but also addresses issues around asylum seekers, forced marriages, domestic violence, and so on.

WHO DO YOU KNOW?

Objective

To encourage a worker to think about how many people they know from different minority ethnic groups and what differences exist between ethnicities.

Participants

Individual work.

Equipment

Paper and pen.

Time

10 minutes.

Task

1. The worker is asked to think about how many people they know or have met in the past (either through work or in their personal life) who were from a different ethnic group.

2. The worker lists the different ethnic origins on a sheet of paper – leaving a gap in between each one.

3. The worker then thinks about whether there are any differences between the person he or she was thinking about and him- or herself.

4. On a separate sheet of paper, the worker explains the differences (if any).

Feedback

1. The worker shares his or her written work with the line manager.

2. General discussion about difference, individuality and equality.

© Jacki Pritchard 2007

WHAT MORE DO YOU NEED TO KNOW?

Objective

To encourage a worker to think about their lack of knowledge regarding minority ethnic groups.

Participants

Individual work.

Equipment

Paper and pen.

Time

10 minutes.

Task

1. The worker is asked to think about service users with whom he or she is working now or has worked in the past who had a different ethnic background.

2. The worker makes a list of what he or she knows about that minority ethnic group.

3. The worker makes another list regarding things he or she does not know and feels he or she should know.

4. The worker makes a list of other minority ethnic groups about whom he or she knows very little.

Feedback

1. The worker shares his or her written work with the line manager.

2. General discussion about where to obtain information (e.g. use of books, articles, the internet, national and local organisations).

Note for trainer

It should be made clear to the worker before undertaking this exercise that he or she will not be criticised for any lack of knowledge.

 © Jacki Pritchard 2007

WHAT IS ABUSE IN RELATION TO MINORITY ETHNIC PEOPLE?

Objective

To get participants to think how people from minority ethnic groups can be abused.

Participants

Work in small groups.

Equipment

Flipchart paper and different coloured pens.

Copies of the *No Secrets* definition of abuse – Handout 3.3.

Time

20 minutes in small groups.

Task

1. Participants are asked to think about the word 'abuse' and what it means to them.

2. Participants discuss situations they know or have heard about where a person from a different minority ethnic group has been a victim of abuse.

3. A sentence is written about the abusive situation.

Feedback

1. Each group will feed back their examples of abuse. Other groups are asked whether they would agree this is a form of abuse.

2. The trainer gives out Handout 3.3 and general discussion follows.

© Jacki Pritchard 2007

WHAT IS DISCRIMINATION?

Objective

To encourage participants to think about the different forms of discrimination.

Participants

Small groups.

Equipment

Flipchart, paper and pens.

Copies of Handout 12.2.

Time

20 minutes.

Task

1. Participants are asked to list the different ways in which a person from a minority ethnic group can experience discrimination.

2. Each group will then write a definition of discrimination.

Feedback

1. Each group will feed back their lists and definitions.

2. Participants are given Handout 12.2.

3. General discussion about discrimination.

© Jacki Pritchard 2007

WHAT IS DISCRIMINATORY ABUSE?

Objective

To encourage participants to think about how they would define discriminatory abuse.

Participants

Large group.

Equipment

Flipchart, paper and pens.

Copies of Handout 12.3.

Time

30 minutes.

Task

1. The trainer asks the group to think back to work situations where they know a minority ethnic person (service user or colleague) has been discriminated against in some way.

2. The trainer asks participants to share their experiences, which are then listed on the flipchart paper by the trainer.

3. As each situation is put forward, the trainer asks the group to discuss whether this could be a form of discriminatory abuse.

4. Participants are given Handout 12.3.

5. General discussion about discriminatory abuse.

6. The group and trainer write a definition of discriminatory abuse which could be used in a policy or practice guidance (this should not be more than three sentences).

Note for trainer

1. During this exercise it is important for the trainer to encourage the participants to be explicit when they share their experiences. For example, saying a racist comment was made is not good enough; the exact words which were used need to be known.

2. The main objective is for the trainer to have got the group to write a definition of discriminatory abuse by the end of the exercise. This is *not* about writing the different forms of discriminatory abuse; Exercise 12.6 is designed to do this.

© Jacki Pritchard 2007

FORMS OF DISCRIMINATORY ABUSE

Objective

To encourage workers to be specific about what constitutes discriminatory abuse.

Participants

Small groups.

Equipment

Flipchart, paper and pens.

Time

20 minutes.

Task

1. Groups are told they have been given the job of writing a vulnerable adult/adult abuse policy.

2. Today they have to write the section in the policy which is concerned with listing the forms of discriminatory abuse.

Feedback

1. Groups will feed back their lists.

2. General discussion about similarities and differences in the lists compiled.

Note for trainer

The trainer needs to make it very clear that the task is *not* about writing a definition of discriminatory abuse. Specific detail is needed about each action and behaviour which would constitute discriminatory abuse.

© Jacki Pritchard 2007

ABUSE OR NOT ABUSE?
(BLACK AND MINORITY ETHNIC PEOPLE)

Objective

To make participants think about what constitutes abuse in relation to people from minority ethnic groups.

Participants

In small groups.

Equipment

Copies of Handout 12.5.

Time

Groups spend 30 minutes undertaking the exercise.

Task

1. Groups will consider each scenario in turn. They have to reach a consensus regarding whether this is a case of abuse or not.

2. If the consensus of opinion is that it *is* abuse, the group has to consider whether in addition to discriminatory abuse any other categories of abuse are taking place.

Feedback

1. Participants remain sitting in their groups. The trainer takes one scenario at a time and goes around asking each group what their consensus of opinion was.

2. If there was a disagreement *within* the group, the trainer will ask participants to explain what they discussed. Where there are differences *between* the groups, the trainer will ask the groups to debate; that is, put forward their arguments.

Note for trainer

This exercise is suitable for all workers across the disciplines and will get participants to think about discriminatory abuse occurring in a variety of settings.

ABUSE OR BAD PRACTICE?
(BLACK AND MINORITY ETHNIC PEOPLE)

Objective

To make participants think further about what constitutes abuse in an institution.

Participants

In small groups.

Equipment

Copies of Handout 12.6.

Time

Groups spend 30 minutes undertaking the exercise.

Task

1. Groups will consider each scenario in turn. They have to reach a consensus regarding whether this is a case of abuse *or* bad practice.

2. If the consensus of opinion is that it *is* abuse, the group has to decide into which category or categories of abuse they would put the action/behaviour.

Feedback

1. Participants remain sitting in their groups. The trainer takes one scenario at a time and goes around asking each group what their consensus of opinion was.

2. If there was a disagreement *within* the group, the trainer will ask participants to explain what they discussed. Where there are differences *between* the groups, the trainer will ask the groups to debate; that is, put forward their arguments.

Note for trainer

It must be made clear when explaining the purpose of the exercise that the groups cannot say the scenario is both abuse and bad practice. The main purpose of the exercise is to get participants thinking about when bad practice crosses that fine line to become abuse.

 © Jacki Pritchard 2007

SYSTEMIC ABUSE

Objective

To make participants think about what constitutes systemic abuse.

Participants

In small groups.

Equipment

Flipchart paper and pens.

Time

15 minutes.

Task

1. Participants are asked to think about minority ethnic people they have known through work or in their personal lives.

2. Groups list examples where a minority ethnic person has been abused by the system rather than a person.

Feedback

1. Groups feed back their lists.

2. The trainer encourages people to agree or disagree with the examples cited.

3. General discussion about systemic abuse.

Note for trainer

Participants often find this exercise difficult to begin with, so it is helpful if the trainer can give a few examples to start off. Participants need to be encouraged to think about specific systems relating to benefits, health care, assessments, fees, and so on.

© Jacki Pritchard 2007

ALERT OR NOT TO ALERT?
(BLACK AND MINORITY ETHNIC PEOPLE)

Objective

To get participants to think about whether to make an alert.

Participants

Individual work; work in pairs.

Equipment

Copies of Handout 12.7.

Time

5 minutes' individual work; 10 minutes' discussion in pairs.

Task

1. Each participant is given a copy of Handout 12.7.

2. Participants answer the questionnaire.

3. Participants work in pairs and discuss their answers.

Feedback

1. Participants talk about the scenarios where they were not sure what they would do.

2. Pairs feed back if they have had disagreements about what they would do.

3. General discussion about alerting.

© Jacki Pritchard 2007

ANTI-DISCRIMINATORY PRACTICE

All service users should be treated equally regardless of:

- age

- gender

- race

- culture

- religion

- sexuality

- disability.

© Jacki Pritchard 2007

DEFINITIONS OF DISCRIMINATION

- Unfair treatment of a person, racial group or minority.

- Action based on prejudice.

- To treat a person or particular group of people differently, especially in a worse way from the way in which you treat other people, because of their skin colour, religion or sex.

© Jacki Pritchard 2007

DISCRIMINATORY ABUSE

Definition from *No Secrets*

Discriminatory abuse – including racist, sexist, that based on a person's disability, and other forms of harassment, slurs or similar treatment.

From: Department of Health (2000) *No Secrets. Guidance on Developing and Implementing Multi-Agency Policies and Procedures to Protect Vulnerable Adults from Abuse.* London: Department of Health, p.9.

Some examples

- Derogatory comments

- Harassment

- Being made to move to a different resource/service based on age

- Denied medical treatment on grounds of age or mental health

- Not providing access

© Jacki Pritchard 2007

HUMAN RIGHTS ACT 1998: THE ARTICLES

Article 2:   Right to life

Article 3:   Prohibition of torture

Article 4:   Prohibition of slavery and forced labour

Article 5:   Right to liberty and security

Article 6:   Right to a fair trial

Article 7:   No punishment without law

Article 8:   Right to respect for private and family life

Article 9:   Freedom of thought, conscience and religion

Article 10:   Freedom of expression

Article 11:   Freedom of assembly and association

Article 12:   Right to marry

Article 14:   Prohibition of discrimination

Article 16:   Restrictions on political activity of aliens

Article 17:   Prohibition of abuse of rights

Article 18:   Limitation on use of restrictions on rights

 © Jacki Pritchard 2007

ABUSE OR NOT ABUSE?
(BLACK AND MINORITY ETHNIC PEOPLE)

1. A home carer says to a new colleague: 'I have to go in to three lots of coloureds now.'

2. A care worker asked Mr Cara, a Sikh man, not to wear his religious symbols when visiting the care home because residents did not like to see them.

3. An Asian man has come into a residential unit for rehabilitation. He says that he does not want any women to help him with personal care tasks. He is told there are no male workers in the unit.

4. A group of teenagers shout at a Croatian woman: 'Go back home you sponger.'

5. A Scottish woman is placed in a care home. One care worker is always making jokes about Scottish people being 'tight with money' in earshot of this service user.

6. Luncheon club staff say they cannot provide Kosher food for Samuel, who is Jewish.

7. An asylum seeker cannot speak English very well. A support worker loses patience with him and says she has not got time to waste on him. She then gives him very little attention and spends more time with other asylum seekers who are better at understanding and speaking English.

8. After Mrs Patel's husband died, her eldest son and his family moved into her house. Mrs Patel is now forced to live in the attic room and her son manages all her finances.

9. Home carers refer to a Chinese man as 'Mr Take-Away'.

10. A Latvian woman has been abused and is going to be interviewed. The community psychiatric nurse brings a Russian interpreter to the interview.

11. It is Ramadan so Mrs Udin needs to fast during the day and then eat at certain other times (before dawn and after sunset). Staff in the care home say she has to eat at the set mealtimes.

12. Saul is a young African Caribbean man who has mental health problems. At a day centre whenever he sits down next to Kate (who is white) she moves to sit somewhere else.

© Jacki Pritchard 2007

ABUSE OR BAD PRACTICE?
(BLACK AND MINORITY ETHNIC PEOPLE)

- Stella Goldberg, who is Jewish, lives in a care home. She wants to go to the Synagogue on a Friday evening. She is told no one can accompany her because there is a shortage of staff.

- Zak is a 28-year-old African Caribbean who has mental health problems. He is serving a short prison sentence for non-payment of fines. He has been the victim of several assaults from some other prisoners who found out he was gay. The prison officers have turned a blind eye to the incidents.

- Genevieve has moderate learning disabilities and attends college for cookery classes. The tutor refers to her as 'the coloured one'.

- A young woman who cannot speak English was admitted to hospital after she was found on the street suffering with hypothermia. She is left lying on a trolley in casualty for 12 hours. No one tries to find out what nationality she is.

- Mrs Bennett is an 80-year-old African Caribbean woman, who attends a day centre. She has asked that workers call her Mrs Bennett. The workers continue to call her by her first name.

- A Muslim man needs to say his prayers. A domestic comes in to say she is going to clean his room. He asks her to come back later, but she insists she has to clean now.

 © Jacki Pritchard 2007

ALERT OR NOT TO ALERT?
(BLACK AND MINORITY ETHNIC PEOPLE)

1. Mrs Maxwell attended the Seventh Day Adventist Church luncheon club once a week. She had always been a very lively woman but over a period of six months she started to present as being very depressed and lethargic. On several occasions she burst into tears for no reason; she told the volunteers she was just tired because she was not sleeping very well. Today she has come in with a black eye and a cut on her cheek. She says she fell over.

    Yes ☐ **No** ☐ **Don't know** ☐

2. The community psychiatric nurse visited Raqia regularly after she had been diagnosed as having schizophrenia. On one occasion she walked into the lounge and saw Raqia's father physically forcing her to get down onto a prayer mat.

    Yes ☐ **No** ☐ **Don't know** ☐

3. A family have requested that if their mother dies on the ward when they are not present, no one outside their religion should touch her body until the family are present. The woman does die in the middle of the night. A nurse, Kay, walks into the room and finds another nurse, Gill, tending to the body. When Kay tells her to stop Gill says she forgot about the family's wishes and asks Kay not to tell anyone what she has done.

    Yes ☐ **No** ☐ **Don't know** ☐

4. Mike, a social worker, is doing an assessment on Mrs Begum who is 81 years old. During the course of their conversation Mrs Begum talks about her family and it becomes clear from what she is saying that her grand-daughter is being forced into a marriage. The grand-daughter is currently locked in her bedroom and is due to fly to Pakistan in a few days' time.

    Yes ☐ **No** ☐ **Don't know** ☐

5. Jodie is a new home carer and she is currently shadowing Joan, who has worked as a home carer for many years. Jodie is shocked at some of the comments Joan has made during the course of the first morning. She has made racist comments about Somalian families and openly said she 'hates' asylum seekers.

    Yes ☐ **No** ☐ **Don't know** ☐

© Jacki Pritchard 2007

CASE STUDY: ZOE (AGED 23)

Zoe is African Caribbean and has learning disabilities. All her life she has been cared for by her family, who refused to let her go into residential care on a permanent basis. Zoe has a large extended family who are very involved in helping her parents. She goes in to a unit for respite care once every six weeks.

It is difficult to communicate with Zoe, but people who know her well believe they can understand her and what she wants or needs. Staff at the residential unit agree with the family; it just takes time to get to know Zoe and her ways. She has never presented any real problems for staff until very recently.

Zoe has become very aggressive towards staff in the unit and when the manager discussed this with the family they said they were also seeing changes in her behaviour at home. They had put this down to the fact another cousin had arrived from Jamaica and was staying in the house; Zoe does not react well to change in routine. They agreed to see how things went over the next few weeks.

At home Zoe seemed calmer to a degree, but definitely not as she always had been. However, when she went in for her next respite stay her behaviour became very aggressive again. When she returned home her parents noticed that her finger nails were broken and some of her underwear was missing. The manager of the unit could not throw any light on either matter.

Once again Zoe settled back at home but her mother noticed that she was doing odd things. She kept finding bits of paper and tissues in her knickers. Zoe was taken to the GP when she missed her period. After tests, she was found to be pregnant.

© Jacki Pritchard 2007

CASE STUDY: MIRANDA (AGED 26)

Miranda is African Caribbean and lives on her own in a bedsit. She had a very unhappy childhood and was always considered 'to be stupid'. In fact, she has very moderate learning disabilities. When she was 13 years old her mother took her back to Jamaica because her parents had divorced. Miranda was very unhappy there because she missed her siblings (she is the youngest of ten children) and then she was sexually abused by her mother's partner.

When she was 16 she returned to England and it was at this time she started to drink heavily, although her mother had let her drink substantial amounts from a very early age. Miranda worked in a hospital as a kitchen assistant for several years, but gave up the job when her father, to whom she was very close, died. Her drinking increased and she created large debts as well as not paying her rent and other bills. She also started getting into fights on the street and appeared in court on two occasions charged with assault. Her brother then became ill with cancer and died a year after her father. Miranda's drinking increased even more.

A social worker became involved after Miranda was violent again in a public place and had to be sectioned. Miranda said that the voices from the people in the walls of her bedsit told her not to pay her bills so that she could buy her drink. After discharge from hospital, Miranda stayed with one of her sisters and seemed well for a time. She then returned to live in her bedsit.

Miranda always felt very lonely. She had no friends of her own age and her sisters were all married and had little time for her. So she started visiting people in the care home which was located directly opposite her bedsit. Staff in the home became aware that some residents were giving Miranda money to go shopping for them, but then other residents were complaining that money was going missing. The care workers (not the residents) started making accusations that it must be Miranda who was stealing.

CASE STUDY: NASIR BEGUM (AGED 19)

Nasir was born in England; his older siblings had all been born in Pakistan. He had always been considered by family members to be 'different' and as he got older he was called 'the rebel'. He did not conform to what was expected of him. In his early teenage years he spent most of his time with his friends who were not part of the Asian community. He refused to go to the mosque and often truanted from school. He also started drinking alcohol. He left school when he was 16 and had various jobs, but did not stick at anything for very long.

When he was 18 years old Nasir was physically attacked in a nightclub and he sustained a brain injury. He remained in hospital for a long time but eventually came home to live with his parents, who were very reluctant to accept advice and support from professionals who specialised in brain injury. A solicitor and a case manager had become involved because many things needed to be sorted out regarding compensation and Nasir's care if he was to return home rather than live in a residential setting.

After he returned home Nasir became more and more depressed. His friends who visited him told the support workers that Nasir was being made to do things which he would never have wanted to do before his injury. His parents were making him pray and forcing him to eat halal meat – all of which he had rejected previously.

© Jacki Pritchard 2007

CASE STUDY: JOSEF (AGED 29)

Josef was an asylum seeker. He had been in England for two years. He had been homeless and then lived in various places. He eventually moved in with Mrs Barr, who offered accommodation to people who were 'in any difficulty'. Two other asylum seekers were living in the house when Josef moved in.

Josef had a lot of health problems and he was eventually diagnosed as having leukaemia. His health deteriorated rapidly and it became clear he was terminally ill. When he went to hospital medical staff were concerned about Josef – not just because of the leukaemia but because he was very frail and unkempt. He always wore the same clothes; he smelt of urine and faeces; his skin was rough and dirty. He often presented with bruises, but the medics thought this was due to the leukaemia. When asked about his accommodation Josef said he was well looked after by his friend, Mrs Barr. He said 'she give me room for very good price and I do jobs for her'.

One day Josef collapsed at home and Mrs Barr called for an ambulance. When the paramedics arrived they saw how Josef was living. The three asylum seekers were living in a very small room which had just three mattresses in it. There was no carpet or curtains. A bucket was placed in one corner of the room.

CASE STUDY: MR AND MRS AHMED (BOTH IN THEIR SEVENTIES)

Mr and Mrs Ahmed were homeless. After living in England for many years they decided to return to live in Pakistan. However, things did not work out as they expected and so they came back to live in England again. They stayed with relatives for a while, but that did not work out either. A family member took them to the local social services office and left them there. They were put in a residential home as emergency placements.

Mr and Mrs Ahmed were both very frail and had health problems. Mr Ahmed is an amputee and also diabetic. Mrs Ahmed has angina, an overactive thyroid and anaemia. There were no other black service users in the home, so they felt very isolated; especially Mrs Ahmed who spoke no English at all. None of the family ever visited them. Other service users were very unwelcoming to them and sometimes made racist remarks.

The staff in the home really liked the Ahmeds because they were a very friendly couple – always laughing and smiling – who welcomed the help they were receiving. It took weeks to sort out their housing problem and, while they were in the home, staff noticed that Mr and Mrs Ahmed started to spend a lot of time in their room. They refused to come downstairs for meals. It was also very obvious to staff that Mrs Ahmed was crying a great deal; her eyes were always swollen and they could hear her crying in the toilet. The couple still seemed devoted to each other; staff were convinced it was not a problem between Mr and Mrs Ahmed themselves. When asked how they could help, Mr Ahmed said his wife was just 'too sensitive' and would not elaborate any further.

© Jacki Pritchard 2007

CASE STUDY: MR RODRIGUEZ (AGED 69)

Mr Rodriguez had been in a private residential home for three years. The manager of the home made a referral to the local social services area office asking for a reassessment, because he said staff could not cope any longer and Mr Rodriguez needed a nursing home. The referral was passed between two older persons' teams and by the time the case was allocated Mr Rodriguez had been admitted to hospital with pneumonia.

When the social worker went to see Mr Rodriguez in hospital she was horrified at what she saw. He had massive bruises on both arms; and there were marks around his neck. The social worker immediately talked to the sister and staff nurse on the ward. They said Mr Rodriguez also had two large, deep pressure sores on his buttocks. They went on to comment that it was obvious that Mr Rodriguez had been 'neglected and battered'. They talked quite openly about what they thought had happened to Mr Rodriguez but added they did not want to be quoted on that.

The social worker said she would have to speak to her manager and she thought an adult abuse investigation would probably take place. The two nurses said that they would deny they had said anything because the owner of the home was a retired nurse, well known in the community, and several consultants referred many patients to him.

They also informed the social worker that Mr Rodriguez could not be interviewed because he was being given large doses of morphine. Apparently he had been having morphine while in the home.

| **APPENDIX 1.1**
ROCHDALE ADULT PROTECTION ALERT
MONITORING FORM | CONFIDENTIAL

Inter-agency Policy Procedure for the Protection of Vulnerable Adults in Rochdale Metropolitan Borough

This form should be completed by the Responsible Manager for each separate alert of abuse.

DATE OF ALERT: _____

NAME OF ALERTER: _____

ADDRESS: _____

_____

CONTACT NO: _____

REGARDING:
NAME: _____

ADDRESS: _____

_____

DATE OF BIRTH: _____

DETAILS OF ALERT:

_____

_____

_____

_____

OUTCOME: *(tick as applicable)*

Information only ☐

Guidance/Advice given ☐

Investigation ☐ (if so, complete Monitoring Form)

Other ☐ (specify)

CALL TAKEN BY: _____

TEAM: _____

COMPLETED FORM TO BE RETURNED TO:
PROTECTION OF VULNERABLE ADULTS ADMIN ASSISTANT, PEINE HOUSE, HIND HILL STREET, HEYWOOD, OL10 1JZ

WORKING together

APPENDIX I.2
ROCHDALE ADULT PROTECTION
MONITORING FORM

CONFIDENTIAL

Inter-agency Policy Procedure for the Protection of Vulnerable Adults in Rochdale Metropolitan Borough

This form should be completed by the Responsible Manager for each separate incident of alleged abuse at the Case Conference stage or at the conclusion of the investigation. Please return the form to: Protection of Vulnerable Adults Admin Assistant, Peine House, Hind Hill Street, Heywood, OL10 1JZ.

Do not give names of vulnerable adult or alleged abuser on this form.

Name and agency of Responsible Manager:

DETAILS OF VULNERABLE ADULT

Date of Birth	Township of home address (see coding sheet)	N S P H M
Ethnic Origin (see coding sheet)	**Gender**	Male / Female

Case category of vulnerable adult (please tick)

☐ Mental illness ☐ Physical disability
☐ Hearing impairment ☐ Learning disability
☐ Visual impairment ☐ Other (please specify)

Is the person already known to any agency, particularly Social Care Services? ☐ Yes ☐ No / New Referral

Are there any indications of the Vulnerable Adult having any problems with (please tick)

☐ Alcohol ☐ Drugs ☐ Finances ☐ Other (please specify)

DETAILS OF ALLEGED ABUSER

Gender Male / Female / Unknown

Relationship of alleged abuser to Vulnerable Adult

Is the alleged abuser a Vulnerable Adult Yes / No

Case category of alleged abuser (please tick all relevant boxes)

☐ Mental illness ☐ Physical disability
☐ Hearing impairment ☐ Learning disability
☐ Visual impairment ☐ Other (please specify)
  ☐ None

Are there indications of the alleged abuser having any problems with

☐ Alcohol ☐ Drugs ☐ Finances ☐ Other (please specify)

If the alleged abuser is a staff member or volunteer, place one tick in each column

Status of alleged abuser **Sector in which alleged abuser works**
☐ Paid staff ☐ Voluntary
☐ Volunteer ☐ Local Authority / Healthcare Trust
☐ Other (please specify) ☐ Private / Independent
  ☐ Other (please specify)

Where does the alleged abuser live? (please tick)
☐ With the victim ☐ Elsewhere

Page 1 of 2

CONFIDENTIAL

WORKING together

APPENDIX 1.2
ROCHDALE ADULT PROTECTION MONITORING FORM

DETAILS OF ALLEGED ABUSE

Category of alleged abuse (please tick all relevant boxes)
- ☐ Physical
- ☐ Enforcement against a persons wishes (eg Forced Marriages)
- ☐ Negligence or Acts of Omission
- ☐ Psychological
- ☐ Discriminatory
- ☐ Financial or Material
- ☐ Sexual
- ☐ None

Setting of alleged abuse (please tick)
- ☐ Victim's home
- ☐ Day Centre
- ☐ Abuser's home
- ☐ Hospital
- ☐ Res. Care Home
- ☐ Nursing Home
- ☐ Other eg Public Place (please specify)

Brief details of alleged abuse

DETAILS OF INVESTIGATION

Date of referral or of allegation | **Date investigation started** / **Date investigation completed**

Were the Police informed? Yes / No

Job title of care manager/identified health professional who conducted the investigation

Which other agencies were involved
1.   4.
2.   5.
3.   6.

Has a case conference been convened? Yes / No   **Please give date**

Who chaired the Case Conference?

Were the allegations of abuse confirmed by the investigation / case conference?
- ☐ Yes
- ☐ No
- ☐ Uncorroborated

Category of abuse confirmed by the investigation / case conference (please tick)
- ☐ Physical
- ☐ Psychological
- ☐ Financial or Material
- ☐ Enforcement against a persons wishes (eg Forced Marriages)
- ☐ Sexual
- ☐ Negligence or Acts of Omission
- ☐ Discriminatory
- ☐ None

SUMMARY OF RECOMMENDATIONS OF THE INVESTIGATION / CASE CONFERENCE

For the victim
- ☐ Relocation to another address
- ☐ Additional services (please specify)
- ☐ Referral to another agency (please specify)
- ☐ Other (please specify)

For the alleged abuser
- ☐ Relocation to another address
- ☐ Legal action / prosecution
- ☐ Referral to another agency (please specify)
- ☐ Other (please specify)

Please give brief details of conclusion of the investigation / case conference

Signature: | **Date:**

APPENDIX 1.3
LINCOLNSHIRE ELECTRONIC RECORDING
OF ADULT ABUSE ALLEGATIONS

Adult Protection - Form AA Part 1

Register No (Office Use).....................

Vulnerable Adult Information:

Name   **Swift Number**
Address
Postcode
Date of Birth   **Gender**
Ethnic Origin   **Primary Service User**

Nature of Alleged Abuse 1

Nature of Alleged Abuse 2

Nature of Alleged Abuse 3

Brief Outline of Allegation (incl. Date and setting where alleged abuse occurred):

Alerter Information:

Alerter Name   **Type of Alerter**   **If Other Please Specify**
Address
Postcode

Alleged Perpetrator Information:

Name   **Type of Alleged Perpetrator**
Address
Postcode

Record of initial contacts:

Date	Agency	Contact Name

Others at risk?   **Who?**
Others Aware of allegations (Not those already listed in initial contacts)

Liaison Officer Information: Date Appointed:

Name
Address
Postcode   **Tel**

Decision to Investigate   **First Strategy Meeting Date**

Investigation Officer(s)

Agency	Contact Name	Contact Telephone

Signed   **Date of completion of Part 1**

APPENDIX 1.3
LINCOLNSHIRE ELECTRONIC RECORDING
OF ADULT ABUSE ALLEGATIONS

Adult Protection - Form AA Part 2
Complete the following only if Further Investigation is carried out.

Joint Investigation
Agency 1
Agency 2

Investigation Activities: Complex Case ☐

Activity	Tick any Applicable	Date	Further Details/People involved etc *(Optional)*
Strategy Meeting 1	☐		
Strategy Meeting 2	☐		
Case Conference	☐		
Medical Examination	☐		
Police Interview	☐		
Service provider	☐		
Other Details:	☐		

Outcomes of Investigation:

Outcomes	Tick any Applicable	Outcomes	Tick any Applicable
Legal Proceedings	☐	Enforcement (RHA 1984)	☐
Service User Moved	☐	Action Refused	☐
Perpetrator Moved	☐	Increased Service	☐
Increased Monitoring	☐	Medical Treatment	☐
Carer Support	☐	Service User Deceased	☐
Other Details	☐	No Further Action	☐

Copy Of Action Plan Attached

Contact Details for further Enquiries:
Name
Address
Postcode

Signed   **Date of completion of Part 2**
Investigation Completion Date

APPENDIX I.4
NORTH WALES INVESTIGATION OR ASSESSMENT REPORT

9. Investigation or Assessment Report

The report of the investigation/assessment forms part of the file on the adult protection case – it is therefore an official document covered by rules of disclosure. This means it will be made available to the defence if legal proceedings are taken.

Likely contents	Likely information
Details of the alert	Who raised the alert, how, when.
Outline of this allegation and any previous allegations	What exactly was alleged.
Pen picture of vulnerable adult and his or her circumstances/situation, social networks	The vulnerable adult's needs and their immediate and wider personal and social situation.
Assessment of vulnerable adult: capacity, consent, other legal issues	Include who was consulted and when, and his or her opinion, in relation to capacity/consent, legal issues.
Information about alleged perpetrator (if applicable)	Brief and relevant information.
Description of investigation strategy/process (e.g. who and what was involved, level of cooperation received from agencies/people involved)	Brief and factual. Include a list of who provided information (written information, interviews etc.), when and where.
Evaluation of evidence	See Toolkit: Evaluating evidence
Assessment of seriousness of alleged abuse	Address immediate concerns *and* underlying issues (e.g. threats, less overt bullying or humiliation). See Toolkit: Evaluating seriousness
Recommendations: future action, risks	This may include recommending formal action, additional/different supports, more/different monitoring, etc.
Likely/possible cause[s] of abuse	Abuse is complex. Consider reasons about why abuse may have arisen (e.g. individual responsibility of perpetrator): the care setting – its regime, management, training and support available to staff; wider context (e.g. resource shortfalls, services don't meet user needs); family dynamics and relationships.
Opinion and conclusions	What you conclude from this investigation/assessment; what should be learned about prevention, etc.

Section 9 of the North Wales Toolkit is in the North Wales Policy and Procedures for the Protection of Vulnerable Adults, which was adapted from Protecting Vulnerable Adults: Interagency policy, procedures and practice guidance for responding to alleged abuse and inappropriate care of vulnerable adults in the South East Wales area. South East Wales Executive Group; published September 2003.

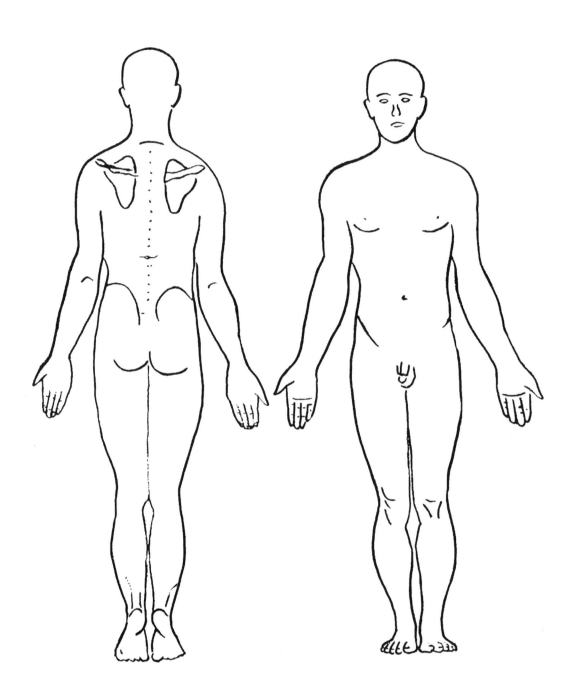

Name of service user:

DOB or ID code:

Date and time injury witnessed:

Name of worker(s):

Job title(s):

Date and time form completed:

Signature(s):

APPENDIX 2.2
BODYMAPS – FEMALE (FRONT AND BACK VIEWS)

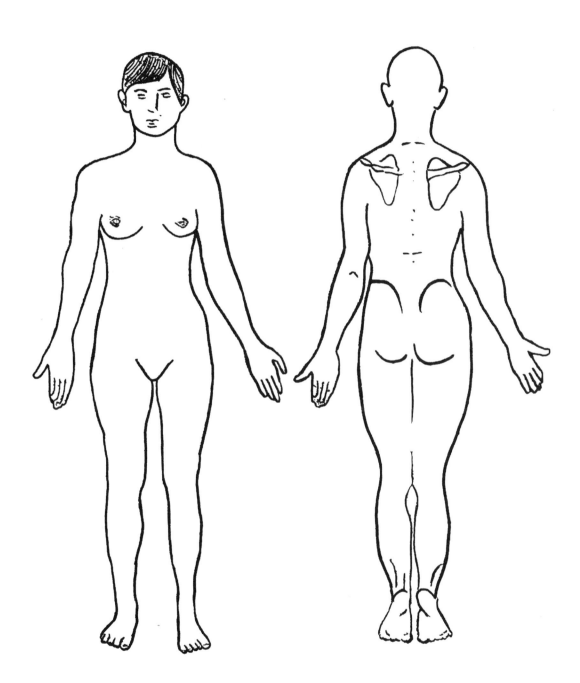

Name of service user:

DOB or ID code:

Date and time injury witnessed:

Name of worker(s):

Job title(s):

Date and time form completed:

Signature(s):

APPENDIX 2.3
BODYMAPS – (SIDE VIEWS)

Name of service user:

DOB or ID code:

Date and time injury witnessed:

Name of worker(s):

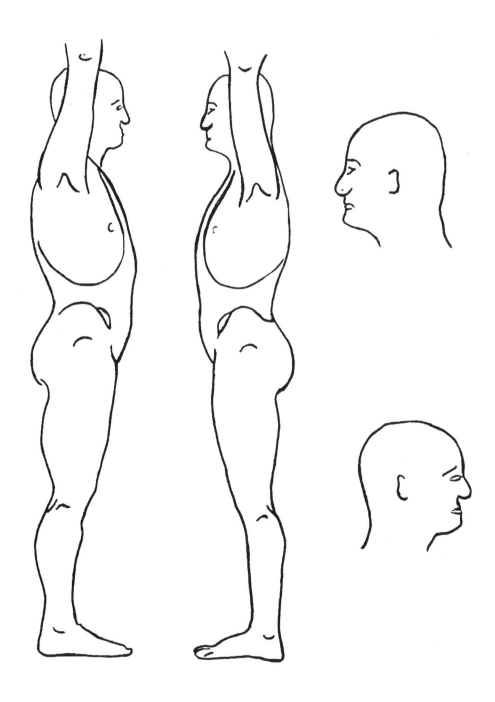

APPENDIX 3.1: RISK ASSESSMENT TOOL

Name of service user	ID Code

Alleged/suspected/proven categories of abuse

Name of worker(s) and job title completing the risk tool:

---

1   Risk-taking actions

ⓘ *What does the service user want to do?*

---

2   Benefits

ⓘ *Why does the service user want to take the risk? What will s/he get out of it?*

---

3   Hazards

ⓘ *Can be anything, e.g. person, behaviour, situation which stops the benefit or causes the danger.*

4   **Dangers**

(i) *The worst feared outcomes/harms. Relate to definition of significant harm.*

1

2

3

4

5

6

7

8

9

10

11

12

© Jacki Pritchard 2007

5 Prediction/Likelihood			
1	2	3	4 ⓘ *The worst feared outcomes/harms. Relate to definition of significant harm.*
DANGER	EVIDENCE	PRESENTED BY	PREDICTION
1			
2			
3			
4			
5			
6			

© Jacki Pritchard 2007

5 **Prediction/Likelihood**

1	2	3	4
DANGER	**EVIDENCE**	**PRESENTED BY**	**PREDICTION**
7			
8			
9			
10			
11			
12			

© Jacki Pritchard 2007

6 **Conflict box**	ⓘ *To be used when a person disagrees with a decision or grading.*
Name of person	Explain what s/he disagrees with

7 | **Development of protection plan**

ⓘ *Detail needed about objectives, agencies, personnel, roles, responsibilities, tasks, contact, method of working, monitoring tools, writen records*

© Jacki Pritchard 2007

---

8 **Grading of case**

Low ☐   Moderate ☐   High ☐

---

9 **Date of review**

Date _____   Time _____

---

10 **Signatures**

Name	Job title/relationship	Signature	Date
	Service user		
	Worker		
	Manager		

Risk tool designed by Jacki Pritchard, March 2005

© Jacki Pritchard 2007

Action on Elder Abuse
Astral House
1268 London Road
London SW16 4ER
Tel: 020 8765 7000
Fax: 020 8679 4074
Helpline: 0808 808 8141
E-mail: enquiries@elderabuse.org.uk
Website: www.elderabuse.org.uk

Ann Craft Trust (ACT)
Centre for Social Work
University Park
Nottingham NG7 2RD
Tel: 0115 951 5400
Fax: 0115 951 5232
E-mail: ann-craft-trust@nottingham.ac.uk
Website: www.anncrafttrust.org

Association for Residential Change (ARC)
Arc House
Marsden Street
Chesterfield
Derbyshire S40 1JY
Tel: 01246 555043
Fax: 01246 555045
E-mail: contact.us@arcuk.org.uk
Website: www.arcuk.org.uk

British Institute of Learning Disabilities (BILD)
Campion House
Green Street
Kidderminster
Worcestershire DY10 3PP
Tel: 01562 723010
Fax: 01562 723029
E-mail: enquiries@bild.org.uk
Website: www.bild.org.uk

Carers UK
Ruth Pitter House
20–25 Glasshouse Yard
London EC1A 4JT
Tel: 020 7490 8818
Fax: 020 7490 8824
CarersLine 0808 808 777
E-mail: info@carersuk.org
Website: www.carersuk.org

Counsel and Care

Twyman House

16 Bonny Street

London NW1 9PG

Tel: 020 7241 8555

Fax: 020 7267 6877

Advice: 0845 300 7585

E-mail: advice@counselandcare.org.uk

Website: www.counselandcare.org.uk

Department for Constitutional Affairs (formerly the Lord Chancellor's Department)

Selborne House

54 Victoria Street

London SW1E 6QW

Tel: 020 7210 8500

E-mail: dcaweb.comments@dca.gsi.gov.uk

Website: www.dca.gov.uk

Department of Health

Richmond House

79 Whitehall

London SW1A 2NS

Website: www.Department of Health.gov.uk

Help the Aged

207–221 Pentonville Road

London N1 9UZ

Tel: 020 7278 1114

Fax: 020 7278 1116

E-mail: info@helptheaged.org.uk

Website: www.helptheaged.org.uk

Home Office

Direct Communications Unit

2 Marsham Street

London SW1P 4DF

Tel: 020 7035 4848

Fax: 020 7035 4745

E-mail: public.enquiries@homeoffice.gsi.gov.uk

Website: www.homeoffice.gov.uk

PAVA (Practitioners Alliance Against the Abuse of Vulnerable Adults)

PO Box 127

Ryde PO33 9AE

E-mail: siteenquiry@pavauk.org.uk

Website: www.pavauk.org.uk

Public Guardianship Office

Archway Tower

2 Junction Road

London N19 5SZ

Tel: 0845 330 2900

Fax: 0870 739 5780

E-mail: custserv@guardianship.gsi.gov.uk

Website: www.guardianship.gov.uk

Respond
3rd Floor
24–32 Stephenson Way
London NW1 2HD
Tel: 020 7383 0700
Fax: 020 7387 1222
Helpline: 0808 808 0700
E-mail: admin@respond.org.uk
Website: www.respond.org.uk

Victim Support
Cranmer House
39 Brixton Road
London SW9 6DZ
Tel: 020 7735 9166
Fax: 020 7582 5712
E-mail: contact@victimsupport.org.uk
Website: www.victimsupport.org.uk

Voice UK
Wyvern House
Railway Terrace
Derby DE1 2RU
Tel: 01332 295775
Fax: 01332 295670
Helpline: 0845 122 8695
E-mail: voice@voiceuk.org.uk
Website: www.voiceuk.org.uk

Women's Aid Federation of England
Head Office
PO Box 391
Bristol BS99 7WS
Tel: 0117 944 44 11
Fax: 0117 924 1703
Helpline: 0808 2000 247
E-mail: info@womensaid.org.uk
Website: www.womensaid.org.uk

Jacki Pritchard Productions

In all the years I have been training I have tried to introduce a variety of training methods into my courses in order to maintain participants' interest throughout the day. Abuse is a very emotive subject and a training course can be hard going because there is so much information for participants to assimilate in a short space of time. I am fortunate in that I still work with abuse victims and I can talk about 'real' cases. The cases studies I use in training and in my writing are based on real situations (although obviously hugely disguised). In addition I think it is important that people are trained using visual aids; using parts of television documentaries can be helpful but training videos can offer a trainer and course participants a lot of different things.

I developed the 'Working with Adult Abuse' series because I wanted to give organisations a complete training package (not just basic awareness); that is, covering all aspects of abuse and investigations together with specialist subjects. My objective was to meet different needs. First, I know many organisations struggle with budgets and cannot afford to bring in expert trainers to train large numbers of staff. Second, I know many managers and workers are being given extra responsibilities, many of which include delivering training. If they have not attended a training the trainers course or have expertise in a subject area, then they need good training resources.

The JPP videos (also available in DVD format) will complement this manual (although it is *not* necessary to purchase the videos in order to use the manual), so some explanation is needed about them. The videos in the 'Working with Adult Abuse' series present information and theory creatively with the use of illustrative case studies. They may be used in a range of ways to train staff:

- Staff groups may watch a video as part of a staff meeting.

- An individual worker may borrow the video to watch at home.

- The video can be used on a training course – watching it straight through as stated or a trainer may develop exercises around the case studies.

How to use a JPP video and training manual

Some trainers may wish to show participants the video straight through; others may prefer to stop at intervals and introduce exercises, handouts, discussion questions from this manual. At crucial points in the video there is a ten-second counter, so the trainer knows when to stop the video (if they want to!). In addition exercises from this training manual can be utilised around the case studies in the video.

Each video contains:

- presentation of theory and knowledge around the subject area

- case studies which illustrate the information given and points being made

- discussion questions

- exercises

- learning points.

The videos in the 'Working with Adult Abuse' series are:

WAA1: What is Adult Abuse?	(50 minutes)
WAA2: Recognising Adult Abuse	(50 minutes)
WAA3: Investigating Adult Abuse	Two-video set
(Video 1: 32 minutes; Video 2: 44 minutes)	
WAA4: Case Conferences	(57 minutes)
WAA5: The Abuse of Older People	Two-video set
(Video 1: 60 minutes; Video 2: 30 minutes)	
WAA6: The Abuse of Black and Minority Ethnic People	(75 minutes)

For more information contact:

Jacki Pritchard Productions Ltd
Units G9 and G10
The Globe Business Centre
Penistone Road
Sheffield S6 3AE
Tel: 0114 270 1782
Fax: 0114 270 6019
E-mail: info@jackipritchardproductions.co.uk
Website: www.jackipritchardproductions.co.uk

References

Action on Elder Abuse (2006) *Adult Protection Data Collection and Reporting Requirements.* London: AEA.

ADSS (1991) *Adults at Risk.* Lancaster: Association of Directors of Social Services.

ADSS (2005) *Safeguarding Adults: A National Framework of Standards for Good Practice and Outcomes in Adult Protection Work.* London: Association of Directors of Social Services.

Baker, A.A. (1975) 'Granny battering.' *Modern Geriatrics 5*, 8, 20–4.

BILD (2007) 'Investigation finds widespread institutional abuse of people with learning disabilities at an NHS trust in Cornwall.' *BILD comment.* Kidderminster: British Institute of Learning Disabilities. Available at (www.bild.org.uk/01headlines.htm#cornwall).

Brearley, C.P. (1982a) *Risk and Ageing.* London: Routledge and Kegan Paul.

Brearley, C.P. (1982b) *Risk in Social Work.* London: Routledge and Kegan Paul.

Brent Multi Agency Adult Protection Committee (2006) *Annual Report 2005.* London: Brent Council.

Brown, H. (1994) 'Lost in the system: Acknowledging the sexual abuse of adults with learning disabilities.' *Care in Place 9*, 2, 145–7.

Brown, H. and Turk, V. (1992) 'Defining sexual abuse as it affects adults with learning disabilities.' *Mental Handicap 20*, 2, 44–55.

Brown, H., Stein, J. and Turk, V. (1995) 'Report of a second two year incidence survey on the reported sexual abuse of adults with learning disabilities: 1991 and 1992.' *Mental Handicap Research 8*, 1, 1–22.

Brown, H., Skinner, R., Stein, J. and Wilson, B. (1999a) *Aims for Adult Protection: The Alerter's Guide and Training Manual.* Brighton: Pavilion Publishing.

Brown, H., Skinner, R., Stein, J. and Wilson, B. (1999b) *Aims for Adult Protection: The Investigator's Guide and Training Manual.* Brighton: Pavilion Publishing.

Burgner, T. (1998) *Independent Longcare Inquiry.* Buckingham: Buckinghamshire County Council.

Burston, G.R. (1975) 'Granny battering.' *British Medical Journal 3*, September, 592–3.

Burston, G.R. (1977) 'Do your elderly patients live in fear of being battered?' *Modern Geriatrics 7*, 5, May, 54–5.

Butler Committee, Home Office and Department of Health and Social Security (1975) *Report of the Committee on Mentally Disordered Offenders.* Cmnd. 6244. London: HMSO.

Camden and Islington NHS Trust (1999) *Beech House Inquiry.* London: Camden and Islington NHS Trust.

Crown Prosecution Service (2006) 'The principles we follow.' Crown Prosecution Service. www.cps.gov.uk/principles.html

Croydon Multi Agency Adult Protection Committee (2006) *Annual Report April 2005 – March 2006.* London: Borough of Croydon.

Department of Health (1989) *Homes Are For Living In.* London: Department of Health.

Department of Health (1992) *Confronting Elder Abuse*. London: HMSO.

Department of Health (1993) *No Longer Afraid: The Safeguard of Older People in Domestic Settings*. London: HMSO.

Department of Health (2000a) *No Secrets: Guidance on Developing and Implementing Multi-Agency Policies and Procedures to Protect Vulnerable Adults from Abuse*. London: Department of Health.

Department of Health (2000b) *'No Secrets' Guidance on Developing Multi-Agency Policies and Procedures to Protect Vulnerable Adults from Abuse*. Health Service/Local Authority Circular HSC 2000/007. London: Department of Health.

Department of Health (2005) 'Over 700 people barred from working with vulnerable adults.' Press release, 26 July (www.Department of Health.gov.uk/PublicationsAndStatistics/PressReleases/PressReleasesNotices/fs/en?CONTENT_ID=4116557&chk=Sv5GFC).

Department of Health (2006a) 'Workers to be registered to tackle elder abuse.' London: Department of Health. Press release, 7 February. Online at www.Department of Health.gov.uk.

Department of Health (2006b) *Protection of Vulnerable Adults Scheme in England and Wales for Adult Placement Schemes, Domiciliary Care Agencies and Care Homes: A Practical Guide*. Revised. London: Department of Health.

Devon Adult Protection Committee (2006) *Annual Report 2006*. Exeter: Devon Adult Protection Committee.

Eastman, M. (1984) *Old Age Abuse*. London: Age Concern.

Elliot, M. (1993) *Female Sexual Abuse of Children: The Ultimate Taboo*. Harlow, Essex: Longman.

Foundation for People with Learning Disabilities (2003) 'Statistics on learning disabilities.' Factsheet, 11 July (www.learningdisabilities.org.uk/page.cfm?pagecode=ISBISTBI).

Gelles, R.J. (1997) *Intimate Violence*. Third edition. Thousand Oaks, CA: Sage.

Gelles, R.J. and Cornell, C.P. (1985) *Intimate Violence in Families*. Beverley Hills, CA: Sage.

Gelles, R.J. and Straus, M.A. (1988) *Intimate Violence*. New York: Simon and Schuster.

Healthcare Commission and Commission for Social Care Inspection (2006) *Joint Investigation into the Provision of Services for People with Learning Disabilities at Cornwall Partnership NHS Trust*. London: Commission for Healthcare Audit and Inspection.

Hildrew, M.A. (1991) 'New age problem.' *Social Work Today 22*, 49, 15–17.

Home Office (1998) *Speaking Up for Justice: Report of the Interdepartmental Working Group on the Treatment of Vulnerable or Intimidated Witnesses in the Criminal Justice System*. London: Home Office.

Home Office (1999) *Action for Justice*. London: Home Office Communication Directorate. Revised 2002.

Home Office (2001a) *Human Rights Act: An Introduction*. London: Home Office Communication Directorate.

Home Office (2001b) *Study Guide: Human Rights Act 1998*. London: Home Office Communication Directorate.

Home Office (2002) *Achieving Best Evidence in Criminal Proceedings: Guidance for Vulnerable or Intimidated Witnesses including Children*. London: Home Office Communication Directorate.

Home Office (2005) *Offender Management Caseload Statistics*. London: Research, Development and Statistics Directorate.

Ingram, R. (2001) 'Is it a domestic? Or is it adult abuse?' In J. Pritchard (ed.) *Good Practice with Vulnerable Adults*. London: Jessica Kingsley Publishers.

Kemshall, H. (1997) *Management and Assessment of Risk in the Probation Service*. London: Home Office/Association of Chief Probation Officers.

Kemshall, H. (1998) *Risk in Probation Practice*. London: Ashgate.

Kemshall, H. and Pritchard, J. (eds) (1997) *Good Practice in Risk Assessment and Risk Management 2: Protection, Rights and Responsibilities*. London: Jessica Kingsley Publishers.

Lincolnshire Adult Protection Committee (2006) *Annual Report 2005–2006*. Lincoln: Lincolnshire County Council.

Lord Chancellor's Department (1997) *Who Decides? Making Decisions on Behalf of Mentally Incapacitated Adults*. London: The Stationery Office.

Lord Chancellor's Department (1999) *Making Decisions: The Government's Proposals for Making Decisions on Behalf of Mentally Incapacitated Adults*. London: The Stationery Office.

National Assembly for Wales (2000) *In Safe Hands*. Cardiff: National Assembly for Wales.

Newport Area Adult Protection Committee (2006) *Annual Report 2005–2006*. Newport: Newport County Council.

North Wales Vulnerable Adults Forum (2005) *North Wales Policy and Procedures for the Protection of Vulnerable Adults.* North Wales: North Wales Vulnerable Adults Forum.

Pring, J. (2003) *Silent Victims: The Continuing Failure to Protect Society's Most Vulnerable and The Longcare Scandal.* London: Gibson Square Books.

Pritchard, J. (1995) *The Abuse of Older People.* Second edition. London: Jessica Kingsley Publishers.

Pritchard, J. (1996) *Working with Elder Abuse: A Training Manual for Home Care, Residential and Day Care Staff.* London: Jessica Kingsley Publishers.

Pritchard, J. (2000) *The Needs of Older Women: Services for Victims of Elder Abuse and Other Abuse.* Bristol: The Policy Press.

Pritchard, J. (2001a) *Becoming a Trainer in Adult Abuse Work.* London: Jessica Kingsley Publishers.

Pritchard, J. (2001b) *Male Victims of Elder Abuse: Their Experiences and Needs.* London: Jessica Kingsley Publishers.

Pritchard, J. (2002) 'The abuse of older men.' *Journal of Adult Protection 4,* 3, 14–23.

Pritchard, J. (2003a) *Support Groups for Older People Who Have Been Abused: Beyond Existing.* London: Jessica Kingsley Publishers.

Pritchard, J. (2003b) *Training Manual for Working with Older People in Residential and Day Care Settings.* London: Jessica Kingsley Publishers.

Pritchard, J. and Sainsbury, E. (2004) *Can You Read Me? Creative Writing with Child and Adult Victims of Abuse.* London: Jessica Kingsley Publishers.

ReSisters (2002) *Women Speak Out.* Leeds: ReSisters.

Saradjian, J. (1996) *Women Who Sexually Abuse Children.* Chichester: John Wiley and Sons.

Sinason, V. (ed.) (1994) *Treating Survivors of Satanist Abuse: An Invisible Trauma.* London: Routledge.

Sinclair, I. (ed.) (1988) *Residential Care: The Research Reviewed.* London: HMSO.

Skills for Care (2006) *A Manager's Guide to Developing Strategic Uses of National Occupational Standards.* Leeds: Skills for Care.

Steinmetz, S.K. (1978) 'The battered husband syndrome.' *Victimology 2,* 499–509.

Straus, M. (1999) 'The controversy over domestic violence by women.' In X.B. Arriaga and S. Oskamp (eds) *Violence in Intimate Relationships.* Thousand Oaks, CA: Sage Publications.

Straus, M.A. and Gelles, R.J. (1986) 'Societal change and change in family violence from 1975 to 1985 as revealed by two national surveys.' *Journal of Marriage and the Family 48,* 465–479.

Straus, M.A., Gelles, R.J. and Steinmetz, S.K. (1980) *Behind Closed Doors: Violence in the American Family.* Garden City, NY: Anchor.

Tomlin, S. (1989) *Abuse of Elderly People: An Unnecessary and Preventable Problem.* London: British Geriatrics Society.

TOPSS (2001) *The First Six Months: A Registered Manager's Guide to Induction and Foundation Standards.* Leeds: Training Organisation for the Personal Social Services.

UNESCO (2002) *Universal Declaration on Cultural Diversity Conference, 21 February.* Pairs: United Nations Educational, Scientific and Cultural Organization. Available at www.unesco.org/education/imld_2002/ universal_decla.shtml.

Wagner Committee (1988) *Residential Care: A Positive Choice.* London: HMSO.

Statutes

Care Standards Act 2000

Children Act 1989

Crime and Disorder Act 1998

Criminal Justice Act 1991

Data Protection Act 1998

Freedom of Information Act 2000

Local Authority and Social Services Act 1970

Human Rights Act 1998

Mental Capacity Act 2005

Mental Health Act 1983

NHS and Community Care Act 1990

Protection from Harassment Act 1997

Youth Justice and Criminal Evidence Act 1999

Statutes are now published by the Stationery Office Ltd (previously HMSO Publications): www.tso.co.uk

Subject Index

Author Index

Action on Elder Abuse 31, 76, 331, 332

ADSS (Association of Directors of Social Services) 14, 29, 32, 41

Baker, A.A. 30, 308

BILD (British Institute of Learning Disabilities) 333

Brearley, C.P. 258, 271

Brent Multi Agency Adult Protection Committee 332

Brown, H. 332

Burgner, T. 60, 331

Burns, B. 290–1

Burston, G.R. 30, 308

Butler Committee 257–8

Camden and Islington NHS Trust 60

Cornell, C.P. 99, 311

Crown Prosecution Service 278

Croydon Multi Agency Adult Protection Committee 332

Department of Health (DH) 14–15, 21, 29, 30–3, 37, 43–5, 61–2, 73, 75–8, 93, 95, 172, 179–80, 244, 257–8, 308, 330–1, 353, 357, 373

Devon Adult Protection Committee 332

Eastman, M. 43, 76, 99, 308, 310

Elliot, M. 99, 311

Foundation for People with Learning Disabilities 333

Gelles, R.J. 99, 310–11

Healthcare Commission and Commission for Social Care Inspection 331

Hildrew, M.A. 30

Home Office 29, 32, 39, 52, 59, 179–81, 188, 199, 257–8, 358

Ingram, R. 103

Kemshall, H. 257

Lincolnshire Adult Protection Committee 332, 387–8

Lord Chancellor's Department 42, 44, 73, 78, 174, 186, 245, 257, 260, 269

National Assembly for Wales 14, 21, 29, 31, 39

Newport Area Adult Protection Committee 332

North Wales Vulnerable Adults Forum 389

Pring, J. 331

Pritchard, J. 13, 19, 119, 139, 192, 226, 289, 310–11, 393–9

ReSisters 334

Saradjian, J. 99, 311

Sinason, V. 49

Sinclair, I. 60

Skills for Care 14, 105

Stein, J. 332

Steinmetz, S.K. 99, 310–11

Straus, M.A. 99, 310–11

Tomlin, S. 308

TOPSS (Training Organisation for the Personal Social Services) 61, 105

Turk, V. 332

UK Voice 31

UNESCO 356

Wagner, G. 60

413